talking the TALK German

SUE PURCELL

Series Editor: Alwena Lamping

Published by BBC Active, an imprint of Educational Publishers LLP, part of the Pearson Education Group, Edinburgh Gate, Harlow, Essex CM20 2JE, England.

First published 2017.
5 4 3 2 1

ISBN 978-1-4066-8470-4

Publisher: Debbie Marshall
Development editor: Doris Hermann-Ostrowski
Layout: Reality Premedia Services
Cover design: Two Associates
Cover photograph: © Richard Boll/GETTYIMAGES
Illustrations: © Mark Duffin
Project editor: Emma Brown
Proofreading: Sigrid Koehler
Audio producer: Colette Thomson, Footstep Productions Ltd.

Printed and bound by Neografia, Slovakia.

The Publisher's policy is to use paper manufactured from sustainable forests.

contents

introduction

Talking the TALK German is BBC Active's latest addition to the bestselling **TALK** series. It is about social conversation: not just small talk but getting to know people and their lives, sharing information, opinions and anecdotes, making plans, talking about aspirations and obligations - and more.

An **audio component** complements the book. It is available for you to download from: www.bbcactivelanguages.com/TTG.

Who is **Talking the TALK** for?

It's for people of all ages who are learning German or who are familiar with the basics, and whose ambition is to be able to chat to people in German, whether someone they've met on holiday, a business contact, extended family, a fellow enthusiast, a neighbour or anyone else.

The contents are also ideal for someone who has followed a course but would like to update their German and extend the range of what they can say.

How does it work?

It is based on the principles of successful conversation. Everyday conversation hangs on a relatively small number of **core linguistic structures** which provide the framework for what we want to say.

The potential of the framework is realised by building on it, so **personalised vocabulary building** is a priority. This book contains hundreds of examples, using **varied and contemporary language**.

Conversation works better if you have the **strategies to keep it flowing**. And it's easier when you're confident that what you're saying sounds **natural and up to date**, and when you know that you'll be **readily understood**.

Is it easy to use?

The approach is hands-on, to enable you to adapt what you're learning so that it's **personal and relevant** to you.

Content is presented in **manageable steps**, with page headings showing clearly what the focus is. Core linguistic structures are generously illustrated and explained with the hallmark **TALK** clarity. Focused **wordbanks**, placed just where you need them, allow you to practise, adapt and **personalise the language structures**: there are frequent suggestions on how you might do this.

The design allows learning German to fit into a busy lifestyle: this is a book that can be dipped into a page or two at a time. The pages are grouped into 11 chapters, each of which ends with conversations that bring the language you're learning to life and a checkpoint which serves as revision and as an aid to remembering the contents.

How does the audio fit in?

The German presenters of the audio have clear aims:

- **helping you to pronounce German correctly**, since conversation is more enjoyable when both sides understand each other without endless repetition. They guide you through the sounds of German, focusing on the ones that English speakers sometimes struggle with. They do this with material selected from each chapter, **reinforcing the core language structures**. They're supported in the book by **how to sound German**, a guide to the sounds and stress patterns of German.
- **developing your listening skills**, since conversation is as much to do with listening as talking. Each chapter ends with informal conversations between the presenters; these are printed in your book on the **Talking the TALK** page, and the **Audio Support Pack** offers suggestions on how to make the most of them.

How do I access the audio?

To download the audio go to: www.bbcactivelanguages.com/TTG.

For maximum flexibility, you can download the complete script including the conversations, and you can download the conversations separately, entirely in German, for intensive listening.

The **Audio Support Pack** is also available from the website above. It includes full transcripts plus guidance and activities on how to make the most of the conversations.

BBC Active would like to thank all the language tutors who contributed to the planning of **Talking the TALK**. The concept is based on your suggestions and feedback.

the main differences between German and English

There are many similarities between German and English, but there are fundamental differences too. It helps to be prepared for those.

Familiarity with grammatical terms will help you to understand explanations of how German works. There's a full list on pages 172–175.

- German has three words for ***you***, **du**, **ihr**, **Sie**, depending on who you're talking to. So when you come across a sentence or a question containing ***you***, be aware that there are two other, slightly different, versions.
- Every German noun is written with a capital letter, even in the middle of a sentence: **der Mann** *the man*, **die Stadt** *the town*.
- For the **plural**, i.e. more than one, German nouns don't add *-s* as in English. Some add -**e**, some -**n**, some -**en**, some -**er**, some also an umlaut. Others don't change at all: **Hund/Hunde** *dog/s*, **Katze/Katzen** *cat/s*, **Bild/Bilder** *picture/s* **Hand/Hände** *hand/s*, **Lehrer/Lehrer** *teacher/s*. As the plural isn't always guessable, it's usually provided in dictionaries.
- Most words linked to a noun have to be masculine, feminine or neuter to **agree** with it: **der Wein** *the wine*, **die Wurst** *the sausage*, **das Bier** *the beer*. An adjective in a dictionary has no ending, but when you use it before a noun it gets an ending to agree with the gender, case and number (singular, plural) of the noun: **ein guter Wein** *a good wine*, **eine gute Wurst** *a good sausage*, **ein gutes Bier** *a good beer*.
- **Case** refers to the role that a word is playing in a sentence. There are four **cases**: the **nominative** is used for the subject of the verb, the **accusative** for the direct object, the **dative** for the indirect object and the **genitive** to indicate possession. Each case has different word endings associated with it. In English, apart from the **'s** ending to show possession, it's only pronouns whose forms change depending on their role in the sentence: *I/me*, *she/her*, but in German, changes in case endings apply to all parts of speech that accompany nouns and pronouns, such as adjectives, articles and possessives.
- Some verbs in German are **separable**. They're made up of a prefix and a main part: **ankommen** *to arrive*. In certain circumstances, the prefix separates from the main part and moves to the end of the sentence: **Otto kommt morgen an** *Otto's arriving tomorrow*. Some English two-part verbs are similar e.g. *to switch on*, *to write down*: *I'm writing the information down* **Ich schreibe die Informationen auf**.

word order

One striking difference between the two languages is the order of words in a sentence. Both have clear rules about this aspect but they're not the same.

The golden rule in German is that the verb is the second element in a statement.
Ich fahre manchmal nach Berlin *I sometimes go to Berlin* has the subject **ich** *I* as the first element, and the verb **fahre** *go* as the second.
It's also correct to say **Manchmal fahre ich nach Berlin** with **manchmal** *sometimes* as the first element and the verb **fahre** as the second. But it isn't correct to use the order *I sometimes go to Berlin* because the verb would be the third element.

This doesn't mean that the verb is necessarily the second ***word***.
Am Wochenende fahre ich nach Berlin. *At the weekend I'm going to Berlin.*

When there are two verbs in a sentence, the second goes to the end.
Ich möchte nach Berlin fahren. *I'd like to go to Berlin.*
Ich muss nach Berlin fahren. *I must go to Berlin.*
The same applies to a past participle: **Ich habe Berlin besucht.** *I have visited Berlin.* And the verb is also sent to the end by words such as **weil** *because.*

In a question starting with a question word, the verb is the second element:
Woher weißt du das? *How do you know that?*

But in a *yes/no* question, the verb comes first, as in English.
Sind Sie hier im Urlaub? *Are you here on holiday?*
Müsst ihr jetzt gehen? *Must you leave now?*

There are some unusual characters in the German alphabet: the vowels **a**, **o** and **u** can add an **umlaut ä, ö, ü**, which changes their pronunciation slightly. The letter **ß**, called **eszett**, or **sharp s** is pronounced *ss*, and is used after long vowel sounds: **der Fußball** *football*, **die Größe** *size*, **die Straße** *street*.

To key in **ä, ö, ü, ß** on your tablet or phone, hold your finger on the basic vowel or *s* on the keyboard then slide it to the version you want from the options that appear. In Word, you can either select Insert → Symbol → More symbols, or use keyboard shortcuts using Alt and the number pad.

ä Alt 132 ö Alt 148 ü Alt 129 ß Alt 225

how to sound German

The sounds and rhythm of German are similar to those of English, so it's entirely feasible for an English speaker to speak German with an accent easily understood by native speakers, regardless of where in Germany, Austria or Switzerland they come from.

The starting point is listening to as many different voices and accents as possible. There are different levels of listening: more often than not you're listening in order to understand ***what***'s being said, but you can also train yourself to listen in order to hear ***how*** something is being said. It doesn't even matter that you don't understand everything, what you're doing is getting a feel for the rhythm and overall sound of German. When you hear many Germans speaking English, you'll recognise that same rhythm - and this is what you're aiming to recreate.

German sounds are not difficult for English speakers if you

- know how to pronounce the letters of the German alphabet and key combinations of letters. This takes relatively little time because the sounds are broadly consistent and don't vary much from one word to the next, unlike English;
- practise and keep practising until what you say is what you hear. It's not enough to say things in your head; you need to say them out loud so that your speech organs – e.g. vocal cords, tongue, lips, teeth, soft and hard palate – are working and adapting to German sounds.

The Talking the TALK audio download, available from www.bbcactivelanguages.com/TTG, is there to support you. But before sampling the audio, have a look at the next few pages, which summarise the fundamentals of pronunciation, stress and rhythm.

vowels

In English, vowels sound very different according to which word they're in:
a: cart, care, paw, woman
o: one, bone, done, gone

In German, vowels have more consistent sounds. They can be short or long, and they sound similar to the way they sound in these English words.

a	cat, cart
ä	chaos
e	net, chaos. It's never silent at the end of a word like the English *have* or *like*, but is pronounced like **er** in mother.
i	in, machine/bee
ie	see
o	hot; when long, a sound somewhere between **o** in go and in more.
ö	burn, but said with your lips pursed. It's often represented in English as **oe**: Goethe.
u	put, but with your lips more rounded. When long, as in cool.
ü	this sound doesn't exist in English, but if you position your lips to say **oo** and, without moving them say **ee**, you'll get there.
y	in the middle of a word, e.g. **typisch** *typical*, sounds like **ü**; at the end of a word it sounds the same as in English: **Hobby, Baby**.

Unlike English, double vowels keep the same essential sound of a single: **Meer** *sea* sounds similar to the English *mare*, **Boot** *boat* to *bought*.

However, the following combinations of vowels have their own sound.

au	as in cow: **Haus** *house* sounds like *house*
äu	as in boy: **Kräuter** *herbs* sounds like *kroyter*
ai	as in lie or rye: **Mai** *May* sounds like *my*
ei	as in lie or rye: **klein** *small* sounds like *incline*
eu	as in boy: **Deutsch** *German* sounds like *Doytsh*

When you come across a new word written down, you can tell a vowel has a long sound if it's followed by **h**, as in **Jahr** *year*, **sehen** *to see*. And you know it's short if it's followed by two or more consonants: **dann** *then*, **Geld** *money*; or when it's a final syllable: **Frage** *question*, **immer** *always*.

consonants

Most consonants sound similar in German and English, but some are different.

c	before **a**, **o**, **u**, **k**, **l** or **r**: **k** as in **kick**
c	before **ä**, **e** or **i**: **ts** as in **puts**
ch	after **a**, **o** or **u**: **ch** as in **loch**
ch	after other letters: **h** as in **Hugh**, but breathed out much more vigorously.
g	as in golf, except in words ending **-ig**, when **g** sounds like the soft German **ch**. You sound the **g** in the combination **gn**: **gnädige Frau** *madam* is pronounced *g-nay-digguh.*
kn	**k** is pronounced when before **n**: **Knie** *knee: k-n-ee-ye.*
j	y in yes
qu	**kv**: **Qualität** is pronounced *kval-it-ait.*
r	is always pronounced at the beginning of a word or syllable. It is silent at the end (as in **Vater, vorkommen**). In northern Germany the back of the tongue is raised towards the roof of the mouth (but not touching it), and the **r** sound is produced in the throat, sounding like a gentle gargle. In southern Germany and Austria **r** is produced much further forward in the mouth, with the tongue vibrating against the ridge behind the top front teeth. It sounds like a Scottish rolled **r**.
s	usually sounds like **z**: **Sie** you is said *zee*. At the end of a word, it's pronounced **s**: **alles** *everything*, **Bus** *bus* – even when that word is part of a compound word: **Busfahrer** *bus driver.*
sch	**sh** as in wash and **sh**oe
sp and st	at the beginning of a word or syllable are pronounced **shp** and **sht**, but elsewhere they're pronounced **sp** and **st**.
th	t as in tea
tsch	**tch** as in pi**tch**
v	usually **f** as in four, but in some common words such as **Universität**, **November** it's pronounced like an English **v**.
w	v as in vase
z	**ts** as in pu**ts**

Position in a word can make a difference to how you pronounce **b**, **d** and **g**. At the end of words, they're pronounced as *p*, *t* and *k*: **gelb** *yellow* sounds like *gelp*, **Bad** *bath* like *bat* and **Zug** *train* like *tsuk*.

stress

Broadly speaking, the majority of German words are stressed on the first syllable: **Österreich** *Austria*, **langweilig** *boring*, **Name**.
If a word begins with **be-**, **er-**, **ent-**, **emp-**, **ge-**, **ver-**, **zer-**, then the stress is on the second syllable: **verstehen** *to understand*, **besonders** *especially*, **Entschuldigung** *excuse me*, **genug** *enough*.
The stress is on -**ier**- in verbs ending -**ieren**: **studieren** *to study*, **interessieren** *to interest*.
The stress is usually on the final syllable for words of foreign origin ending **-ie -ion, -ist, -tät**: **Biologie**, **Theorie**, **Funktion**, **Stadion**, **Polizist**, **Tourist**, **Elektrizität**, **Universität**.

If not affected by the rules above, words from other languages often keep their original stress: **Appetit**, **Computer**, **Hotel**, **Garage**.
They also tend to keep their original pronunciation:
English: **Job**, **Jazz**, **chatten** *to chat online*
French: **Journalist**, **Garage**, **Chef**, **Ingenieur**.

intonation/rhythm

Pronunciation is about more than individual words. It involves the rhythm and intonation of whole sentences: how the voice rises and falls, and how it varies when registering different emotions.

Luckily, German and English intonation patterns are not too dissimilar. Very broadly speaking, in German a falling intonation is used for statements, commands and questions introduced by a question word. A rising intonation is typically used for yes/no questions. A level intonation is often used for formulaic utterances, such as greetings. Intonation can vary, however, depending on context and on speakers' attitudes to their words and their listeners. Getting the intonation right is largely a matter of listening and imitating. Watch also how people's mouths and faces move, and what gestures they make when they speak.

eins
first impressions

Germans are much less formal than in the past, and the word that used to be associated with Germany, **Ordnung** *order, orderliness*, is not so apparent these days. Nevertheless, Germans still appreciate efficiency and appropriateness, and value others doing things properly and showing respect. This idea permeates all aspects of life, including language.

As in most languages, the way you talk to people in German is affected by social context, age, hierarchy and respect. But in German, levels of formality are built right into the language. For example, it's important to choose the right version of *you* so that you don't unknowingly get off on the wrong foot. Traditional greetings and titles are integral to **gute Umgangsformen** *good manners*; a casual **Hi** is appropriate only in very informal situations.

First impressions matter.

choosing between du, Sie and ihr

Unlike English, which has only one word for *you*, German has three: **du, Sie** and **ihr**, and they're not interchangeable.

du is used for friends, children and family members. It can only be used to address one person.

Sie is used to address people you've just met, whether one person or more than one. It's always written with a capital **S**. Adults use **Sie** with each other until they agree to use **du**.

ihr is the plural of **du**.

The verb changes according to which one you're using:

Where do you live?	*Are you ...?*
Wo wohnst du?	**Bist du Laura?**
Wo wohnen Sie?	**Sind Sie Frau Schindler?**
Wo wohnt ihr?	**Seid ihr Laura und Dominik?**

Widespread use of **du** is becoming more acceptable, especially in southern Germany, and is the norm on social media and among groups of young people. But if you use **du** straightaway with an older person or an official, they might well perceive it as over-familiarity. If you're starting a conversation and you're not sure whether to use **du** or **Sie**, opt for **Sie**. If **du** is more appropriate, someone will soon suggest **Wollen wir uns nicht duzen?** *Let's use* ***du****, let's not be so formal.*

Sie is also the German for *they*, but in the 18th century it was adopted as a respectful way of addressing social equals and superiors. For hundreds of years before that, **Ihr** was used as the polite form of *you*.

addressing someone properly

Formality isn't confined to a choice of **du** or **Sie**. The use of surnames rather than first names communicates respect: using a person's title and surname is the norm, far more so than in English.

If you're on **Sie** terms, you'll almost certainly be using a person's surname:

Herr Schmidt *Mr Smith*; **Frau Meier** *Mrs/Ms Meier*

Fräulein, *Miss*, is considered old-fashioned these days.

If a German has an academic title, then it's used in addition to **Herr** and **Frau. Doktor** and **Professor** are used for men and women.

Herr Doktor Schneider; Frau Professor Winter

Once you get to know Dr Schneider and Professor Winter, you can drop their surnames and just use their titles: **Herr Doktor, Frau Professor.**

You'll hear a wider range of professional and academic titles used in Austria, e.g. **Herr Diplom Ingenieur** for an engineer with a post-graduate degree; **Frau Magister** for a master's graduate.

Just as in English, German does not use *sir* and *madam* when addressing strangers. Germans would call after someone: **Hallo, Sie da! Sie haben was verloren**. Literally, *Hello, you there! You've lost something.*

Austrians, however, do use **Gnädige Frau** *madam* and **Mein Herr** *sir.*

Guten Morgen, gnädige Frau. *Good morning, madam.*

Vielen Dank, mein Herr. *Thank you, sir.*

And Germans do often address a group of people as **meine Damen und Herren: Herzlich willkommen, meine Damen und Herren.** *Welcome, ladies and gentlemen.*

Formerly, you called out **Herr Ober** and **Fräulein** to attract the attention of a waiter or waitress in a restaurant, but nowadays a simple **Hallo, Entschuldigung** *excuse me*, is enough.

terms of endearment

The equivalent of *darling* in German is **Schatz** *treasure*, **Schätzchen** *little treasure* or **Liebling** *favourite*, used by both men and women. More informally there's **Schnucki** *sweetie pie*. Germans also go in for calling their loved ones by animal names: **Hase/Hasi** *hare*, **Maus/Mäuschen** *mouse/little mouse*, **Bär/Bärchen** *bear/little bear.*

Don't be offended if your German beloved calls you **Dickerchen** *little dumpling*. Although it comes from the word **dick** *fat*, it really is a term of endearment.

greeting people with confidence

hello

Guten Morgen. *Hello. Good morning.*
Guten Tag. *Hello. Good afternoon.*
Guten Abend. *Hello. Good evening.*
Grüß Gott. *Hello.* (southern Germany)
Hallo. *Hi.*
Servus. *Hi.* (in southern Germany)

Guten Morgen, Guten Tag and **Guten Abend** are fairly formal and often used together with the person's name: **Guten Tag, Frau Weber**. More informally, the **Guten** can be dropped, so you might simply hear **Morgen!**
Hallo is friendly and suitable for most situations; it's also used to catch someone's attention. There's also **Hi**, common among young people and very informal, as is **Servus**.

It's normal to shake hands in business and formal situations. Kissing – twice, once on each cheek – is common among good friends, or they might give each other a hug.

how are you?

Wie geht es dir/Ihnen? *How are you?* **(du/Sie)**
Wie geht's? *How's it going?*
Gut, danke. *Fine, thank you.*
... und dir/Ihnen? *... and you?* **(du/Sie)**
When young people meet, they often ask each other **Alles klar?** *What's up?* lit. *Is everything clear?*

The above are not the casual *Hi, how are you?* that's often said in English with no expectation of a reply – they require an answer. While **Gut, danke** is perfectly adequate, there are alternatives:

Danke, mir geht's gut. *Thanks, I'm fine.*
Mir geht es sehr gut, danke. *I'm very well, thank you.*
Gut, und selbst? *Fine, and you?*
Super. *Great.*
Nicht schlecht. *Not bad.*
Nicht so gut. *Not so good.*
Geht so. *OK. So-so.*
Könnte schlechter sein. *Could be worse.*
Schlecht. *Bad.*

farewells

Auf Wiedersehen. *Goodbye.*
Auf Wiederschauen. *Goodbye.* (southern Germany and Austria)
Auf Wiederhören. *Goodbye.* (on the phone)
Tschüss. *'Bye.*
Gute Nacht. *Goodnight.*
Träum was Schönes. *Sweet dreams.*

Auf Wiedersehen/Wiederschauen is formal and can be used at any time of day. Its literal and original meaning is *until we see each other again*. You will also hear the Italian **Ciao** *'bye*, sometimes written the German way **Tschau**. The southern German greeting **Servus** can also mean *'bye*.

Schönen Tag and **Schönen Abend** can be used when parting. They mean *have a good day/evening*. In Germany, you may hear an additional **noch**, which can mean *still* or *also* but in this context doesn't add anything to the meaning: **Schönen Tag noch**.

Tschüss Luca.
Auf Wiedersehen, Herr Winkler.
Auf Wiederhören, Frau Doktor.
Tschau Stefan. Schönen Tag noch.
Gute Nacht, Schatz (*darling*). **Träum was Schönes.**
Ich wünsche dir/Ihnen einen schönen Abend. *I hope you have a nice evening.*
Danke für den wunderschönen Abend. *Thank you for a lovely evening.*

see you ...

Bis morgen. Bis später. *See you tomorrow. See you later.*
Bis bald. *See you soon.*
Bis dann./Bis gleich. *See you.*
Wir sehen uns ... *See you ...*
  ... im Büro. *... in the office.*
  ... beim Mittagessen. *... at lunch.*
  ... nach dem Abendessen. *... after dinner.*
  ... heute Abend. *... this evening.*
  ... nächste Woche. *... next week.*
Okay. *OK.*

meeting people

Just as in English, the key words for introductions come from the verb **sein** *to be*, an essential verb to know.

ich bin	*I am*	**wir** sind	*we are*
du bist	*you are*	**ihr** seid	*you are*
er ist	*he, it is*	**sie** sind	*they are*
sie ist	*she, it is*	**Sie** sind	*you are*
es ist	*it is*		

introducing yourself

Ich bin Jon/Jessica. *I'm Jon/Jessica.*
Ich bin nicht Laura/Oskar. *I'm not Laura/Oskar.*
Ich bin hier im Urlaub. *I'm here on holiday.*
Ich bin geschäftlich hier. *I'm here on business.*
Ich heiße Jon/Jessica. *My name's Jon/Jessica.*
Mein Name ist Jon/Jessica. *My name is Jon/Jessica.*
Mein Familienname ist Collins. *My surname is Collins.*

Nicht *not* is used before names but you need **kein** (m) or **keine** (f and pl) before an ordinary noun:
Wir sind nicht Herr und Frau McDonald. *We're not Mr and Mrs McDonald.*
Er ist kein Tourist/Sie ist keine Touristin. *He/She's not a tourist.*
Wir sind keine Touristen. *We're not tourists.*

responding

Sehr erfreut. *Very pleased to meet you.*
Freut mich, dich kennenzulernen. *Pleased to meet you.* **(du)**
Es freut mich, Sie kennenzulernen. *I'm pleased to meet you.* **(Sie)**
Ebenfalls. *Likewise. Pleased to meet you too.*
(Sehr) angenehm. *I'm delighted to make your acquaintance.* (very formal)
Herzlich willkommen. *A warm welcome. Welcome.*

finding the right person

Bist du Hannah? *Are you Hannah?*
Sind Sie Herr Wolff? *Are you Mr Wolff?*
Frau Davies, nicht wahr? *Mrs Davies, isn't it?*
Seid ihr die MacLeods? *Are you the MacLeods?*

spelling names

You'll often be asked how you spell your name or want to know how someone else spells theirs. The key question is **Wie schreibt man das?** Literally, *How is it written?*

If you're speaking face to face and it's convenient to do so, you can just say **Das schreibt man** *that's written* and write your name down. Otherwise, on the phone for instance, you'll need to spell it out using the names of the letters in German, beginning **Ich buchstabiere**, literally *I spell.*

how to say the letters in German

a *ah*	b *beh*	c *tseh*	d *deh*
e *eh*	f *ef*	g *geh*	h *hah*
i *ee*	j *yot*	k *kah*	l *el*
m *em*	n *en*	o *oh*	p *peh*
q *kuh*	r *air*	s *ess*	t *teh*
u *uh*	v *fow*	w *veh*	x *iks*
y *ipsilon*	z *tsett*		

Doppel-m *Double m*

Mein Name ist Williams. Ich buchstabiere: veh, ee, Doppel-el, ee, ah, em, ess.
Mein Name ist Joseph. Ich buchstabiere: yot, oh, ess, eh, peh, hah. Aber alle nennen mich Joe. *My name is Joseph. I'll spell it: j, o, s, e, p, h. But everyone calls me Joe.*

Two dots over a vowel is called an umlaut:
ä a-Umlaut
ö o-Umlaut
ü u-Umlaut

ß is **scharfes s** (literally *sharp s*) or **eszett** (literally *s-z*)

It's well worth working out how to spell out your own name in German and committing it to memory.

introductions

You can introduce someone with **das ist** *this is.*

wordbank

Das ist ...	**Das ist ...**
mein Mann *my husband*	**meine Frau** *my wife*
mein Großvater *my grandfather*	**meine Großmutter** *my grandmother*
mein Vater *my father*	**meine Mutter** *my mother*
mein Bruder *my brother*	**meine Schwester** *my sister*
mein Sohn *my son*	**meine Tochter** *my daughter*
mein Stiefsohn *my stepson*	**meine Stieftochter** *my stepdaughter*
mein Onkel *my uncle*	**meine Tante** *my aunt*
mein Cousin *my cousin* (m)	**meine Cousine** *my cousin* (f)
mein Schwiegersohn *my son-in-law*	**meine Schwiegertochter** *my daughter-in-law*
mein Schwiegervater *my father-in-law*	**meine Schwiegermutter** *my mother-in-law*

Das ist mein Kollege Jack. *This is my colleague Jack.*
Das ist meine Kollegin Laura. *This is my colleague Laura.*
Das ist mein Freund Oskar. *This is my friend Oskar.*
Das ist meine gute Freundin Mila. *This is my good friend Mila.*
Das ist meine Verlobte Anna. *This is my fiancée Anna.*
Das ist Frau Klein, meine Nachbarin. *This is Mrs Klein, my neighbour.*
Oliver ist mein jüngerer/älterer Bruder. *Oliver is my younger/older brother.*
Und das ist Richards Schwester. *And this is Richard's sister.*
Das ist Anton, Peters Lebenspartner. *This is Anton, Peter's (civil) partner.*

In German an apostrophe isn't needed before **s** to show possession: **Marias Mann** *Maria's husband,* **Richards Schwester** *Richard's sister.* More colloquially, you might hear **von** *of* used instead: **der Partner von Tobias** *Tobias's partner, the partner of Tobias.*

To introduce more than one person you use **das sind.**
Das sind meine Kinder. *These are my children.*
Das sind meine Eltern. *These are my parents.*
Das sind meine Freunde Heinrich und Natascha. *These are my friends Heinrich and Natascha.*

A more formal way of introducing someone is with **darf ich ... vorstellen** *may I introduce ...* The person you're introducing needs to be in the accusative case, but you only need to remember this if it's a single male as otherwise the word for *my* is the same as in the nominative case (see page 177).

Darf ich meinen Mann vorstellen? *May I introduce my husband?*
Darf ich meine Kollegin vorstellen? *May I introduce my colleague* (f).
Darf ich meine Schwestern vorstellen? *May I introduce my sisters?*

You can add **Ihnen** *to you* **(Sie)**.
Darf ich Ihnen meine Kollegin Laura vorstellen? *Let me introduce (to you) my colleague Laura.*
Darf ich Ihnen meinen Vater vorstellen? *May I introduce my father to you?*

If you're talking to people you call **du** or **ihr, Ihnen** is replaced by **dir** or **euch.**
Darf ich dir meinen Bruder Erik vorstellen? *May I introduce my brother Erik to you?*
Darf ich euch meine Frau vorstellen? *May I introduce my wife to you?*
Darf ich dir meine Kollegen Jan und Anselm vorstellen? *Let me introduce (to you) my colleagues Jan and Anselm.*

Vorstellen is an example of a separable verb. In the present tense, **vor** separates off and moves to the end.
Ich stelle dir meinen Freund Max vor. *Let me introduce my friend Max.*
Ich stelle dir meine Lebenspartnerin Pia vor. *Let me introduce my (civil) partner Pia.*
Ich stelle euch Oskar vor: wir sind Sandkastenfreunde. *Let me introduce Oskar: we're childhood friends.* lit. *sandpit friends*
German has many separable verbs that work on the same principle, explained on page 51.

Practise introducing members of your family and circle of friends. Photos are useful props; you can point at people and say who they are.

Include some detail, such as my younger sister, my older cousin, my good friend. Remember to match mein and meine to the right genders and to use the accusative case if you're using vorstellen to introduce one male: darf ich meinen Cousin vorstellen? Make sure you can introduce yourself too and spell your name.

It's much more effective if you do all this out loud rather than in your head. And when you've finished, write down two or three of your introductions.

basic courtesies

Entschuldigen Sie, bitte
Entschuldigung *Excuse me*
Verzeihung

Verzeihen Sie mir, bitte. *Excuse me, forgive me*
Macht nichts. *It doesn't matter.*
Keine Ursache. *Don't worry about it* (lit. *no reason to apologise*).

There are several ways of saying *thank you*. Simplest is **danke** *thank you*. To express more heartfelt thanks, there's also:
danke schön *thank you very much*
vielen Dank *many thanks*
ich bedanke mich *many thanks* (lit. *I express my thanks*)
ich danke dir/euch herzlichst *thank you so much* **(du/ihr)**
ich danke Ihnen herzlich *thank you very much* **(Sie)**

bitte *please*
Bitte is a very useful word. In addition to meaning *please*, it is also the response to **danke,** the equivalent of *don't mention it*. **Bitte schön** is the response to **danke schön.**
It's also used in the sense of *please do, after you, here you are, at your service,* and *can I help you?* when said by a shop assistant or waiter.
Darf ich? *Excuse me, May I?* (e.g. when you want to come in, squeeze past)
Bitte *of course, go ahead.*

Other ways of responding to **danke** and **danke schön** include:
Gern geschehen. *My pleasure.*
Nichts zu danken. *Don't mention it.*
Kein Problem. *No problem.*
You'll also hear **gern** or **gerne,** both meaning *gladly, of course* and used interchangeably.
Entschuldigung, kannst du mir helfen? *Can you help me?* **Gerne.** *Sure, Of course.*

Störe ich Sie gerade? *Am I disturbing you?* **Nein, gar nicht.** *Not at all.*
Mach es dir bequem/Macht es euch bequem/Machen Sie es sich bequem. *Make yourself/yourselves comfortable.* **(du, ihr, Sie)**
Bitte bediene dich/bedient euch/bedienen Sie sich. *Help yourself/ yourselves.* **(du, ihr, Sie)**

talking the talk

The **Talking the Talk** page towards the end of each chapter sets out the transcript of the informal conversations between the presenters on the audio.
Listen to the conversation first – at least a couple of times – before you read it here. Assuming that you have worked through the chapter, you'll probably be able to get the gist and pick out some details. At the same time you'll be getting familiar with the rhythm of German.
Don't stop at that. You'll find practical ideas in your Audio Support Pack on how to make the most of these conversations, how to use them to develop your listening skills.

Volker	Claudia, darf ich dir meinen Cousin Tobias und meine Cousine Miriam vorstellen?
Claudia	Sehr erfreut.
Volker	Und das ist meine Tante Anna.
Anna	Sehr erfreut.
Claudia	Es freut mich, Sie alle kennenzulernen. Herzlich willkommen!

Jan	Und das ist meine Tochter Mia.
Claudia	Hallo, Mia.

Volker	Darf ich euch meinen Onkel vorstellen? ... Und das ist meine gute Freundin Julia. Julia, ich stelle dir Claudia vor.
Julia	Sehr erfreut.
Frau	Das ist mein Sohn Markus.
Volker	Freut mich, dich kennenzulernen, Markus. Wie geht's?
Markus	Gut danke. Und dir?
Julia	Entschuldigung. Wo ist Jan?

checkpoint 1

1. How would you greet someone at 8 p.m.?
2. What is the response to **danke schön**?
3. Would you use **du** or **Sie** when speaking to a close friend's elderly grandmother?
4. When might you hear **Auf Wiederhören**?
5. If someone trying to squeeze past you on a crowded bus said **Darf ich?** what would you say in response?
6. One way of telling someone your name is **Mein Name ist** ... What's another way?
7. At a party, would you say **Herzlich willkommen** or **Sehr erfreut** when you are introduced to your host?
8. What word for *my* is missing in this sentence, said as you introduce your friend Max: **Darf ich euch .... Freund Max vorstellen**?
9. Is your daughter's husband your **Stiefsohn** or your **Schwiegersohn**?
10. How would you attract the attention of a waiter in a restaurant?
11. When you leave a shop, is the sales assistant more likely to say **Guten Tag** or **Schönen Tag** to you?
12. If a friend replies **Schlecht** to your question **Wie geht's?** would it be more appropriate to commiserate or give them a high five?
13. Which word would you add to **Ich bin .... Rachel** to mean *I am not Rachel*?
14. How do you write the letter of the German alphabet **eszett**?
15. If you were introducing your two sisters to someone, would you say **Das ist meine Schwester** or **Das sind meine Schwestern**?
16. Which one of these expressions wouldn't you use if you wanted to offer your heartfelt thanks: **danke schön, nichts zu danken, vielen Dank**?
17. If someone says to you **Darf ich meine Kollegen vorstellen?** are they introducing one colleague or more than one?
18. Given that you'd say **Wo wohnst du?** to ask one friend where they live, how would you ask two friends the same thing?
19. If someone says to you at a party **Bedienen Sie sich**, what are you being invited to do?
20. What two small differences would you make to write the English *Anna's partner* in German?

zwei
getting to know people

Germans are welcoming and friendly but not gushingly so. They make a clear distinction between their public and private selves, and don't tend to strike up conversations with strangers on the bus or train. They go in more for **reservierte Freundlichkeit**, a cautious or reserved friendliness.

You will get to know people though, and this implies that you'll be telling them about yourself and answering questions. It's well worth becoming thoroughly familiar with the words you need to do this and practising some complete sentences.

A good conversation is a two-way process which involves asking as well as answering questions. Closed questions such as *Do you work here?* or *Have you been there before?* can result in simple *yes* or *no* answers. Open questions, on the other hand, elicit more information; this type of question uses words such as **wo** *where?*, **wann** *when?*, **warum** *why?*

You'll probably need to establish early on that you're keen to speak German, otherwise people may be equally keen to practise their English on you.
Könnten wir bitte auf Deutsch sprechen? *Could we speak in German?*
Ich möchte auf Deutsch sprechen. *I'd like to speak in German.*
Ich möchte lieber auf Deutsch sprechen. *I'd prefer to speak in German.*
Ich möchte mein Deutsch üben. *I'd like to practise my German.*
Ich brauche mehr Übung. *I need more practice.*

asking questions

When using a question word, the verb goes straight after it without words like *is/do/does/did:* **Wo arbeitet er?** *Where does he work?*

Wann **ist sein/ihr Geburtstag?** *When's his/her birthday?*
Wann habt ihr geheiratet? *When did you get married?*
Wann fahren sie weg? *When are they leaving?*
Bis wann sind Sie hier? *Until when are you here?*

Wie **geht's?** *How are things? How are you?*
Wie alt sind Ihre Kinder? *How old are your children?* **(Sie)**
Wie heißt deine jüngere Schwester? *What's your younger sister called?*
Wie sagt man ... auf Deutsch? *How do you say ... in German?*
Wie lange bleibst du noch hier? *How much longer are you staying here?*
Wie ist das Hotel? *What's the hotel like?*

Wie viel **Gepäck haben Sie?** *How much luggage have you got?*
Um wie viel Uhr treffen wir uns? *What time are we meeting?*

Wie viele **Kinder haben Sie?** *How many children have you got?*
Wie viele Leute werden da sein? *How many people will be there?*

Wievielmal/Wie viele Male **wart ihr schon in Berlin?** *How many times have you been to Berlin before?*
Wievielmal/Wie viele Male haben Sie sich schon getroffen? *How many times have you already met?*

Was **willst du?** *What do you want?*
Was wollen wir machen? *What shall we do?*
Was meinst du? *What do you think?*
Was ist passiert? *What's the matter? What's happened?*

Was für ein **Zimmer möchten Sie?** *What sort of room would you like?*
Was für eine Gegend ist das? *What sort of area is it?*
In was für einer Gegend wohnt ihr? *What sort of area do you live in?*
Mit was für einem Zug möchten Sie fahren? *What sort of train would you like to travel by?*
Was für Leute kommen hierher? *What sort of people come here?*

Wo **bist du/sind Sie geboren?** *Where were you born?*
Wo ist Ihre Kollegin? *Where is your colleague (f)?*

If movement to a place is involved, then *where* is **wohin**. *Where from* is **woher**.
Wohin gehst du heute Morgen? *Where are you going (to) this morning?*
Wohin wollen wir uns setzen? *Where shall we sit?*
Woher kommen Sie? *Where are you from? Where do you come from?*
Woher wissen Sie das? *How do you know that?* lit. *from where*
Woher kennst du ihn? *How do you know him?*

Wohin and **woher** can separate out.
Wo gehst du heute Morgen hin? *Where are you going (to) this morning?*
But **woher** only separates with verbs of motion, and it affects the meaning.
Wo kommen Sie her? *Where have you (just) come from?*

Combined with prepositions, **wo** loses the meaning *where*:
Worauf warten wir? *What are we waiting for?*
Worüber sprecht ihr? *What are you talking about?*

Warum gefällt euch diese Gegend? *Why do you like this area?* **(ihr)**
Warum ist Theo nicht mitgekommen? *Why hasn't Theo come too?*
Warum hat der Zug Verspätung? *Why is the train delayed?*

wer (nom), **wen** (acc), **wessen** (gen), **wem** (dat)? *who? whom? whose?*
Wer ist der Hauptgeschäftsführer? *Who's the CEO?*
Wer sind die Leute da drüben? *Who are those people over there?*
Wer ist an der Reihe? *Whose turn is it?*
Wen kennst du in Österreich? *Who(m) do you know in Austria?*
Wessen Schlüssel sind das? *Whose keys are these?*
Mit wem bist du gekommen? *With whom did you come?*

Welcher/Welche agrees with the noun it refers to.
Welches Lied gefällt dir? *Which song do you like?* **(du)**
Welche Filme gefallen dir? *Which films do you like?* **(du)**
Welchen Fußballverein unterstützt ihr? *Which football team do you support?*
Wir haben viele Kuchen. *We have a lot of cakes.*
    Welchen möchten Sie? *Which one would you like?*
    Welche möchten Sie? *Which ones would you like?*

breaking the ice

To meet people and put your German into practice you might want to start a conversation, whether with someone staying next door, attending the same business meeting, standing in a queue, sitting next to you in a concert or restaurant, or admiring the same view.

Sind Sie hier im Urlaub? *Are you here on holiday?*
Sind Sie geschäftlich hier? *Are you here on business?*
Sind Sie hier wegen der Meisterschaften? *Are you here for the championships?*
Sind Sie hier auf der Messe/Ausstellung? *Are you here for the trade fair/the exhibition?*
Sind hier immer so viele Leute? *Are there always so many people here?*
Ist es nicht schön hier? *Isn't this a beautiful place?*
Was für eine Aussicht! *What a view!*
Seid wann sind Sie hier in Wien? *How long have you been here in Vienna?*
Bist du/seid ihr/sind Sie zum ersten Mal hier? *Is this the first time you've been here?*
Sind wir nicht im gleichen Hotel? *Aren't we at the same hotel?*
Wie heißt dieses Gebäude da drüben? *What's the name of that building over there?*
Kann ich dir/euch/Ihnen helfen? *Can I lend a hand?* **(du/ihr/Sie)**
Hast du eine Ahnung, wo man Karten kaufen kann? *Any idea where you buy tickets?*
Was für ein herrliches Wetter! *What amazing weather!*
Ist dieser Platz frei? *Is this seat free?*
Macht es dir/euch Spaß? *Are you having fun?* **(du/ihr)**
Das Programm ist sehr interessant, nicht wahr? *It's an interesting programme, isn't it?*

Adding **nicht wahr** (sometimes shortened to **nicht**) or **oder** to your question is like adding an English question tag such as *isn't it? does she? aren't you? won't they? haven't we? didn't it?*
Sie arbeiten hier, oder?/Sie arbeiten hier, nicht wahr? *You work here, don't you?*
Sie arbeiten nicht hier, oder? *You don't work here, do you?*
You'll also hear **gell** used colloquially in southern Germany.
Das ist die Führerin, gell? *That's the guide, right?*

sharing information

As you get to know people, the more information you tend to share and the more detail you get into.

To talk about nationality, German uses nouns (Englishman), not adjectives (English).

A man says **Ich bin ...** *I'm ...*
Amerikaner American, **Australier** Australian, **Brite** British, **Engländer** English, **Ire** Irish, **Kanadier** Canadian, **Schotte** Scottish, **Waliser** Welsh.

A woman says **Ich bin ...** *I'm ...*
Amerikanerin American, **Australierin** Australian, **Britin** British, **Engländerin** English, **Irin** Irish, **Kanadierin** Canadian, **Schottin** Scottish, **Waliserin** Welsh.

Meine Mutter ist Schottin. *My mother is Scottish.*
Mein Partner ist Franzose/Meine Partnerin ist Französin. *My partner* (m/f) *is French.*
Unsere Schwiegertochter ist Schweizerin. *Our daughter-in-law is Swiss.*
Mein Ex ist Österreicher/Meine Ex ist Österreicherin. *My ex* (m/f) *is Austrian.*
Mein Urgroßvater war Deutscher. *My great-grandfather was German.*
Meine Großmutter war Deutsche. *My grandmother was German.*
Meine Neffen/Meine Nichten/Meine Schwiegereltern sind Deutsche. *My nephews/nieces/in-laws are German.*

You use **sein** *to be* (page 18) when talking about your personal life too.

Ich bin ...
ledig, unverheiratet *single*, **in einer Beziehung** *in a relationship*, **verlobt** *engaged*, **verheiratet** *married*, **in einer Lebenspartnerschaft lebend** *in a civil partnership*, **getrennt lebend** *separated*, **geschieden** *divorced*, **verwitwet** *widowed*
hetero *straight*, **homo, schwul** *gay*, **lesbisch** *lesbian*, **bi, bisexuell** *bisexual.*

Ich bin alleinerziehender Vater/alleinerziehende Mutter. *I'm a single father/mother.*
Wir sind Pflegeeltern. *We're foster parents.*
Wir sind zusammen. *We're going out with each other.* lit. *We're together.*

Wie alt bist du? *How old are you?*
Ich bin einundzwanzig (Jahre alt). *I'm 21 (years old).*
Meine Mutter ist achtzig (Jahre alt). *My mother is 80 (years old).*
Wirklich? Sie sieht viel jünger aus. *Really? She looks much younger.*
Wie alt sind Ihre Kinder? *How old are your children?* **(Sie)**
Die Zwillinge sind sieben. *The twins are seven.*
Sie sehen älter als sieben aus. *They look older than seven.*

haben *to have*

To talk about your family, you'll need the verb **haben** *to have.*

ich habe	*I have (got)*	**wir** haben	*we have*
du hast	*you have*	**ihr** habt	*you have*
er hat	*he has*	**sie** haben	*they have*
sie hat	*she has*	**Sie** haben	*you have*
es hat	*it has*		

Hast du Kinder? *Do you have children?*
Haben Sie Enkel? *Have you got any grandchildren?*

Ich habe/wir haben ... *I/we have ...*
- **... einen Bruder/eine Schwester.** *... a/one brother, sister.*
- **... vier Brüder/Schwestern/Geschwister.** *...four brothers/sisters/siblings.*
- **... einen Sohn/eine Tochter.** *... a son/a daughter.*
- **... drei Söhne/Töchter/Kinder.** *... three sons/daughters/children.*
- **... zwei kleine Kinder.** *... two young children.*
- **... zwei Adoptivtöchter.** *... two adopted daughters.*
- **... drei erwachsene Kinder.** *... three grown up children.*
- **... einen Enkel/eine Enkelin/ein Enkelkind.** *... a grandson/a granddaughter/a grandchild.*
- **... ein Enkelchen.** *... a tiny little grandson/granddaughter.*
- **... fünf Enkel.** *...five grandchildren.*

Ich habe/Wir haben keine Kinder. *I/We don't have children.*
Sie hat keinen Bruder. *She hasn't got a brother.*

Haben isn't, of course, restricted to talking about family members. It's one of the most used verbs in German, essential in all sorts of contexts.

Sie hat ein großes Haus mit Garten *She's got a large house with a garden*
... aber das Haus hat keine Terrasse. *... but the house doesn't have a terrace.*
Wir haben ein deutsches Auto. *We've got a German car.*
Haben Sie Haustiere? *Have you got any pets?*
Wir haben einen Hund und zwei Katzen. *We have a dog and two cats.*
Ich habe Kopfschmerzen. *I've got a headache.*
Das Baby hat Schluckauf. *The baby's got hiccups.*
Sie hat blaue Augen. *She has blue eyes.*
Er hat ein goldenes Herz. *He's got a heart of gold.*
Sie hat ein Elefantengedächtnis. *She's got a memory like an elephant.*

German often uses **haben** + noun where English uses a different verb.
Hunger haben *to be hungry* **Durst haben** *to be thirsty*
Angst haben *to be afraid* **Recht haben** *to be right*
Unrecht haben *to be wrong* **Heimweh haben** *to be homesick*
gute/schlechte Laune haben *to be in a good/bad mood*
Lust haben *to want to, to feel like*

Ich habe keine Angst. *I'm not scared.*
Sie haben Recht. *You're right.*
Ich habe so einen großen Durst. *I'm really thirsty.*
Unser Hund hat Heimweh, der Arme. *Our dog's homesick, poor thing.*
Sie hat immer gute Laune. *She's always in a good mood.*
Habt ihr Lust, ins Café zu gehen? *Do you feel like going to the café?*

And you'll also come across **haben** in several everyday expressions, where the English equivalent doesn't feature the word *have.*
Was hast du denn? *What's up? What's the matter?*
Hast du was? *Is anything up? Is there anything the matter?*
Wann hast du Urlaub? *When's your holiday?*
Den Wievielten haben wir heute?/Welches Datum haben wir heute? *What's the date today?*
Wir haben den Fünfzehnten. *It's the 15th.*

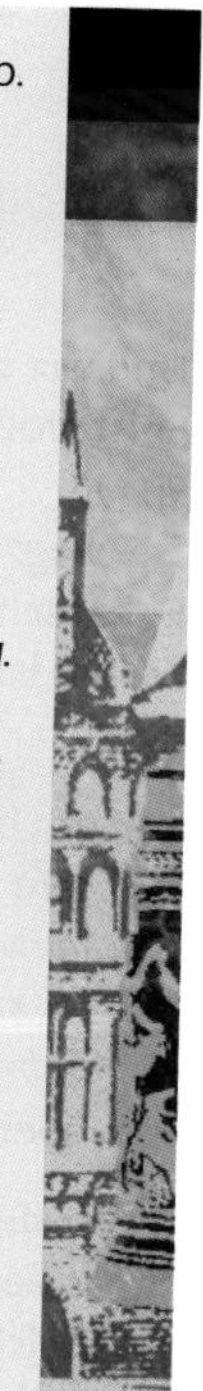

describing people

You need adjectives to describe people.
Wie ist Nils/Klaudia? *What's Nils/Klaudia like?*
Nils ist lieb und freundlich. *Nils is lovely and friendly.*
Klaudia ist immer heiter. *Klaudia is always cheerful.*
Wie sind Ihre Kollegen? *What are your colleagues like?*
Sie sind meistens kompetent. *They're mostly competent.*

When adjectives are followed by a noun, their endings might need to change (page 178).
Mein lieber Freund Leon. *My dear friend Leon.*
Ich habe nette Kollegen. *I have nice colleagues.*
Seine Tochter ist ein heiteres Mädchen. *His daughter's a cheerful girl.*
Wer ist der dünne Mann/die dünne Frau da drüben? *Who's the thin man/woman over there?*

Und wie sieht er/sie aus? *And what does he/she look like?*
Er ist groß. Er ist zwei Meter/ein Meter neunzig groß. *He's tall. He's 2 m/1 m 90 tall.*
Sie wiegt ungefähr siebzig Kilo. *She weighs about 70 kg.*
Er hat schwarze/braune/blaue Augen. *He has black/brown/blue eyes.*
Sie hat lange/kurze/glatte/lockige Haare. *She has long/short/straight/curly hair.*

You can bring your descriptions to life with:

- **sehr** *very*, **nicht sehr** *not very*, **echt** *really*, **ganz** *quite*, **ziemlich** *rather, fairly* **ein bisschen** *a bit*, **äußerst** *extremely*, **so** *so*, **gar nicht** *not at all*, **super** *super, really*, **nicht besonders** *not particularly*, **unglaublich** *unbelievably.*
- **über** *ultra* tacked to the front of an adjective e.g. **überintelligent**

Sie ist super nett. *She's really nice.*
Jonas sieht echt cool aus. *Jonas looks really cool.*
Er ist nicht sehr ehrgeizig. *He's not very ambitious.*
Sie sind nicht besonders begeistert. *They're not particularly keen.*
Karl ist ein bisschen zurückhaltend. *Karl's a bit quiet/reserved.*
Er ist echt intelligent. *He's seriously intelligent.*
Monika ist sehr hübsch, aber so dünn. *Monika is very pretty but so skinny.*
Meine Frau? ... sie ist unglaublich geduldig! *My wife? ... she's incredibly patient!*

wordbank

Try describing a few people – family, friends or celebrities. Use these adjectives and/or look others up in a dictionary. Don't forget to use extras such as sehr, **very**, *ein bisschen* **a bit**, *super or über,* **really, ultra.**

groß *tall*
stämmig *stocky, thickset*
kräftig *strong, burly*
übergewichtig *overweight*
dick *fat*
rundlich *plump, chubby*
blond *blond*
schön *beautiful, handsome*
gut aussehend *good-looking*
fähig *capable, able*
klug *clever*
nett *nice*
freundlich *friendly, kind*
selbstsicher *confident*
gelassen *calm, easy-going*
höflich *polite*
taktvoll *tactful*
zurückhaltend *cautious, reserved*
großmütig *generous*
geduldig *patient*
fleißig *hardworking*
naiv *naïve*
optimistisch *optimistic*
dynamisch *dynamic*
heiter *cheerful*
süß *sweet, cute*
schüchtern *shy*
gutherzig *kind-hearted*
zuverlässig *reliable, trustworthy*
treu *faithful, loyal*
einfühlsam *understanding*
begabt *gifted, talented*
froh *happy*

klein *short, small*
schlank *slim*
musculös *muscular*
dünn *thin, skinny*
zierlich *petite, dainty*
dunkel *dark*
hübsch *pretty*
schlampig *scruffy*
dumm *dumb, stupid*
blöd *silly*
gemein *nasty, mean*
aggressiv *aggressive*
reserviert *reserved*
ängstlich *anxious*
unhöflich *rude*
taktlos *tactless*
impulsiv *impulsive*
selbstsüchtig *selfish*
stur *stubborn, pig-headed*
faul *lazy*
schlau *shrewd, smart*
pessimistisch *pessimistic*
cool *laid-back*
unverfroren *insolent*
frech *cheeky*
kühn *bold*
sensibel *emotionally sensitive*
verantwortungslos *irresponsible*
freimütig *frank, outspoken*
gefühllos *insensitive*
kunstverständig *artistic*
glücklich *happy, fortunate*

gut im Sport/in Sprachen *good at sport/languages*

talking about places

Wo wohnst du/wohnt ihr/wohnen Sie? *Where do you live?*
Wo lebst du/lebt ihr/leben Sie? *Where do you live?*
Wo genau? *Where exactly?*
Wo in England ist das genau? *Whereabouts in England is it?*
Ist das eine große Stadt? *Is it a big town/city?*
Was für eine Stadt ist das? *What sort of town is it?*
Wie ist die Landschaft/Gegend? *What's the landscape/region like?*

Wohnen and **leben** both mean *to live*. You can use both to talk about where you live and who you live with but only **leben** in the wider sense of living as opposed to dwelling/residing. **Wohnen** also means *to stay*.
Wo wohnst du? *Where do you live? Where are you staying?*
Wo lebst du? *Where do you live?*
Ich wohne/lebe in München. *I live in Munich.*
Wir wohnen in einem Bauernhaus. *We're living/staying in a farmhouse.*
Ich wohne/lebe in der Nähe vom Bahnhof. *I live near the station.*
Ich wohne/lebe allein. *I live alone.* **Ich wohne/lebe mit meiner Familie.** *I live with my family.*
Wir wohnen/leben zusammen. *We're living together.*
Ich lebe gut. *I live well.*

Sind Sie in einem Hotel/in einer Wohnung? *Are you in a hotel/an apartment?*
In welchem Hotel sind Sie? *Which hotel are you staying at?*
Wo ist der Campingplatz? Wo befindet sich der Campingplatz? *Where's the campsite?*
Wie groß ist der Wohnkomplex? *How big is the complex?*
Wie ist das Dorf/die Stadt/das Hotel? *What's the village/town/hotel like?*

Gibt es **ein Schwimmbad/einen Tennisplatz?** *Is there a pool/a tennis court?*
Gibt es **einen Spielplatz für kleine Kinder?** *Is there a play area for young children?*
Was für Services und Einrichtungen gibt es? *What services/facilities are there?*
Es gibt kein **Schwimmbad**/keine **Restaurants.** *There's no swimming pool; there are no restaurants.*

Die Gegend, wo wir wohnen, ist ... Unsere Gegend ist ... *The area we live in is ... Our area is ...*

... im Nordosten Englands, im Nordosten des Vereinigten Königreichs. *... in the north east of England/of the UK.*
... in der Grafschaft Cornwall/West Yorkshire. *... in the county of Cornwall/ West Yorkshire.*
... entfernt/städtisch/bergig. *... remote/urban/mountainous.*

Die Stadt, wo ich wohne, ist ... Meine Stadt ist ... *The town where I live is ... My town is ...*

zwischen Cambridge und London. *... between Cambridge and London.*

Der Ort ist ... *The place is ...*

... groß/ziemlich klein. *... big/quite small.*
... voller Menschen/ruhig. *... crowded* (lit. *full of people)/tranquil.*
... aufstrebend. *... up and coming.*
... ein verschlafenes Nest. *... a real backwater.*

Es ist ... Das Hotel ist ... *It is ... The hotel is ...*
... (gast)freundlich und gut ausgestattet. *... welcoming and well-equipped.*
... sehr sauber/ziemlich heruntergekommen. *... spotless/somewhat run-down.*
... gepflegt/ein bisschen verwahrlost. *...well-kept/a bit neglected.*
Es hat auf jeden Fall schon bessere Tage gesehen. *It's definitely seen better days.*
Da kommen wir gerne wieder her. *We always like coming back here.*
Vermeiden Sie es um jeden Preis! Ein schrecklicher Ort. *Avoid at any price! A dreadful place.*

Der Campingplatz/Der Ferienort ... *the campsite/resort ...*

... liegt hundert Meter vom Strand. *... is 100 metres from the beach.*
... ist sonnig/schattig. *... is sunny/shaded.*
... ist sandig/schlammig. *... is sandy/muddy.*

Es gibt viel zu tun. *There's plenty to do.*
Es gibt einen Spielplatz und einen Tennisplatz. *There's a playing field and a tennis court.*

wordbank

Use some of these adjectives to describe places, for example where you live, where someone you know lives, where you last went to on holiday or even somewhere you saw in a film. Bring your descriptions to life with sehr, ziemlich, etc. and words like aber **but, however;** *auch* **also,** *jedoch* **however;** *zudem* **what's more.**

winzig *tiny,* **klein** *small,* **eng** *narrow, cramped*
groß *big,* **ungeheuer** *huge,* **riesig** *enormous*
weitläufig *broad, spacious,* **geräumig** *spacious,* **bequem** *comfortable,* **offen** *open*

neu *new,* **alt** *old*
modern *modern,* **uralt** *ancient,* **historisch** *historic*
altmodisch *dated,* **verfallen** *dilapidated*

ruhig *quiet,*
lebendig *lively,* **belebt** *bustling,* **überfüllt** *congested, busy*

entfernt *remote,* **ländlich** *rural, rustic*
bewaldet *wooded,* **hügelig** *hilly,* **bergig** *mountainous*
zerklüftet *rugged,* **steil** *steep,* **flach** *flat,* **steinig** *stony, rocky*

städtisch *urban*
industriell *industrial,* **zentral** *central,* **touristisch** *touristy*

sonnig *sunny,* **schattig** *shady*
trocken *dry,* **schlammig** *muddy,* **sandig** *sandy,* **luftig** *airy*

sauber *clean,* **makellos** *immaculate,* **luxuriös** *luxurious*
gut ausgestattet *well-equipped,* **gepflegt** *well-kept,* **unverdorben** *unspoilt*
schmutzig *dirty,* **spartanisch** *basic,* **verwahrlost** *neglected,* **verschmutzt** *polluted*

fantastisch *fantastic,* **faszinierend** *fascinating*
wunderschön *superb, wonderful*
grandios *imposing, impressive,* **bezaubernd** *charming*
malerisch *picturesque*

how to remember words

It's all very well having a bank of words to refer to - but how do you remember them?

The key to transferring a word to your long-term memory is to consciously **do something with it**. What you do depends on how you personally learn best - try some of these suggestions and see which suit you.
Don't try and learn too many words at the same time. Aim for about seven or eight at a time, ideally with a connection between them.

- Listen to the words online. If you enter *quiet in German* or *translate into German quiet*, the first search result is likely to be a box containing **ruhig**. Click on the speaker icon and listen to how it's said – as many times as you want. Try it with *historic* and *industrial* to hear where the stress is in the German.
- Say the words out loud – several times. Some people swear by doing this last thing at night, then again the next morning.
- The way words look on a page can make them easier to remember. If you have a visual memory, the unusual arrangement of the words opposite should help you. If so, use a similar technique for your own notes.
- Don't always think in individual words. Sometimes a group of words, e.g. **voller Menschen** *crowded*, **es hat schon bessere Tage gesehen** *it's seen better days* can be more memorable.
- Write words down. It doesn't matter whether you write them on paper or key them in. Keep them in manageable groups rather than an endless list. Highlight words that you think will be the most useful to you (but don't discount others since you never know what someone else is going to say).
- Learn tricky words first. You're going to remember words like **modern**, and **zentral** anyway, so leave them until last.
- Use associations, no matter how silly, to help you remember words. For example, the German for *expensive* is **teuer**, so you could think of one of Toyah Willcox's, or La Toya Jackson's, expensive outfits. For **schlammig** *muddy*, think of slamming something down in the mud.
- Use the words. Use the ones opposite as suggested, but don't stop there. Whenever you're out and about, think of an adjective to describe the places you see. It could be factual: **klein, alt, bergig**; or it could be subjective: **wunderschön, faszinierend**.

a bit of a mouthful!

If you find some German words a mouthful, you're in good company. In his essay **Die schreckliche deutsche Sprache** *The awful German language*, Mark Twain said, "Some words are so long that they have a perspective", and he described them as processions of letters marching majestically across the page, not real words.

In English, when two words are combined to form another term, they frequently remain as two words, or are hyphenated: *swimming pool, great-grandmother*. In German, the two words combine to form one, often long, word:

der Bier**keller** *beer cellar*
der Technologie**park** *technology/science park*
der Urgroß**vater** *great-grandfather*
die Urgroß**mutter** *great-grandmother*
die Schneeball**schlacht** *snowball fight*
das Schwimm**bad** *swimming pool*
das Luxus**hotel** *luxury hotel*
das Bananen**brot** *banana bread*

Some of them can become very long

die Freundschafts**bezeigung** *gesture of friendship*
der Entwicklungs**prozess** *development process*
die Lebensversicherungs**gesellschaft** *life insurance company*
das Elektrizitätsversorgungs**unternehmen** *electric utility company*
die Nahrungsmittel**unverträglichkeit** *food intolerance*
der Bestechungs**skandal** *corruption scandal*
die Fallschirmspringer**schule** *parachuting school*

German doesn't only combine nouns. Where English uses an adjective and a noun, German often prefers to combine two nouns:

der Politikwissen**schaftler** *political scientist* (male)
die Politikwissen**schaftlerin** *political scientist* (female)
die Touristen**stadt** *touristy town*
das Industrie**gebiet** *industrial area*
die Riesen**stadt** *mega-city* (**der Riese** is *giant)*

The gender of a compound word is the same as the gender of its final noun. It's **das Bier** *beer* and **der Keller** *cellar*, so *beer cellar* is **der Bierkeller**. **Hotel** is neuter so **das Luxushotel** *is also neuter.*

Platz (~es, Plätze) m **1** square **Potsdamer** ~ Potsdam Square; **2**. field **Kampf~** *battlefield;* **Spiel~** *playing field.* **3** course: **Golf~** *golf course.* **4** court: **Basketball~** *basketball court;* **Tennis~** *tennis court.* **5** pitch: **Fußball~** *football pitch;* **Hockey~** *hockey pitch.*

m indicates that **Platz** is a masculine noun. The genitive singular and nominative plural are indicated by ~**es** and **Plätze**. So **Kampfplatz, Spielplatz, Golfplatz, Basketballplatz, Tennisplatz, Fußballplatz** and **Hockeyplatz** are all masculine, like **Platz**.

German numbers (pages 190–191) also combine to form single words:
neunundneunzig *99*
einhundertachtunddreißig *138*
fünfhunderttausend *500,000*

And should you ever want to say a number in the thousands with a range of digits, such as 7,596 or 84,235, you'll need
siebentausendfünfhundertsechsundneunzig
vierundachtzigtausendzweihundertfünfunddreißig

Until 2013, the longest legitimate word in German was **das Rindfleischetikettierungsüberwachungsaufgabenübertragungsgesetz** which translates as *law on beef label monitoring*. The word became redundant when the law came off the statute books.
The longest word, with 36 letters, in the authoritative Duden dictionary is **Kraftfahrzeughaftpflichtversicherung**, which means *automobile liability insurance*. **Kraftfahrzeug** is vehicle, and it's often abbreviated to **Kfz** on signs and documents.

Much of what is written about very long German words is apocryphal.
From 1992-96 the word **die Donaudampfschiffahrtselektrizitätenhauptbetriebswerkbauunterbeamtengesellschaft** with 79 letters, meaning *Society for the Subordinate Officials of the Head Office of the Danube Steamship Electricity Services*, was in the record books as the longest word in the world, but there is no evidence that this society ever existed.

talking the talk

Sophie Wer ist Jan?

Volker Jan ist mein jüngerer Bruder. Er ist achtundzwanzig Jahre alt. Er ist schon geschieden. Er hat ein Kind, ein Mädchen, meine Nichte. Sie heißt Mia. Sie ist so unglaublich süß.

Nathalie, seine Ex-Frau, ist Französin und wohnt in der Nähe von Colmar. Mia wohnt mit Nathalie. Jan wohnt allein in Freiburg. Das ist ungefähr fünfzig Kilometer von Colmar. Er hat ein kleines Haus. Das Haus hat keinen Garten, aber es hat eine kleine Terrasse. Freiburg ist eine sehr schöne alte Stadt, sehr historisch.

Sophie Und wie ist Jan?

Volker Er ist sehr intelligent, aber nicht sehr ehrgeizig. Er hat immer gute Laune. Er ist super nett.

Sophie Und wie sieht er aus? Ist er groß?

Volker Er ist ein Meter neunzig groß. Und er ist schlank. Er hat kurze blonde Haare und blaue Augen. Er ist achtundzwanzig Jahre alt, aber er sieht viel jünger aus.

Volker Und du, hast du Geschwister?

Sophie Ja, ich habe einen Bruder. Er heißt Andreas. Er ist fünfundzwanzig Jahre alt und arbeitet in London. Er hat keine Kinder aber er hat viele Haustiere – einen Hund und drei Katzen.

verb practice 1

1 Fill the gaps with the correct forms of **sein** *to be* (page 18), and say what the sentences mean.

a **Mein Bruder........ geschieden.**
b **Wir........ keine Engländer.**
c **Kati........ sehr stur.**
d **Paul und sein Bruder........ Zwillinge.**
e **........Sie Österreicher?**
f **Das Hotel........ sauber und bequem.**
g **Ich........ nicht besonders religiös.**
h **........ ihr verheiratet?**
i **Wie alt........ Ihre Kinder?**
j **Du........ Schottin, nicht wahr?**

2 Now do the same using **haben** *to have.*

a **Ich........ blaue Augen, aber mein Bruder........ braune Augen.**
b **Ingrid........ keine Lust, ins Restaurant zu gehen.**
c **Wie viele Geschwister........ du?**
d **Mein Mann........ schlechte Laune.**
e **Wie viel Gepäck........ ihr?**
f **Du........ zwei Kinder, nicht wahr?**
g **Meine Eltern........ einen kleinen Garten.**
h **........Sie Hunger? Möchten Sie einen Kuchen?**

3 How would you ask these questions in German?

a Is she Canadian or American?
b Are Nadja and Anja twins?
c Does the hotel have a pool?
d Markus is gay, isn't he?
e Are you thirsty? [**du**, **ihr** and **Sie**]
f Is there a terrace?

Have a go at writing about yourself. Include all the information you can but keep it structurally simple. Use ich bin +nationality, your relationship status, your age, what you look like; use ich habe and ich habe kein(e) with at least five nouns, e.g. siblings, children, pets, house; ich wohne + where you live. Now make a list of the questions you would need to ask to get this information from other people.

checkpoint 2

1 What's an alternative word for **nicht wahr** to mean *isn't it, is she, aren't you etc.* at the end of a question?

2 Is **wohnt** or **lebt** the right word for *lives* in **Mein Sohn ..... in einer Parallelwelt.** *My son lives in a parallel universe*?

3 How might you offer to lend your good friend a hand?

4 **wo**, **warum**, **welcher**, **was für**, **wie viele**, **was**, **wer**, **wie viel**, **wann**, **wie**. Rearrange these question words into the order *who, which, why, what, when, where, how, how many, how much, what sort of.*

5 Which of the above question words means *What ... like* in *What's he like/What's it like*?

6 How do you turn **das Hotel hat eine Sauna** *the hotel has a sauna* into *the hotel hasn't a sauna*?

7 If someone says to you **Ich habe Heimweh,** are they likely to be feeling cheerful or a bit down?

8 What does **Lust haben** mean?

9 If **Sie ist Schweizerin** is *She's Swiss*, what's *He's Swiss*?

10 Would you go to a doctor or a dentist if you had **Zahnschmerzen**?

11 If Frau Weber is **ziemlich freundlich** and Frau Müller is **äußerst freundlich**, which of them is the friendlier?

12 *Garden* in German is **der Garten** and *terrace* is **die Terrasse**. What do you think *garden terrace* is, and what gender is it?

13 Which of these means *happy* or *fortunate*: **ängstlich, glücklich, höflich, schrecklich**?

14 If someone asks you **Welchen Kuchen möchtest du?** are they talking about one cake or more than one?

15 What do you need to add to **wir wohnen** to say *we're living together*?

16 Sort these adjectives into pairs with opposite meanings: **alt, kurz, lang, ledig, neu, riesig, sauber, schmutzig, verheiratet, winzig.**

17 What's the difference between **Wir haben den Zwanzigsten** and **Wir sind zwanzig Jahre alt**?

18 How do you tell people you'd like to speak in German?

drei
what do you do?

What do you do? is one of the first questions that tends to be asked when people are getting to know each other.

The subject isn't, of course, confined to the workplace. That said, you may be among the growing number who do have business dealings with Germans, and many people who wouldn't even contemplate tackling negotiations in German would still love to be in a position to chat informally with their counterparts, between meetings, over a meal or in the bar.

It's tempting to suppose that all you need is the language to say what you do and explain your particular role, plus some questions. But when you ask the questions, you need to understand the replies, so don't be too selective in the vocabulary you learn. If you're neither a lawyer nor a postman you're never going to want to say **ich bin Rechtsanwalt** or **ich bin Briefträger** ... but somebody might well say it to you and expect you to understand.

Business hierarchy is more in evidence in German than in English-speaking countries. Professional titles are more prevalent; introductions are likely to consist of a surname or a full name, together with the role in the company. Even if the culture in the places you visit seems to you to be casual, it's as well not to assume that immediate informality will break the ice quickly and forge strong relationships: uninvited use of **du** and first names may instead take some people out of their comfort zone.

what you do

Typical conversations about work start with questions like:
Was sind Sie von Beruf? *What do you do? What's your job?*
Was machen Sie beruflich? *What do you do? What's your job?*
Was arbeiten Sie? *What do you do? What's your job?*
The answer might begin with **Ich bin ...** or **Ich arbeite als ...** *I work as ...* followed by the job. **Ein/eine** *a(n)* are not used with jobs.

> **Ich bin Lehrer, Designer.** *I'm a teacher, a designer.*
> **Ich arbeite als Sporttherapeut in einem Fitnesscenter.** *I work as a sports therapist in a fitness centre.*

For the feminine form, most jobs add **-in** to the masculine:
der Manager, die Managerin *manager*
der Polizist, die Polizistin *police officer*
der Architekt, die Architektin *architect*
der Ingenieur, die Ingenieurin *engineer*

Some feminine forms add an umlaut:
Der Koch, die Köchin *cook*
der Arzt, die Ärztin *doctor*
der Zahnarzt, die Zahnärztin *dentist*
der Rechtsanwalt, die Rechtsanwältin *lawyer*

Some masculine forms ending in **-e** lose that **-e** before adding **-in**:
der Fluglotse, die Fluglotsin *air traffic controller*

If the masculine form ends in -**mann**, the feminine ends in **-frau**:
Der Geschäftsmann, die Geschäftsfrau *businessman/woman*
der Kaufmann, die Kauffrau *trader*

There are a few exceptions:
Er ist Auszubildender; sie ist Auszubildende *he/she is a trainee, an apprentice*
Angestellter/Angestellte *employee* (m/f)
and its compounds:
Büroangestellter/Büroangestellte *office worker* (m/f)
Bankangestellter/Bankangestellte *bank clerk* (m/f)

Some traditionally female occupations are based on feminine nouns. German cannot simply change the gender of these words to make them refer to men, so has coined new words based on **pflegen** *to care for* and **helfen** *to help.*

> **die Krankenschwester, der Krankenpfleger** *nurse*
> **das Kindermädchen, der Kinderpfleger** *nanny*
> **die Hebamme, der Geburtsspfleger/Geburtshelfer** *midwife*
> **die Tagesmutter, der Tagesvater** *childminder*
> **das Model** *(catwalk) model* refers to both sexes, and it's **der/die Geistliche** for *clergyman/woman*

wordbank

Ausbilder *instructor*
Bankier *banker*
Bauarbeiter *builder*
Berater *counsellor*
Börsenmakler *stockbroker*
Briefträger *postman*
Choreograph *choreographer*
Computerwissenschaftler *computer scientist*
Consultant *consultant*
Dekorateur *decorator*
Dozent *lecturer*
Fahrer *driver*
Küchenchef *chef*
Künstler *artist*
Maler *painter*
Musiker *musician*
Pilot *pilot*
Politiker *politician*
Polizist *policeman*
Programmierer *programmer*
Feuerwehrmann *fire fighter*
Flugbegleiter *flight attendant*
Forscher *researcher*
Fußballspieler *footballer*
Grafikdesigner *graphic designer*
Historiker *historian*
Immobilienmakler *estate agent*
Journalist *journalist*
Klempner *plumber*
Kosmetiker *beautician*, usually **Kosmetikerin**
(Personal) Trainer *(personal) trainer, coach*
Reiseverkehrskaufmann *travel agent*
Rettungsschwimmer *lifeguard*
Sänger *singer*
Schriftsteller *writer*
Verkäufer *salesperson*
Wächter *security guard*
Wissenschaftler *scientist*

jobs you can guess

A large group of nouns end in **-ologe**, and are the equivalent of English nouns ending *-ologist*: **der Radiologe, die Radiologin; der Biologe, die Biologin; der Geologe, die Geologin; der Kardiologe, die Kardiologin.** And several English words have been fully assimilated into German e.g. **der Job, das Consulting, der Boss, der Babysitter, der Designer.**

not the 9 to 5

Ich bin ... *I'm ...*

- **... selbstständig.** *... self employed, I have my own business.*
- **... freiberuflicher Fotograf.** *... a freelance photographer.*
- **... Hausfrau und Mutter.** *... a stay-at-home mother.*
- **... Hausmann.** *... a stay-at-home father.*
- **... Student(in).** *... a student.*
- **... Auszubildende(r).** *... an apprentice.* (f/m)
- **... Praktikant(in).** *... a trainee, an intern.*
- **... zwischen zwei Arbeitsstellen.** *... between jobs.*
- **... arbeitslos.** *... unemployed.*
- **... auf der Suche nach Arbeit.** *... job hunting.*
- **... Rentner(in).** *... retired.*
- **... im vorzeitigen Ruhestand.** *I've taken early retirement.*

Ich arbeite ... *I work ...*

- **... von zu Hause.** *... from home.*
- **... freiberuflich.** *... freelance.*
- **... Vollzeit/Teilzeit.** *... full-time/part-time.*
- **... karitativ.** *I volunteer/ do charity work.*

Ich arbeite nicht. *I don't work.*

To talk about other people, you use ist **is** or arbeitet **works**. Think about a few friends or family members who don't follow a 9-to-5 lifestyle and say out loud what they do. For instance, Mein Sohn ist auf der Suche nach Arbeit; Meine Mutter ist Rentnerin; Mein Partner ist freiberuflicher Designer; Meine Frau arbeitet Vollzeit/arbeitet nicht.

Ich mache ein Jahr Auszeit. *I'm taking a gap year/a year out.*
Ich mache ein Sabbatjahr. *I'm taking a sabbatical (year).*
Ich habe meiner freiwilligen Entlassung zugestimmt. *I've taken voluntary redundancy.*
Ich helfe meiner Tochter. *I help my daughter.*
Wir kümmern uns um die Enkel. *We look after our grandchildren.*

When you've covered verb endings (page 50), you'll be able to convert these to talk about other people too.

work talk

In welcher Firma arbeiten Sie? *For which firm do you work?*
Die Firma means firm or company in any field. A large multinational company is **das Unternehmen**, so if you know that a person works for a large company you can ask: **In welchem Unternehmen arbeiten Sie?**

Ich arbeite bei + dative case ... *I work for ...*
... **NATO/bei Siemens.** *NATO/Siemens.*
... **Robert Bosch GmbH.** *Robert Bosch Ltd* (**GmbH** stands **for Gesellschaft mit beschränkter Haftung**, *company with limited liability*. **Die Gesellschaft** means *corporation*)
... **Carl Zeiss AG** *Carl Zeiss PLC;* **AG** stands for **Aktiengesellschaft** *corporation limited by share ownership*, where **Aktien** means *shares.*

Was ist Ihr Fachgebiet? *What's your field?*
Ich arbeite im Personalbereich. *I work in HR.*
Ich arbeite im Pressebüro. *I work in the media office.*
Ich arbeite in der Verwaltung. *I'm in admin.*
Ich leite die Qualitätskontrolle. *I head Quality Control.*
Ich leite die Abteilung. *I run the department.*
Ich leite ein Team von acht Technikern. *I lead a team of eight technicians.*
Ich bin stellvertretender Geschäftsführer/stellvertretende Geschäftsführerin. *I'm deputy director/assistant manager.* (m/f)
Ich bin Projektkoordinator. *I'm a projects co-ordinator.*
Ich bin Vorarbeiter. *I'm supervisor, foreman.*
Ich bin Abteilungsleiter. *I'm head of department.*
Ich bin Hausmeister. *I'm a caretaker.*

Was genau ist deine/Ihre Funktion? *What exactly is your role?* **(du, Sie)**
Ich bin für die Computertechnik zuständig. *I'm responsible for the computer system.*
Ich bin für die Unternehmenswebsite zuständig. *I look after the company website.*
Ich bin fürs/für das Lager(haus) verantwortlich. *I'm in charge of the warehouse.*
Ich befasse mich mit Arbeitssicherheit. *I deal with Health and Safety.*
Ich bin direkt dem Chef unterstellt. *I answer directly to the boss.*

where you work

Wo arbeitest du/arbeiten Sie? *Where do you work?*

Ich arbeite ... *I work ...*
in **London** *in London*, **in Köln** *in Cologne*, **in Wien** *in Vienna*

in ... *in* ... (followed by the dative case)
einer Arztpraxis *a surgery*
einem Bioladen *a health-food shop*
einem Büro *an office*
einem Callcenter *a call centre*
einem Feinkostladen *a delicatessen*
einer Fabrik *a factory*
einer Gärtnerei *a nursery/garden centre*
einer Grundschule *a primary school*
einem Industriegebiet *an industrial estate*
einer internationalen Bank *an international bank*
einer Kanzlei *a lawyer's office*
einer karitativen Organisation *a charity*
einem Kindergarten *a nursery, kindergarten*
einem Krankenhaus *a hospital*
einer Nachrichtenagentur *a news agency*
einem Pharmaunternehmen *a pharmaceutical plant*
einem Softwareunternehmen *a software company*
einem Supermarkt *a supermarket*
einer Tierhandlung *a pet shop*
einem Fitnesscenter *a gym, fitness centre*
einem Weingut *a winery*
einer Werkstatt *a repair shop, garage*
einem Wettbüro *a betting shop*

When **in** is followed by **dem**, it's often shortened to **im**:
im Einzelhandel *in retail*
im Gesundheitssektor *in the health sector*
im Tourismussektor *in tourism*
im Ministerium für Umwelt *in the Ministry of the Environment*
im öffentlichen Sektor *in the public sector*
in der Forensik *in forensics*
in der Landwirtschaft *in agriculture*
in der Öffentlichkeitsarbeit *in public relations*

auf ... *on* ... + dative case

einem Bauernhof *on a farm* **einer Baustelle** *on a building site*

an *on/at* + dative case is used with institutes and universities. **Am** is short for **an dem**.

an der Universität *at the university*
am Goethe Insitut *at the Goethe Institute*

... and how long you've been doing something

Wie lange machst du/machen Sie das schon? *How long have you been doing that?*
Although English uses *have been doing*, German uses the present tense *are doing* because the action is still going on. To talk about the length of time you've been doing something (*since* or *for*), you use **seit** or **schon seit** followed by the dative case, or **schon** followed by the accusative case.

Ich arbeite als Zollbeamter seit ... *I've been a customs officer for ...*
... sechs Monaten. *... six months.*
... anderthalb Jahren. *... a year and a half.*
... mehr als zehn Jahren. *... more than ten years.*

Ich arbeite hier (schon) seit ... *I've been working here since ...*
... letztem Jahr. *... last year.*
... September. *... September.*
... zweitausenddreizehn *.... 2013.*

Ich mache diese Arbeit schon ... *I've been doing this work for ...*
... zwanzig Jahre. *... for twenty years.*
... lange. *... for a long time.*
... länger, als ich denken kann. *... for longer than I care to remember.*

Try saying what you, your family or friends do and the places where you all work. Use ich bin, ich arbeite, er/sie ist **he/she is**, *er/sie arbeitet* **he/she works** *als/in/bei: Meine Mutter ist Zahnärztin; sie arbeitet in einem Krankenhaus; mein Partner ist Programmierer; er arbeitet in einem deutschen Unternehmen/bei BMW.*

how verbs work

Ich arbeite *I work* and **ich wohne** *I live* come from **arbeiten** *to work* and **wohnen** *to live*. These are infinitives, which are the forms used in a dictionary – and nearly every German infinitive has the ending **-en**. Removing that **-en** leaves you with a stem, **arbeit-**, **wohn-**, to which you add different endings, according to who is carrying out the action of the verb.

Present tense endings for almost every verb in German are:

ich *I*	-e
du *you*	-(e)st*
er/sie/es *he/she/it*	-(e)t*
wir *we*	-en
ihr *you*	-(e)t*
sie *they*	-en
Sie *you*	-en

* The extra (**e**) is used with stems ending in **-t** or **-d** to make the words easier to pronounce: **er wohnt** *he lives* but **er arbeitet** *he works.*

heißen *to be called*	**ich heiß**e *I am called* **sie heiß**t *she is called*
kommen *to come*	**du komm**st, **ihr komm**t, **Sie komm**en *you come/are coming*
machen *to make, do*	**wir mach**en *we do/are doing, make/are making*
warten *to wait*	**du wart**est, **ihr wart**et, **Sie wart**en *you wait/are waiting*

Some verbs undergo a change in the stem in the **du** and **er/sie/es** forms.

essen *to eat*	**ich esse** *I eat*, **du isst** *you eat*, **er isst** *he eats*
geben *to give*	**ich gebe** *I give*, **er/sie gibt** *he/she's giving*
helfen *to help*	**ich helfe** *I help*, **er/sie hilft** *he/she's helping*
fahren *to go, travel*	**ich fahre** *I go*, **du fährst** *you go/are going*
nehmen *to take*	**ich nehme** *I take*, **er nimmt** *he takes/is taking*
sprechen *to speak*	**ich spreche** *I speak*, **sie spricht** *she speaks*

separable verbs

Many German verbs begin with a separable prefix, which in the present tense separates from the main body of the verb and goes to the end of the clause or sentence. Common separable prefixes are: **ab-, an-, auf-, hin-, mit-, vor-, weg-, zu-, zurück-**

ankommen *to arrive*
aufstehen *to get up*
mitkommen *to come along/too*
wegfahren *to leave, depart*
vorstellen *to introduce*
zurückkommen *to come back*

Wir kommen am Dienstag an. *We're arriving on Tuesday.*
Um wie viel Uhr kommt der Zug an? *At what time does the train arrive?*
Ich stehe um 8 Uhr auf. *I get up at 8 o'clock.*
Kommst du mit? *Are you coming with us? Will you join us?*
Ich stelle euch Oskar vor. *Let me introduce Oskar to you.*
Wir fahren morgen weg, aber wir kommen bestimmt nächstes Jahr zurück. *We're leaving tomorrow, but we'll definitely come back next year.*

In the infinitive, the two parts join up again. If **zu** is needed before the infinitive, which it is when the infinitive follows any other verb but a modal (see Chapter 8, starting on page 121), it goes between the prefix and the main body of the verb.
Ich möchte um sieben Uhr aufstehen. *I'd like to get up at 7 o'clock.*
Hast du Lust mitzukommen? *Would you like to come with us?*
Ich habe Angst wegzufahren. *I'm afraid to leave.*

inseparable verbs

Another large group of verbs begin with an inseparable prefix. They never separate. In the present tense, inseparable verbs simply behave like verbs without a prefix. Common inseparable prefixes are: **be-, emp-, ent-, er-, ge-, unter-, ver-:**
bezahlen *to pay for;* **gefallen** *to please;* **empfehlen** *to recommend;* **verstehen** *to understand;* **erkennen** *to recognise*

Verstehst du mich? *Do you understand me?*
Wann und wo bezahle ich die Unterkunft? *When and where do I pay for the accommodation?*
Uns gefällt Konstanz sehr gut. *We like Konstanz very much.*
Natürlich erkenne ich dich. *Of course I recognise you.*
Ich empfehle Ihnen, mit dem Zug zu fahren. *I recommend you go by train.*
Was können Sie uns empfehlen? *What can you recommend to us?*

reflexive verbs

You'll find that some infinitives have **sich** in front of them. These are called reflexive verbs: **sich freuen auf** *to look forward to*
sich interessieren für *to be interested in*
sich langweilen *to be bored*
sich setzen *to sit down*

In the present tense, **sich** changes according to the person doing the action and comes after the verb, which has the same endings as any other verb:

ich freue mich auf	*I look forward to*
du freust dich auf	*you look forward to*
er/sie/es freut sich auf	*he/she/it looks forward to*
wir freuen uns auf	*we look forward to*
ihr freut euch auf	*you look forward to*
sie/Sie freuen sich auf	*they/you look forward to*

Ich interessiere mich für Kunst. *I'm interested in art.*
Warum langweilst du dich? *Why are you bored?*
Setzen Sie sich! *Sit down, take a seat!*
Wir freuen uns auf den Ausflug. *We're looking forward to the excursion.*

Reflexive verbs can be separable:
sich anziehen *to get dressed*
Im Winter ziehen wir uns warm an. *In winter we dress warmly.*
sich ausziehen *to get undressed*
Ich ziehe mich im Badezimmer aus. *I get undressed in the bathroom.*

... or inseparable:
sich befinden *to be located*
sich erinnern an *to remember*
Öffentliche Toiletten befinden sich hinter dem Rathaus. *Public toilets are located behind the town hall.*
Erinnerst du dich an mich? *Do you remember me?*

When a reflexive verb has the literal meaning of doing something to or for oneself, the reflexive pronouns are in the dative case. In practical terms, the only difference is that **mir** is used instead of **mich**, and **dir** instead of **dich**.
Ich mache mir ein Brot zum Mittagessen. *I make (for) myself a sandwich for lunch.*
Willst du dir was kaufen? *Do you want to buy anything for yourself?*

wordbank

These commonly used verbs are arranged by whether they have a prefix.

ändern *to change*
antworten *to answer*
bieten *to offer*
chatten *to chat online*
finden *to find*
folgen *to follow*
fragen *to ask*
sich freuen (über) *to be pleased (about)*
führen *to lead*
hoffen *to hope*
hören *to hear*
ignorieren *to ignore*
kaufen *to buy*
sich kümmern um *to look after, take care of*
lächeln *to smile*
lachen *to laugh*
lassen *to let*
lernen *to learn*
lügen *to lie, tell a lie*
öffnen *to open*
raten *to guess, to advise*
rechnen *to calculate*
reden *to talk, chat*
schließen *to close*
sehen *to see*
spielen *to play*
stellen *to put*
suchen *to look for, search*
treffen *to meet*
wechseln *to change (money)*

separable

abfahren *to leave (of a train)*
anfangen *to start*
annehmen *to accept*
ansehen *to look at*
aufhören *to quit, stop*
ausgeben *to spend*
sich hinlegen *to lie down*
sich umziehen *to get changed*
vorschlagen *to suggest*
sich vorstellen *to imagine*
weggehen/wegfahren *to leave, go away*
zuhören *to listen*
zurückfahren *to go back*

inseparable

sich beeilen *to hurry*
beenden *to finish*
sich befassen (mit) *to deal (with)*
bekommen *to get*
besuchen *to visit*
sich entspannen *to relax*
erklären *to explain, clarify*
erlauben *to allow*
gewinnen *to win*
sich unterhalten *to chat, have a conversation*
unterstützen *to support (team)*
unterrichten *to teach*
verbieten *to forbid*
vergleichen *to compare*
verkaufen *to sell*
verlieren *to lose*
vermeiden *to avoid*
versprechen *to promise*

Choose ten verbs and run through the present tense endings. Try using a few of them in a sentence.

talking the talk

Sophie	Was ist dein Bruder von Beruf?
Volker	Jan? Er ist freiberuflicher Grafikdesigner. Er arbeitet von zu Hause.
Sophie	Und dein Vater? Wo arbeitet er?
Volker	Er arbeitet in einem großen Pharmaunternehmen.
Sophie	Was ist seine Funktion? Ist er Wissenschaftler?
Volker	Nein, er leitet die Marketingabteilung. Er macht diese Arbeit schon fünfzehn Jahre.

Sophie	Und deine Mutter? Arbeitet sie?
Volker	Sie kümmert sich um ihre Mutter. Meine Großmutter ist krank.

Volker	Und dein Bruder Andreas? Was macht er?
Sophie	Er ist Programmierer. Er arbeitet in London in einer deutschen Firma.
Volker	Und deine Eltern?
Sophie	Meine Mutter ist Wissenschaftlerin. Sie arbeitet in einer karitativen Organisation.
Volker	Arbeitet sie Vollzeit?
Sophie	Nein, Teilzeit. Mein Vater war Zahnarzt, aber jetzt ist er im vorzeitigen Ruhestand. Er arbeitet karitativ und hilft Migranten.

verb practice 2

1 Write the correct form of the verbs. Remember that separable verbs separate!

a	**bekommen** *to get*	**du** ....
b	**zurückfahren** *to go back* (sep)	**Sie** ....
c	**sich beeilen** *to hurry*	**wir** ....
d	**verstehen** *to understand*	**ihr** ....
e	**bieten** *to offer*	**es** ....
f	**unterstützen** *to support*	**ich** ....
g	**hoffen** *to hope*	**sie** (=she) ....
h	**anfangen** *to begin* (sep)	**ich** ....
i	**suchen** *to look for*	**wir** ....
j	**zuhören** *to listen*	**er** ....
k	**fragen** *to ask*	**sie** (= they) ....
l	**sich umziehen** *to get changed* (sep)	**ich** ....

2 Which of the following verbs are separable, and which are inseparable?

a **unterbrechen** *to interrupt*
b **besichtigen** *to visit (a building)*
c **anrufen** *to phone*
d **absagen** *to cancel*
e **gebrauchen** *to use*

3 Some verbs have a change in stem in the **du** and **er/sie/es** forms only. Write the **du** form of the verbs below.

a	**treffen** *to meet*	**du**	**er/sie trifft**
b	**versprechen** *to promise*	**du**	**er/sie verspricht**
c	**anfangen** *to begin*	**du**	**er/sie fängt an**
d	**sehen** *to see*	**du**	**er/sie sieht**
e	**ausgeben** *to spend*	**du**	**er/sie gibt aus**

4 Decide whether **mich, dich, sich, uns** or **euch** belongs in the gap:

a **Freust du .... über die Situation?** *Are you pleased about the situation?*
b **Sie kümmern .... um ihre Haustiere.** *They look after their pets.*
c **Langweilt ihr .... ?** *Are you bored?*
d **Erinnern Sie .... an uns?** *Do you remember us?*
e **Ich interessiere .... für Sport.** *I'm interested in sport.*

checkpoint 3

1 Match the people with their workplace: **Arzt, Lehrerin, Klempner, Rechtsanwalt, Dozent, Koch: Grundschule, Universität, Restaurant, Kanzlei, Krankenhaus.**
What does the person left over do?

2 Which word is missing in the sentence **Ich arbeite .... Journalist**?

3 What do you add to this sentence to say you've been working here for 15 years: **Ich arbeite hier .... fünfzehn Jahren.**

4 What do you think the masculine and feminine forms of the German for *meteorologist* are? And what do you think a **Rheumatologe**, an **Archäologe** and a **Psychologe** are?

5 What is another way of asking someone what they do, in addition to **Was machen Sie beruflich?**

6 What's the difference between **ein Ausbilder** and **ein Auszubildender**? What do you think the separable verb **ausbilden** might mean?

7 Is your grandfather or your grandson more likely to be a **Rentner**?

8 How would you tell someone in German that your male partner is self-employed?

9 Where do people employed **im Personalbereich, im öffentlichen Sektor, im Einzelhandel** and **auf einem Bauernhof** work?

10 How would you ask someone what their role is?

11 If a male actor is **ein Schauspieler** in German, what do you think the German for actress is?

12 What German word would you use to translate *for* in *I work for General Foods*?

13 **Abteilungsleiter** means *head of department*, so what sort of head of department is **ein stellvertretender Abteilungsleiter**?

14 Rearrange these words to form a sentence, then say what it means in English: **einer arbeitet meine karitativen Schwester in Organisation.**

15 *I was* is **ich war** in German, so how would you say *I was a teacher*?

16 What do you think **mein Großvater war Polizist** means?

vier
the art of conversation

Once you're past the stage of exchanging basic information with someone, you generally move on to more general conversation. A proper conversation flows without awkward pauses or prolonged silences; it feels comfortable and includes comments and prompts, questions and exclamations.

The general principles – showing interest in the person you're talking to, knowing when to say something, how much or how little to say – are things we do in our first language without much conscious thought, but when you're speaking in a new language and concentrating on finding the right word at the right time, it helps to think about how to achieve them.

Even if you can't always say as much as you'd like, you can still contribute simply by knowing how to keep a conversation going. There are a number of strategies you can use to show that you're properly engaged in a conversation. Gestures, eye contact, a smile, positive body language or a nod at the right time all show that you're actively listening and following what's being said – but they're not nearly as satisfying as being able to offer an exclamation or an appropriate comment.

For the strategies to work, it's important to concentrate your energies on listening to what's being said and to resist the temptation to half listen while you work out what you're going to say next. A conversation is unpredictable and, by the time you're ready with your perfect sentence, the thread might well have moved on.

following what's being said

Following what's being said in German demands extra skills, given that you often have to wait to the end of the sentence to hear the verb, which might well be the key word. Nobody will mind if you ask for help now and again, or ask for the conversation to be slowed down a little.

Entschuldigung/Entschuldigen Sie. *Excuse me.*
Entschuldige mich/Entschuldigen Sie mich. *Excuse me.*
These are perfectly polite, but can be made even more so with **bitte**.
Entschuldigen Sie, bitte. *Excuse me, please. I beg your pardon.*
Verzeihen Sie, bitte. *I beg your pardon, forgive me.* (slightly more formal)

Entschuldigen Sie die Unterbrechung, aber ... *Excuse my interruption, but ...*
Ich verstehe nicht. *I don't understand.*
Ich habe nicht verstanden. *I haven't understood.*
Ich weiß nicht, ob ich richtig verstanden habe. *I don't know if I've understood properly.*
Ich bin nicht sicher, ob ich verstanden habe. *I'm not sure I've understood.*

Ich habe nicht verstanden ... *I haven't understood ...*
Was bedeutet ...? *What does ... mean?*
... bedeutet ..., nicht wahr? *... means ... doesn't it?*

Was hast du/haben Sie gesagt? *What did you say?*
Wiederhole/Wiederholen Sie bitte? *Can you repeat that please?* **(du/Sie)**
Sprich/Sprechen Sie ein bisschen langsamer? *Can you speak more slowly?* **(du/Sie)**
Könntest du bitte erklären? *Would you mind explaining?*
Könnten Sie bitte wiederholen? *Would you mind repeating that?*

You can show you're following by echoing what's been said, before offering a relevant comment or question.
Mein Schwager arbeitet in China. *My brother-in-law works in China.*
In China? Tatsächlich? Wo? *In China? Really? Whereabouts?*

You could use **wirklich, ehrlich** or **echt** in place of **Tatsächlich**.
Wirklich? Was macht er da? *Really? What's he doing there?*

making yourself understood

There will be times when you need to know if you're getting your message across.
Verstehst du mich/Versteht ihr mich/Verstehen Sie mich? *Do you understand me? Am I making sense?*
Ist alles klar? *Is everything clear?*
Lass/Lassen Sie es mich erklären. *Let me explain/clarify.*
Ich weiss nicht, ob ich es gut erkläre. *I don't know if I'm explaining things very well.*

If you're struggling for a word, say so:
Ich habe das Wort vergessen. *I've forgotten the word.*
Ich kann das richtige Wort nicht finden. *I can't find the right word.*
Es liegt mir auf der Zunge. *It's on the tip of my tongue.*
Wie heißt das auf Deutsch? *What's this/that called in German?*
Wie sagt man ... auf Deutsch? *What's the German for ...?*

Man is the equivalent of the English *one*, referring to people in general, usually translated as *you* or *they*. It takes the same verb endings as **er/sie**.
Wie sagt man das auf Deutsch? *How do you say that in German?*
Hier spricht man Dialekt. *They speak a dialect round here.*

Paraphrasing can be very useful.

- **Es ist das Gegenteil von ...** *It's the opposite of ...*
- **Es ist nicht ...** *It isn't ...*
- **Es ist (so) eine Art von ...** *It's a sort of ...*
- **Es ist ein bisschen wie ...** *It's a bit like ...*
- **Er/Sie sieht wie ... aus** *He/She/It looks like ...*
- **Ich kann mich nicht an ihren Namen erinnern. Sie wohnt in Bad Reichenhall. Sie ist schlank und stark geschminkt und sie trägt eine Brille.** *I don't remember her name. She lives in Bad Reichenhall. She's slim, heavily made up, and wears glasses.*
- **Es befindet sich in den Bergen in Oberbayern, südwestlich von Salzburg, richtig abgelegen.** *It's in the mountains in Upper Bavaria, south-west of Salzburg, really off the beaten track.*

If all else fails, you can resort to gestures and mime.
Es war so groß. *It was this big.*
Sein Gesicht war so. *His face was like this.*

educated guesswork

English and German belong to the same language group because they both originate from a single language, often referred to as Common Germanic, which existed two thousand years ago. Being sister languages, English and German share many similarities.

Some words look identical, although their pronunciation differs: **absurd, intelligent, modern, Pause, Sand, Sport, Synonym, Wind.**
Many others are almost identical: **Banane, bizarr, effektiv, exquisit, fabulös, Insekt, perfekt, vulgär.**

Some sounds often correspond in German and English words, so it's always worth making an educated guess:

🇬🇧	🇩🇪	
gh	**ch**	**acht, lachen, Licht, Sicht**
k	**ch**	**brechen, Buch, machen, Milch**
p	**pf** or **f**	**Apfel, Pfeffer, Pfund**
d	**t**	**Bett, Garten, gut, trinken**
t	**tz** or **z**	**Katze, Salz, sitzen, zehn, zwei**
t	**ss** or **ß**	**beißen, Fuß, Nuss, Wasser, weiß**
th	**d**	**Bad, Bruder, danke, Leder, Pfad**

Word endings can provide clues, e.g.
-ic or *-ical* = **-isch: allergisch, praktisch, fantastisch, realistisch**
-ism = **-ismus: Alkoholismus, Sozialismus, Tourismus**

falsche Freunde *false friends*
Not all words mean what they appear to mean, however, e.g.

aktuell *current, recent*
die Art *type, kind*
bald *soon*
brav *good, well-behaved*
delikat *delicious*
das Etikett *label*
eventuell *possible*
familiär *family-related*
fast *almost*
genial *brilliant*
das Handy *mobile phone*
das Menü *set meal*
komisch *weird*
prägnant *succinct*
psychisch *psychological*
sensibel *sensitive*
seriös *respectable*
sympatisch *likeable, nice*

showing empathy

A well-chosen interjection shows that you're listening and understanding the mood of the conversation. To endorse what's being said, you can say:
Ach so! *I see.*
Bravo! Richtig! *Well said! Hear, hear!*
Eben! *That's just it!* **Das stimmt!** *That's right!*
Genau! Haargenau! *Exactly! Spot on!*

Like English, German has expressions that can equally well convey interest, admiration, incredulity, indignation, amusement, amazement, concern, fascination or horror depending on your tone of voice and expression.
Wirklich? *Really?*
Im Ernst? *Seriously?*
Mein Gott! *OMG!* **Ach du liebe Güte!** *My goodness! Goodness me!*
Ach geh! Hör mir auf! Ach, erzähl mir doch nichts! *Get away!*
Was du nicht sagst! Das darf nicht wahr sein! *You don't say! Come on!*
Um Himmels willen! Guter Gott! *Good grief! For heaven's sake!*
Au weia! Oh weh! *Oh dear! Oh no!*
Mein lieber Schwan! Mein lieber Scholli! *Wow! Good heavens!*
Stell dir vor! Also so was! Hätte ich nie gedacht! *Fancy that!*
Wenn doch nur! *If only! I wish!*
Du spinnst! Du machst Witze! *You're joking!*
Meine Güte! Echt! *My goodness! Wow! My word!*
Um Gottes willen! *For goodness' sake!*
Du Glückliche(r)! Du Glückspilz! *Lucky you!* (f/m) **Die Glücklichen!** *Lucky them!*

You may find that younger people say something different from older people. While they might use **Cool!** or **Wow!** for *Great! Fantastic! Amazing!*, older people are more likely to say **Donnerwetter!** or **Echt toll!**

Some expressions are far removed from their literal meaning:
Schwan in the expression **Mein lieber Schwan!** means *swan*. The expression originally comes from Wagner's opera *Lohengrin*.
Du Glückspilz! literally means *you lucky mushroom:* **der Pilz** is *mushroom*.
Eine Schau is a *show* or *exhibition* but **Das ist eine Schau!** means *That's great! Amazing!*
Der Mensch is *person* and **die Kinder** are *children* but **Menschenskinder!** translates as *Good heavens!*

commenting

Sometimes a simple comment such as *What a* ... or *How* ... is all that's required, and you can do this with **was für ein(e)** + noun. Other options are **so ein(e), welche(r), so was/so etwas** and, less commonly, **wie**.

Was für ein Anblick! Was für ein Spektakel! *What a sight/performance!*
So ein Durcheinander! *What a mess!*
So eine Enttäuschung! *What a disappointment!*
Welche Freude! *What (a) joy! What a pleasure! What a delight!*
Was für ein Glück! *What a piece of luck! How lucky!*
Was für eine gute Idee! *What a good idea!*
Was für eine Überraschung! *What a surprise!*
Was für ein Zufall! *What a coincidence!*
So (et)was Blödes! *How silly!*
So (et)was Dummes! *What a nuisance!*
Welche Perfektion! Was für eine Perfektion! *What perfection!*
Wie Schade! *What a pity!*

Another way is to use **wie** *how* with an adjective.
Wie ärgerlich! *What a bore! How annoying!*
Wie großzügig! *How generous!*
Wie gruselig! *How scary!*
Wie langweilig! *What a drag!*
Wie schrecklich! *How dreadful!*
Wie spannend! *How exciting!*
Wie widerlich! Wie scheußlich *How disgusting! How horrible!*

It's useful to have a ready supply of adjectives. As well as following **wie**, they work on their own or they can be used after **so** *so*.
Wunderschön! *Marvellous!* **Unmöglich!** *Impossible!* **Schrecklich!** *Terrible!*
Das ist so gut/furchtbar! *That's so good/terrible!* **Wie süß!** *How cute!* Don't forget words like **sehr, ein bisschen, so, ganz, ziemlich:**
Sehr spannend! *Very exciting!*
Ein bisschen traurig. *A bit sad.*
So seltsam. *So odd.*
Ganz bizarr! *Seriously weird!*
Ziemlich unangenehm. *Rather unpleasant.*

wordbank

Sometimes a well-chosen adjective is all you need to show insight into what's being said and affinity with the speaker.

Herrlich! *Amazing!*
So stressig. *So stressful.*
Wie spannend! *How exciting!*
Unverschämt! *Outrageous!*
Echt komisch! *Seriously weird!*
Sehr traurig. *Very sad.*

Choose at least six of these adjectives and think of situations where you might use them with wie, so, sehr, ganz or ziemlich. Say them out loud.

admiration, appreciation
angenehm *pleasant, nice*
außergewöhnlich *amazing, exceptional*
beeindruckend *impressive*
einzigartig *special, exceptional*
erfreulich *delightful*
erstklassig *superb, first-class*
faszinierend *fascinating*
lustig *jolly, enjoyable*

disapproval
ärgerlich *annoying*
blöd *daft*
dumm *silly, stupid*
enttäuschend *disappointing*

horror, sympathy
gemein *mean, nasty*
grauenhaft *horrible, horrifying*
katastrophal *catastrophic*
tragisch *tragic*

astonishment, amusement
außerordentlich *extraordinary*
erstaunlich *astonishing, amazing*
lächerlich *ridiculous*
unheimlich *eerie, uncanny*
verrückt *crazy, wacky, weird*

general
ausgezeichnet *excellent*
befriedigend *satisfying*
ehrlich *honest*
einfach *simple*
ernsthaft *serious*
günstig *convenient*
mutig *brave*
nützlich *useful*
schwierig *difficult*

The opposite of many adjectives can be formed by adding **un**-: **unangenehm** *unpleasant;* **unerwartet** *unexpected;* **ungewöhnlich** *unusual;* **unglücklich** *unfortunate.*

adding structure and fluency

Conversations tend to include words like *well, anyway, let's see, frankly, however, in fact*. Some of them add structure to what you say, others add emphasis, while some simply bring a natural feel to a conversation. When using some of them, you need to bear German word order rules in mind.

Ja, nein, und and the phrases below don't affect word order at all - it's as if they weren't there.
ach so *I see*
also, also jetzt, nun denn *well then ..., so ..., right then ...*
das heißt, *that is, in other words, the thing is*
doch *but yes* (when contradicting what has just been said)
ehrlich gesagt, offen gesagt *to be honest, frankly*
kurz gesagt *to cut a long story short, in a nutshell*
zum Beispiel *for example*
Lass sehen/Lassen Sie sehen. *Let's see.* **(du/Sie)**

Also, **ich muss mir das überlegen.** *Well, I'll have to think about it.*
Doch, **es war sehr interessant.** *On the contrary, it was very interesting.*
Kurz gesagt, **die Reise war schrecklich**. *To cut a long story short, the journey was terrible.*

Other phrases obey German word order rules, which state that the verb must always come second: not necessarily the second word, but the second element. The following can either come immediately before the verb, in first place, or later in the sentence. They cannot be in the second position in the sentence - that position must be occupied by the verb.

allerdings, jedoch *however, though*
auf alle Fälle, auf jeden Fall *in any case, anyway*
deshalb, deswegen, aus diesem Grunde *so, therefore*
eigentlich, *actually, as a matter of fact*
im Allgemeinen *in general, on the whole*
im Grunde, grundsätzlich *basically*
klar *clearly,* **offensichtlich** *obviously*
noch *still, and yet*
schon *true, certainly*
sogar *even, indeed*
auch *also,* **außerdem, zudem** *what's more, furthermore*
wirklich, in der Tat, tatsächlich *in fact, indeed, really*
wohl *I suppose, indeed*

Ich muss jetzt wirklich gehen. *I really must go now.*
Wir haben allerdings keine Zeit. *We've not got time, though.*
Eigentlich wusste ich nicht. *Actually I didn't know.*
Allerdings haben wir keine Zeit. *We've got no time, though.*
Auf jeden Fall kann ich das Hotel empfehlen. *I can recommend the hotel anyway.*

The following are useful for structuring a more formal discussion:

erstens, zunächst *first of all*
zweitens *secondly*
ich würde sagen *I would say*
kurz gesagt *in short, to cut a long story short*
einerseits *on one hand;* **andererseits** *on the other hand*
zum Schluss *finally, in conclusion*

Filler words, like the ones opposite, never translate neatly between German and English, and there are always a lot of translation possibilities. The context is the important thing.

Wohl *I suppose, indeed* is used when you believe something to be true:
Du bist wohl müde. *You must be tired.*
Sie sind wohl verheiratet. *I expect you're married*
Wohl is also used when you emphatically agree with a statement:
Das kann man wohl sagen. *Indeed it is. You can say that again. You certainly are/did/should.*

Schon, as well as being an adverb meaning *already*, is a filler word indicating agreement, but where you have reservations.
Das ist schon möglich. *That's quite possible.*
Ich glaube schon, (aber ...) *I think so, (but ...)*

Also is a very useful and much-used word. It doesn't mean the English *also*, but means a lot of other things: *so, then, well, well now, right, therefore.*
Also gut! *All right, then! Very well!*
Also wirklich! *Honestly! Really!* (annoyed)
Bis morgen also. *Till tomorrow, then.*
Also, gehen wir? *So, shall we go?*

beer culture

Beer-brewing is one of Germany's oldest traditions and the local beer garden is a favourite place to meet for a convivial get-together. With thousands of different types of beer brewed in Germany at thousands of breweries, there's always plenty to talk about.

Fassbier oder Flaschenbier? *Draught beer or bottled?*
Eine Maß, bitte. *A large beer, please.*
Noch mal. *Another one (of the same).*
Noch ein kleines Bier, bitte. *Another small beer, please.*
Noch ein Kölsch? Oder vielleicht ein Bockbier? Probier mal! *Another Kölsch? Or maybe a Bock? Try it!*
Prost! *Cheers!* **Zum Wohl!** *To your health!*

There's a wide range of cocktails and other drinks at **eine Bar** or **ein Lokal,** whereas for an informal beer-drinking venue you'd go to **eine Kneipe** *pub*, **ein Biergarten** *beer garden* or **ein Bierkeller** *beer cellar.* **Eine Brauerei** is *a brewery*. Long, shared tables are the norm in **Kneipen** *pubs* and **Biergärten** *beer gardens.* Tables marked **Stammtisch** are for regular customers. The untranslatable **Stammtisch** refers to the table or the group of regulars.

Different beers are served in different glasses. **Ein Weizenbierglas** is for **das Weizenbier** *wheat beer*, also called **Weißbier** *white beer.* It's narrow at the bottom and slightly wider at the top. **Eine Maß** or **ein Maßkrug** is a heavy, dimpled glass with a handle that holds a full litre of beer. **Eine Stange** is a slim cylindrical glass for serving the Cologne speciality **Kölsch. Pils** is served in **eine Pilstulpe**, similar to a wine glass, but with a short stem. **Bockbier**, a strong full-bodied beer is served in a bulbous glass with a handle, **ein Henkelglas**. The English word *stein*, an earthenware or decorative tankard, might sound German, but it isn't used in Germany. Germans say **der Steinkrug**. **Der Stein** means *stone*.

Several adjectives are used to describe beer.
ein klares helles Bier *a clear light beer*
dunkles/frisches/kühles/herbes/vollmundiges Bier *dark/fresh/cool/sharp-tasting/full-bodied beer*
Es ist schwer und stark. *It's heavy and strong.*
Es ist stärker als du denkst. *It's stronger than you think.*
So erfrischend! *So refreshing!*

Germans enjoy answering questions about their beers.

Wie viele Biersorten gibt es? *How many varieties of beer are there?*
Wissen Sie, es gibt über fünftausend Biersorten in Deutschland. *Do you know, there are over 5,000 varieties of beer in Germany.*
Theoretisch kann man fast vierzehn Jahre lang jeden Tag ein anderes Bier aus Deutschland trinken. *In theory you can drink a different beer from Germany every day for nearly fourteen years.*

Welches Bier trinken die Deutschen am liebsten? *Which beer do Germans like drinking most of all? Which is the most popular beer among Germans?*
Eigentlich ist Pils die meistgetrunkene Biersorte in Deutschland. *As a matter of fact Pils is the most popular* (lit. *most drunk*) *beer variety in Germany.*

Was ist das Reinheitsgebot? *What is the Purity Law?*
Das Reinheitsgebot steht für Qualität. Nach dem Reinheitsgebot von 1516 sind nur Malz, Hopfen, Hefe und Wasser im Bier - sonst nichts. *The Purity Law stands for quality. In accordance with the Purity Law of 1516 there's only malt, hops, yeast and water in beer - nothing else.*

das Oktoberfest *the Munich Beer Festival*
Wann findet das Oktoberfest statt? *When does the Festival take place?*
Das Oktoberfest beginnt schon im September. *The Festival begins in September.*
Es dauert ungefähr achtzehn Tage. *It goes on for about eighteen days.*
Das Oktoberfest endet traditionell am ersten Sonntag im Oktober. *The Festival traditionally ends on the first Sunday in October.*

ein Trinklied *a drinking song*
Kommt, singt mit! *Come on, join in with the singing.*
> **Ein Prosit, ein Prosit** *A toast, a toast*
> **Der Gemütlichkeit** *to good cheer*
> **Ein Prosit, ein Prosit**
> **Der Gemütlichkeit.**
> **Oans! Zwoa! Drei! G'suffa!** *1, 2, 3, down the hatch!*

Oans! Zwoa! Drei! G'suffa! Was bedeutet das? *'Oans! Zwoa! Drei! G'suffa!'* *What does that mean?*
Das ist eins, zwei, drei, getrunken auf Bayrisch. *That's 1, 2, 3, drunk it, in Bavarian.*

prompting

Simple prompts can be all you need to encourage a conversation to flow.

Ja, und? *And then what?*
Und dann? *And afterwards?*
Wie geht die Geschichte weiter? *How does the story continue?*
Übrigens: die Besprechung ... *Talking of the meeting ...*
Was Andrea betrifft ... *About Andrea ...*

Erzähl/Erzählen Sie mir mal davon. *Tell me about it.*
Erzählen Sie mir von ... *Tell me about ...*
Erzählen Sie mir mal von dem/vom Unfall. *Tell me about the accident.*
Erzählen Sie, was nachher geschehen ist. *Tell me what happened after.*
Erzähl, wie du dahin gekommen bist. *Explain to me how you ended up there.*
Sagen Sie mir Bescheid. *Tell me. Let me know.*
Erklär mir, warum. *Explain to me why.* **(du)**

Connectors that normally join together parts of a sentence can be used inquiringly to prompt.

> **Und?** *And?*
> **Aber?** *But?*
> **Mit anderen Worten?** *In other words?*
> **Zum Beispiel?** *For example?*

And open questions, even at their most basic, promote further conversations. The following can simply stand alone.

Wo? *Where?*
Woher? *Where from?*
Wohin? *Where to?*
Wann? *When?*
Wer? *Who?*
Mit wem? *Who with?*
Warum? *Why?*
Wie? *How?*
Welcher/welche/welches? *Which one (m/f/n)?*
Welche? *Which ones?*
Wie viel? *How much?*
Wie viele? *How many?*

talking the talk

Sophie	Also, hilft dein Bruder seiner Ex-Frau mit dem Kind, mit Mia?
Volker	Ja, er macht ziemlich viel, zum Beispiel wenn die Mutter Nathalie arbeitet.
Sophie	Aber Nathalie wohnt in Frankreich, nicht wahr?
Volker	Das stimmt, aber Colmar ist nur anderthalb Stunden von Freiburg, und Jan arbeitet freiberuflich. Nathalies Mutter hilft ihr auch viel. Und ihre Schwester Susanne hilft auch. Susanne ist Vollzeitmutter, sie hat zwei Kinder, Zwillinge. Ihr Mann ist Bernard Martinez.
Sophie	Bernard Martinez? Der Fußballspieler? Wirklich? Das darf nicht wahr sein! Bernard Martinez ist der Mann von deiner Schwester? Stell dir das vor!
Volker	Nein, du hast nicht verstanden. Susanne ist nicht meine Schwester, sie ist die Schwester von Nathalie, Jans Ex-Frau.
Sophie	Ach, so, alles klar. Fantastisch! Aber die Frau von Bernard Martinez ist Popsängerin, oder?
Volker	Ja, richtig. Die Sängerin Susanne Lambert.
Sophie	Genau. Und jetzt heißt Susanne Lambert Susanne Martinez. Echt! Was für eine Überraschung!

checkpoint 4

1. If someone says to you **Wiederholen Sie, bitte** what will you do?
2. **Lustig** means *enjoyable*; which is stronger **ganz lustig** or **ziemlich lustig**?
3. What's the German word for *excellent*?
4. Is **Toll!** a term of admiration or disapproval?
5. How do you ask if everything is clear?
6. If someone replies, **Das stimmt**, do they agree with you, or not?
7. Which one of the following doesn't mean *really*? **in der Tat, tatsächlich, im Allgemeinen, wirklich**
8. What's the difference between **ich verstehe nicht** and **ich habe nicht verstanden**?
9. What's *for example* in German?
10. Class the following as positive or negative: **wie schrecklich, wie langweilig, wie schön, wie ärgerlich, wie spannend.**
11. How else, apart from **Verzeihen Sie, bitte** could you say *I beg your pardon*?
12. Which of these wouldn't be translated by **Also**? *So, then, well, well now, as well, right then.*
13. How would you say *What is this called in German?*
14. What do you add to **Das Bier ist ....stark.** to mean *This beer is a bit strong*?
15. What sort of children are **brave Kinder**?
16. Does **offen gesagt** or **kurz gesagt** mean *frankly*?
17. How would you say *What does **Stammtisch** mean?*
18. What pronoun is used in **........sagt,** when not specifying anyone in particular, as in the English *you say, we say*?
19. Make an educated guess at the meaning of **Die Omelettpfanne ist leicht und funktionert gut.**
20. If **höflich** means *polite*, what's the German for *impolite*?

fünf
what's happened

A real conversation is unpredictable: it may at times be confined to the here and now but is more likely to weave comfortably between the present, future and past as you chat about what's going on, what your plans are, where you've been and what you've been doing.

Telling people what's been happening, sharing an experience or recounting an anecdote is more straightforward in German than in English. Using *to play* as an example, English has *I played, I have played, I have been playing, I was playing, I used to play, I would (often) play* – whereas spoken German conveys all of these with **ich habe gespielt**. This is called the perfect tense or the conversational past.

Being able to talk about the past brings a whole new dimension to your German, and it's easy to practise. Every so often you can say to yourself what you've been doing, preferably out loud; every day spend a few minutes writing a journal. You'll be using the same structures over and over, and your vocabulary will expand exponentially as you look up any new words you need.

While the perfect tense is largely all you'll need to use while talking, in parts of northern Germany you might hear the imperfect **ich spielte** used instead of **ich habe gespielt.**

what you've been doing

To express in German what you *did, have done, have been doing* or *were doing*, you use the perfect tense, which is in two parts, just like *have + played* in English.

1. the present tense of **haben** *to have*:

ich habe	wir haben
du hast	ihr habt
er/sie/es hat	sie/Sie haben

2. **+ past participle.** In English this often ends in *-ed*, e.g. *worked, watched*, or *-en*, e.g. *eaten;* in German it's the last of the verb forms given in a dictionary, and usually begins with **ge-**. It goes at the end of the sentence.

Ich habe Schach gespielt. *I played/was playing chess.*
Wir haben roten Wein getrunken. *We drank red wine.*

Broadly speaking, German verbs divide into two groups: weak and strong. Strong verbs change their stem vowel in at least one of their verb forms, while weak verbs, by far the biggest group, are usually regular and don't (page 181). The past participle of weak verbs replaces the **-en** of the infinitive with **-t** ...
Heute morgen haben sie Tennis gespielt. *This morning they were playing tennis.*
Ich habe bis elf Uhr gearbeitet. *I worked/was working until 11 o'clock.*
Sie hat früher mit mir gearbeitet. *She used to work with me.*
Wir haben den Namen im Internet gesucht. *We looked up the name on the internet.*
Ihr erstes Auto hat sie vor zwanzig Jahren gekauft. *She bought her first car 20 years ago.*

... whereas the past participle of strong verbs ends in **-en**, and some verbs undergo a change of vowel: **sehen** *to see* → **gesehen, lesen** *to read* → **gelesen, geben** *to give* → **gegeben** ... but **finden** *to find* → **gefunden, sprechen** *to speak* → **gesprochen, trinken** *to drink* → **getrunken, nehmen** *to take* → **genommen.**
Ich habe diesen Aufenthalt sehr gut gefunden. *I've found this stay very pleasant.*
Wir haben den ganzen Tag Deutsch gesprochen. *We spoke/were speaking German all day.*
Gestern habe ich zu viel getrunken. *I drank too much yesterday.*

The past participles of two groups of verbs do not add **ge-**.

- Verbs ending **-ieren**, e,g, **fotografieren** *to photograph*, **studieren** *to study*, **probieren** *to taste*, **reparieren** *to repair*, **sich amüsieren** *to have a good time*, which simply replace the final **-en** with **-t.**
  Ich habe so viele interessante Gebäude fotografiert. *I photographed so many interesting buildings.*
  Er hat an der Technischen Universität Darmstadt studiert. *He studied at Darmstadt Technical University.*
  Ich habe das erste Mal in meinem Leben Sachertorte probiert. *I tasted Sachertorte* (a rich chocolate gateau) *for the first time in my life.*
  Er hat deine Tasche repariert. *He's mended your bag.*
  Ich habe mich auf der Party sehr gut amüsiert. *I had a very good time at the party.*

- Inseparable verbs, e.g. **besuchen** *to visit*, **empfehlen** *to recommend*, **gefallen** *to like*, **verkaufen** *to sell*, **verstehen** *to understand.*
  Wir haben unsere Verwandten besucht. *We visited our relatives.*
  Eine Bekannte hat uns dieses Restaurant empfohlen. *An acquaintance recommended this restaurant to us.*
  Oberammergau hat uns sehr gut gefallen. *We really liked Oberammergau.*
  Entschuldigung, ich habe Sie nicht verstanden. *Sorry, I didn't understand you.*
  Habt ihr schon euer Haus verkauft? *Have you sold your house yet?*
  Der Zug hat sich verspätet. *The train was delayed.*

However, separable verbs, e.g. **abholen** *to pick up*, **anschauen** *to look at*, **vorstellen** *to introduce*, **anrufen** *to telephone*, **fernsehen** *to watch television*, **kennenlernen** *to meet, get to know*, do add **ge-**, which goes between the prefix and the main part of the verb.
Wir haben uns in der Schule kennengelernt. *We met at school.*
Wer hat dich vom Bahnhof abgeholt? *Who picked you up from the station?*
Meine Mutter hat mich vor einigen Minuten angerufen. *My mother rang me a few minutes ago.*
Er hat stundenlang ferngesehen. *He watched television for hours.*

coming and going

All German verbs have two parts in the perfect tense but a large minority replace **haben** with **sein** for the first part.

ich bin	**wir sind**
du bist	**ihr seid**
er/sie/es ist	**sie/Sie sind**

Verbs to do with movement take **sein**:

reisen *to travel*	**Ich bin gereist** *I travelled*
wandern *to hike*	**Ich bin gewandert** *I hiked*
gehen *to go (on foot)*	**Ich bin gegangen** *I went, walked*
fahren *to go (vehicle)*	**Ich bin gefahren** *I went (by vehicle)*
einsteigen *to get on (vehicle)*	**Ich bin eingestiegen** *I got on*
aussteigen *to get off (vehicle)*	**Ich bin ausgestiegen** *I got off*
umsteigen *to change (vehicle)*	**Ich bin umgestiegen** *I changed (e.g. trains)*

In meiner Jugend bin **ich viel** gereist. *I travelled a lot in my youth.*
Er ist **am Wochenende in den Bergen** gewandert. *He went hiking in the mountains at the weekend.*
Gestern Abend sind **wir ins Kino** gegangen. *We went to the cinema yesterday evening.*
Bist **du mit dem Zug** gefahren? *Did you go by train?*
Wir sind **um zwei Uhr** gelandet. *We landed at 2 o'clock.*
Sie sind **um elf Uhr nach Hause** gekommen. *They came home at 11.*
Ich bin **noch nie** geflogen. *I've never flown before.*
Sie sind **am Montag** angekommen, **nicht wahr?** *You arrive d on Monday, didn't you?*
Sie ist **spät** angekommen. *She arrived late.*
Wo sind **Sie** umgestiegen? *Where did you change trains?*
Alle Passagiere sind ausgestiegen. *All passengers got off.*

Not all **sein** verbs relate to physical movement: some relate to a change of state, such as *becoming, growing up, dying* or *being born.*
Die Stadt ist **viel schöner** geworden. *The town has got/become much more beautiful.*
Sind **die groß** gewachsen! *Haven't they grown!*
Er ist **vor gut neun Monaten** gestorben. *He died a good nine months ago.*
Wo bist **du** geboren? *Where were you born?*
The **ge-** of **geboren** is an inseparable prefix, not a past participle marker.

Change of state isn't always easy to recognise. Compare these two:
Ich habe geschlafen (from **schlafen**) *I slept* = the state of being asleep
Ich bin eingeschlafen (from **einschlafen**) *I fell asleep* = a change of state: from being awake to being asleep.

A few verbs that form their perfect tense with **sein** are nothing to do with movement or change of state: **bleiben** *to stay (behind)*, **sein** *to be*, **geschehen/passieren** *to happen*.
Die Kinder sind in der Stadt geblieben. *The children stayed on in the city.*
Mein Mann ist zu Hause geblieben. *My husband stayed at home.*
Die Musik ist sehr laut gewesen. *The music was very loud.*
Wo bist du gewesen? *Where have you been? Where were you?*
Was ist passiert? *What happened? What's happened?*
Was geschehen ist, ist geschehen. *What's happened has happened. It's no use crying over spilt milk.*

wordbank

gestern *yesterday*, **vorgestern** *the day before yesterday*
gestern Morgen/Nachmittag/Abend *yesterday morning/afternoon/evening*
neulich *the other day*, **neulich abends** *the other evening*

am Tag zuvor *the day before*
am Tag vor der Feier *the day before the party*
in der Woche zuvor *the week before*
im Monat/Jahr zuvor *the month/year before*

letzten Sonntag *last Sunday*
letzte Woche *last week*
letzten Monat/Januar/Mai *last month/January/May*
letztes Jahr *last year*
im vorletzten Jahr *the year before last*

vor kurzer Zeit *a short time ago*
vor einer halben Stunde *half an hour ago*
vor drei Tagen/zwei Wochen *three days/a fortnight ago*
(ungefähr) vor einem Monat *(about) a month ago*

sharing an experience

Not all conversations consist of short questions and answers: some questions and prompts call for some detail. This is particularly true of questions such as **Waren Sie schon mal in Bayern?** *Have you ever been to Bavaria?*

Sie waren is the **imperfect** tense of **sein** and is one of a handful of common verbs used in the imperfect in conversation, in preference to the perfect.

ich war	wir waren
du warst	ihr wart
er/sie/es war	sie/Sie waren

The reply **wir waren noch nie in Süddeutschland** *we've never been to southern Germany* shuts down the topic but when the answer is positive, you would normally want to give more detail.
Ich war einmal dort, als ich fünfzehn Jahre alt war. *I was there once when I was 15 years old.*
Wo wart ihr? *Where were you?*
Wir waren in München. *We were in Munich.*
Wir waren zu viert. *There were four of us.*
Mit wem warst du zusammen? *Who were you with?*
Ich war mit einigen Freunden. *I was with some friends.*
Die Gebäude waren spektakulär. *The buildings were spectacular.*

There will be times when you're not simply responding, when you can't wait to share an experience.
Grab the other person's attention:
Was für ein Tag! *What a day!*
Es war ein unvergesslicher Tag. *It was an unforgettable day.*
Du wirst nicht glauben, was geschehen ist! *You won't believe what happened!*

Set the scene by saying when it took place: **neulich** *the other day*, **gestern Morgen** *yesterday morning*, **vor kurzer Zeit** *a short time ago*. And add a sense of continuity with **und dann** *and then* and **nachher** *afterwards*, as well as **und** *and*, **aber** *but* and **weil** *because*.

Create atmosphere with the occasional exclamation:
Was für eine Freude! *What a delight!*
Eine absolute Katastrophe! *An absolute catastrophe!*
Was für ein Glück/Unglück! *What good/bad luck!*

Now describe in about six sentences something that happened or that you did recently.

Another verb you'll often hear in the imperfect is **haben** *to have*:

ich hatte	**wir hatten**
du hattest	**ihr hattet**
er/sie/es hatte	**sie/Sie hatten**

Ich hatte sehr viel Spaß. *I had a great time.*
Hatten Sie einen schönen Urlaub? *Did you have a lovely holiday?*
Wir hatten keine Probleme mit dem Zoll. *We had no problems with customs.*
Hattest du genug Zeit, das Museum zu besichtigen? *Did you have enough time to visit the museum?*
Schade, dass ihr keine Zeit hattet, die Kunstgalerie zu besichtigen. *What a shame that you didn't have time to visit the art gallery.*

Es gab *there was, there were, there has been, there have been* is particularly useful when you're telling someone what happened.
Es gab ein weiteres Problem. *There was another problem.*
Wie viele Leute gab es auf der Feier? *How many people were there at the do?*

Werden *to become* is also often used in the imperfect:
Es wurde schnell dunkel. *It got dark quickly.*
Sie wurden gute Freunde. *They became good friends.*

Other verbs used frequently in the imperfect are **ich wollte** *I wanted to*, **ich konnte** *I was able to* and **ich musste** *I had to*. More on these in Chapter 8.

It isn't incorrect to use the perfect tense of these verbs or of **sein** and **haben** – the choice of tense is often down to regional or personal preference.
Wir haben keine Probleme mit dem Zoll gehabt. *We had no problems with customs.*
Haben Sie einen schönen Urlaub gehabt? *Did you have a lovely holiday?*
Hast du genug Zeit gehabt? *Did you have enough time?*
Gestern bin ich krank gewesen. *I was ill yesterday.*
Wir sind noch nie in Österreich gewesen. *We've never been to Austria.*
Wie viele Leute hat es auf der Feier gegeben? *How many people were there at the do?*
Es hat ein weiteres Problem gegeben. *There was another problem.*
Es hat Paprikahendl mit Nockerl gegeben. *There was chicken paprika and noodles.*

conversation starters

Questions about what someone's been doing are a good way of starting a conversation or moving it along.

Wo bist du geblieben? *Where have you been? Where did you get to?*
Was hast du diese Woche gemacht? *What have you been doing this week?*
Wo wart ihr gestern? *Where were you yesterday?*
Wohin sind Sie am Wochenende gefahren? *Where did you go at the weekend?*
Seid ihr geflogen oder gefahren? *Did you fly or drive?*
Waren Sie in den Bergen? *Were you in the mountains? Have you been in the mountains? Did you go to the mountains?*
Seid ihr in einen Weinberg gegangen? *Did you go to a vineyard?*
Um wieviel Uhr hast du angefangen? *What time did you start?*
Wo habt ihr zu Mittag gegessen? *Where did you have lunch?*
Wo habt ihr beide euch kennengelernt? *Where did you both meet?*

Hast du Glühwein probiert? *Have you tried mulled wine?*
Haben Sie schon deutsches Essen probiert? *Have you tried German food yet?*
Habt ihr was Interessantes auf dem Markt gekauft? *Did you buy anything interesting at the market?*
Habt ihr schon den Kölner Dom besichtigt? *Have you visited Cologne cathedral yet?*
Haben Sie schon das Brandenburger Tor gesehen? *Have you seen the Brandenburg Gate yet?*

schon mal *ever*
Warst du schon mal in der Schweiz?/Bist du schon mal in der Schweiz gewesen? *Have you ever been to Switzerland?*
Waren Sie schon mal auf dem Oktoberfest?/Sind Sie schon mal auf dem Oktoberfest gewesen? *Have you ever been to Munich's Beer Festival?* **Wart ihr schon mal hier?/Seid ihr schon mal hier gewesen?** *Have you ever been here before?*
Hast du schon mal Reh gegessen? *Have you ever eaten venison?*
Haben Sie schon mal Schnaps probiert? *Have you ever tried schnapps?*
Habt ihr schon mal von Tokio Hotel gehört? *Have you ever heard of (the pop group) Tokio Hotel?*

... and delving into the past

When people are getting to know each other, there's usually a mutual interest in finding out about personal background.

Wo bist du geboren? Wo sind Sie geboren? *Where were you born?*
Ich bin in Sachsen geboren. *I was born in Saxony.*
Wo sind Sie aufgewachsen? *Where did you grow up?*
Sind Sie hier in Bayern aufgewachsen? *Did you grow up here in Bavaria?*
Wir sind in Schleswig-Holstein aufgewachsen. *We grew up in Schleswig-Holstein.*
Was hast du studiert? *What did you study?*
Wo haben Sie sich kennengelernt? *Where did you meet?*
Wann habt ihr geheiratet? *When did you get married?*

Wo hast du als Kind gewohnt? *Where did you live when you were a child?*
Wo haben Sie früher gewohnt? *Where did you use to live?*
Wir haben in einem kleinen Dorf am Bodensee gewohnt. *We lived in a little village on Lake Constance.*
Es war ein sehr ruhiger Ort. *It was a very quiet place.*
Fast jeden Winter hat es geschneit. *It snowed nearly every winter.*
... aber im Sommer war es immer warm. *But in summer it was always warm.*

Wir hatten ein kleines Häuschen hoch in den Bergen. Es war sehr schön. *We had a little house high up in the mountains. It was very beautiful.*

Mein Vater war selbstständig und hat meistens zu Hause gearbeitet. Manchmal war er auf Geschäftsreise. *My father had his own business and mostly worked at home. Sometimes he travelled on business.*

Meine Oma und mein Opa haben uns ab und zu besucht. *My granny and grandad visited us now and then.*

Aber sie konnten nicht oft zu uns kommen, weil sie damals ein Restaurant geführt haben. *But they couldn't come to us often because they were running a restaurant at that time.*

Think of at least six sentences in German about when you were growing up and say them out loud.

avoiding ambiguity

Because the perfect tense translates a range of English tenses such as *did, was doing, have done, used to do*, German adds adverbs of time or other expressions to the sentence to signal the timing of an action more precisely and avoid ambiguity.

Wir haben jedes Jahr in demselben Hotel gewohnt. *We would stay at the same hotel every year.*

Das Baby hatte oft Koliken. *The baby often used to get colic.*

Als Kinder haben wir stundenlang ferngesehen! *As children, we used to watch telly for hours on end!*

Früher hat sie bei der Deutschen Bank gearbeitet. *At one time she used to work for Deutsche Bank.*

Er hat den ganzen Nachmittag am Computer gespielt. *He was playing computer games all afternoon.*

Sie hat gerade ein Buch gelesen. *She has (just) been reading a book.*

wordbank

oft *often*, **häufig** *frequently*
gewöhnlich, normalerweise *usually*
regelmäßig *regularly*
eine Weile *for a while*
manchmal *sometimes*
(so) viele Male *(so) many times*, **mehrere Male** *several times*
selten *rarely*, **nie, nimmer** *never*

jeden Tag *every day*, **jede Woche** *every week*
jeden Monat *every month*, **jedes Jahr** *every year*
ab und zu, dann und wann, mitunter *now and then, once in a while*

früher *formerly, at one time*
vor langer Zeit *a long time ago*
damals, zu dieser Zeit *at that time*
in den zweitausendnuller Jahren, im ersten Jahrzehnt dieses Jahrhunderts *in the noughties*
in den zweitausendzehner Jahren *in in the 2010s*
in den neunzehnneunziger Jahren *in the 1990s*
in grauer Vorzeit *in the dim and distant past*
es war einmal *once upon a time*

bringing what you say to life

Adverbs, as their name suggests, add information to verbs: **das passiert oft** *it happens often*, **das ist regelmäßig passiert** *it happened regularly*. They can also add information to adjectives and whole sentences: **sehr gut** *very good*, **leider ist er nicht hier** *unfortunately, he's not here.*

Although some adverbs provide essential information, such as when or where something is done, not all adverbs saying ***how*** something is done are essential to basic communication - but these are the words that can bring to life what you say and make it more interesting to listen to.

German adjectives can also be used as adverbs, unlike English they don't add *-ly*: **schnell** *quick/quickly;* **schlecht** *bad/badly*, **gut** *good/well.*

wordbank

endlich, schließlich *finally*
fast *almost*
gleich *right now*
glücklicherweise *luckily*
hoffentlich *hopefully*
langsam *slow, slowly*
leise *quiet, quietly*
meistens *most of the time*
mittlerweile *in the meantime*
natürlich *naturally, of course*
sofort *immediately*
unglaublich *unbelievably*
vielleicht *perhaps, maybe*
wahrscheinlich *probably*
wieder *again*
zufällig *accidentally, by chance*

The thing to remember about German adverbs is their position in the sentence. They are frequently the first word, and they cannot go between the subject and the verb. The verb is ***always*** in second place.
Hoffentlich wird das Wetter bald wieder besser. *Hopefully the weather will be better again soon.*
Mittags essen wir meistens zu Hause. *We have lunch at home most of the time.*
Glücklicherweise hatten wir genug Zeit, die Ausstellung von Anselm Kiefer zu sehen. *Luckily we had enough time to see the Anselm Kiefer exhibition.*

When there's an adverb of time and an adverb of place in the same sentence, time usually comes first. The usual order is Time - Manner - Place.
Ich gehe zweimal in der Woche ins Fitnessstudio./Zweimal in der Woche gehe ich ins Fitnessstudio. *I go to the gym twice a week.*
Er fährt jeden Tag mit dem Zug nach Düsseldorf/Jeden Tag fährt er mit dem Zug nach Düsseldorf. *He goes to Düsseldorf every day by train.*

coping in a crisis

In an emergency situation you need to know how to get help.

Hilfe! *Help!*
Feuer! *Fire!*
Es ist ein Notfall! *It's an emergency!*
Können Sie mir helfen? *Can you help me?*
Ich brauche Hilfe. *I need help.*

To say what's going on now you use the present tense:

Er kann nicht schwimmen. *He can't swim.*
Sie/Er blutet. *She/He's bleeding.*
Ich bin verletzt. *I'm hurt.*
Es ist ein Asthmaanfall. *It's an asthma attack.*
Ich kann nicht atmen. *I can't breathe.*
Es riecht nach Gas. *There's a smell of gas.*

... but to explain what's already happened, you need the perfect tense, except for **war** *was* and **hatte** *had.*

Ich bin/Er ist hingefallen. *I/He fell.*
Sie ist in Ohnmacht gefallen. *She's fainted.*
Sie ist auf dem Gehweg gestolpert. *She tripped on the pavement.*
Er ist ausgerutscht, weil der Boden nass war. *He slipped because the floor was wet.*
Ich hatte eine Panne. *My car's broken down.*
Es hat ein Unfall/Verkehrsunfall stattgefunden. *There's been an accident/a road accident.*

You use the verb **werden** to say something was done to you. when the emphasis is on the action rather than the person performing the action **Ich wurde beraubt.** *I was robbed. I've been robbed.*
Unsere Freunde wurden beraubt. *Our friends were robbed.*
Ich wurde überfallen. *I was attacked/mugged. I've been attacked/mugged.*
Mein Auto wurde aufgebrochen. *My car was/has been broken into.*
Die Tasche wurde mir aus der Hand gerissen. *My bag was/has been snatched.*
Mein Pass wurde gestohlen. *My passport was/has been stolen.*

saying something *had* taken place

In German, as in English, the only difference between saying something ***has*** happened and ***had*** happened is the tense of *have*. In German you use the imperfect of **haben** or **sein** – **hatte** or **war** – everything else is the same.

Ich hatte vergessen zu tanken. *I had forgotten to fill up with petrol.*
Ich hatte schon warum gefragt. *I had already asked why.*
Hattest du das Buch schon gelesen? *Had you already read the book?*
Er war müde, weil er nicht gut geschlafen hatte. *He was tired because he hadn't slept well.*
Da er sein Portemonnaie verloren hatte, konnte er nicht bezahlen. *Since he had lost his wallet he couldn't pay.*
Du hattest ihn gesehen, nicht wahr? *You had seen him, hadn't you?*
Am Tag zuvor hatten sie bis spät in den Abend hinein gearbeitet. *They had worked late into the evening on the day before.*
Sie hatten die Hälfte schon gegessen. *They had already eaten half.*
Hatten sie sich gut amüsiert? *Had they enjoyed themselves?*
Sie hatten sich hierher beeilt. *They had hurried down here. They had rushed here.*

Ich war vor zwei Monaten hingefallen. *I had fallen two months earlier.*
Warst du schon weggegangen? *Had you already left?*
Sie war mit Thomas angeln gegangen. *She'd gone fishing with Thomas.*
Wir waren vorzeitig angekommen. *We had arrived early.*
Wart ihr gleichzeitig weggefahren? *Had you left at the same time?*
Sie war eingeschlafen. *She had fallen asleep.*
Am Samstag war alles klar geworden. *By Saturday, everything had become clear.*
Das Leben war für sie nicht leicht gewesen. *Life had not been easy for her.*
Um wieviel Uhr waren Sie aufgewacht? *What time had you woken up?*

Old English

English is a Germanic language, so its structure has much in common with German. The Norman invasion 'frenchified' English, but Old English is very similar to modern day German. English past participles used to start with **ge-**, as modern German ones do: *done* was ***gedon***, *gone* ***gegan***, *lived* ***gelifd*** and *said* ***gesægd***.

talking the talk

Sophie Hast du was Interessantes gestern Abend gemacht?
Volker Ich habe mit einem Freund im Fitnessstudio Tennis gespielt. Leider habe ich nicht sehr gut gespielt, aber wir hatten viel Spaß.
Sophie Cool! Und dann was habt ihr gemacht?
Volker Dann sind wir in die Stadt gegangen und haben eine Pizza gegessen und ein Glas Bier getrunken. Ich bin nicht sehr spät nach Hause gegangen, weil ich heute arbeiten musste.
Sophie Ach so!

Volker Und du Sophie, wo warst du gestern Abend? Du bist so schnell weggegangen.
Sophie Ja, ich wollte Oskar sehen. Er hat mich angerufen.
Volker Oskar? Wer ist Oskar?
Sophie Mein Cousin, der Künstler. Er wurde beraubt. Sein Laptop wurde gestohlen.
Volker Was für ein Unglück! Was ist passiert?
Sophie Sein Auto wurde aufgebrochen. Er hat fast seine ganze Arbeit verloren.
Volker Wie schrecklich! Der Arme!

Sophie Oskar und ich sind zusammen aufgewachsen. Wir haben in demselben Dorf gewohnt.
Volker Wo war das?
Sophie Wir haben in den Bergen in Unterammergau in der Nähe von Garmish-Partenkirchen gewohnt.
Volker Eine wunderschöne Gegend.
Sophie Genau. Wir hatten ein schönes Haus in den Bergen. Wir sind immer viel gewandert, und wir waren alle sehr fit. Jeden Winter hat es viel geschneit. Und du, wo bist du geboren?
Volker Ich bin in Karlsruhe geboren, aber als Kind habe ich in Offenburg gewohnt. Wir waren zu viert in einer kleinen Wohnung: ich, mein Bruder Jan und meine Eltern. Es gab keine Berge in Offenburg, aber wir Kinder haben immer viel Spaß gehabt. Wir sind fast jede Woche nach Straßburg gefahren, und damals habe ich sehr gut französisch gesprochen. Leider habe ich jetzt fast alles vergessen!
Sophie Schade!

verb practice 3

1 Write these verbs in the **perfect** tense; they are all regular weak verbs.

a	**hoffen** *to hope*	**ich** ....
b	**tanzen** *to dance*	**wir** ....
c	**sich küssen** *to kiss (each other)*	**sie** (they) ....
d	**sagen** *to say*	**du** ....
e	**glauben** *to believe*	**sie** (she) ....
f	**machen** *to do*	**ihr** ....
g	**lernen** *to learn*	**Sie** ....
h	**schicken** *to send*	**er** ....

2 Change the verbs in the **perfect** tense in these sentences to the **imperfect** and say what they mean.

a **Bist du schon mal in Österreich gewesen?**
b **Es hat viele Probleme gegeben.**
c **Ich habe nicht genug Zeit gehabt.**
d **Gestern Abend ist er müde gewesen.**
e **Ich hoffe, du hast Spaß gehabt.**

3 Which of these verbs would you expect to form their perfect tense with **sein**?

klettern *to climb*; **bezahlen** *to pay for*; **bekommen** *to get*; **laufen** *to run*; **springen** *to jump*; **verkaufen** *to sell*

4 Complete this journal entry for yesterday, putting the verbs in brackets into the perfect tense. They are a mixture of **haben**, **sein**, separable and inseparable verbs. Then translate the entry into English.

Gestern morgen .... ich in die Stadt .... (fahren). Dort .... ich zwei Bücher .... (kaufen). Am Nachmittag .... ich meine Oma .... (besuchen). Wir .... zusammen eine Tasse Kaffee .... (trinken). Ich .... um vier Uhr zu Hause .... (ankommen). Am Abend .... mein Freund und ich ins Kino .... (gehen). Wir .... einen neuen italienischen Film .... (sehen). Der Film .... uns sehr gut .... (gefallen).

checkpoint 5

1 If **bevorzugen** *to prefer* and **entdecken** *to discover* are inseparable weak verbs, what are their past participles?

2 How would you say *I was born in Manchester*?

3 .... **haben wir die Insel besucht.** What needs inserting for the sentence to say *We visited the island the day before yesterday*?

4 How would you tell someone you've lost your wallet?

5 The past participles of which two categories of verbs don't start with **ge-**?

6 Use these phrases in the correct order to write the sentence: We went to Berlin by train last year: **nach Berlin/mit dem Zug/letztes Jahr**.

7 What are these calamities: **ein Unfall, eine Panne, ein Asthmaanfall**?

8 How would you ask somebody (**Sie**) what they did yesterday?

9 Which verb would you use to say *to change trams*: **aussteigen, einsteigen** or **umsteigen**?

10 What's the German for *ago*, and how does its usage differ from English usage?

11 **Geblieben, gewesen, geworden, gesprochen, verstanden** and **aufgewachsen** are the past participles of which strong verbs? What do these verbs mean?

12 Which words need to be added to **Warst du in Zürich?** for the question to mean *Have you ever been to Zurich?* and where do the words go?

13 If you hear **Wo habt ihr euch kennengelernt?** when you're with your partner or friend, what information are you being asked for?

14 What's the difference between **ich habe gesehen** and **ich hatte gesehen**; and between **er ist gegangen** and **er war gegangen**?

15 Put these time expressions in order, starting with the one closest to the present time: **gestern, vor zwei Jahren, vor kurzer Zeit, vorgestern**.

16 What's another way of saying **Was ist geschehen?** *What's happened*?

17 What's the difference in meaning between **Was ist eine Katastrophe?** and **Was für eine Katastrophe!?**

18 Put these adverbs into pairs of opposites: **glücklicherweise, gut, langsam, leider, schlecht, schnell**.

19 Which of the following does ***not*** translate the sentence **Ich habe als Briefträger gearbeitet**: *I worked as a postman, I have worked as a postman, I had worked as a postman, I used to work as a postman*?

sechs
lifestyle choices

Knowing how to say what you like and enjoy - or don't - is something that comes in useful in all sorts of situations, whether you're referring to food or the weather, discussing work, people, places, your interests or your pet hates. It allows you to explain why you'd rather do one thing than another, or simply to express delight when something pleases you (and frustration when you're less than pleased!).

There are various ways of saying what you do and don't like in German. These include **mir gefällt, ich mag, gern**, and **ich finde ... gut.** The one you use depends on what you're talking about.

Like has other meanings too, and consequently there are other German words for it.
wie neu *like new*
eine Frau wie du *a woman like you*
Wie ist er? *What's he like?*
saufen wie ein Loch lit. *to drink like a hole*
sich aufführen wie ein Elefant im Porzellanladen *to behave like an elephant in a china shop*
so *like this/like that*
das Kind sieht seinem Vater nicht ähnlich *the child doesn't look like his/her father*

liking places, clothes or art

When talking about appearance or about external or outer characteristics, you use the verb **gefallen** *to please, to be pleasing*, and the structure of the sentence is quite different to that used in English.

Mir gefällt literally means *pleases me, is pleasing to me.*
You can begin with **mir** or the thing you like. The verb always comes second.
Mir gefällt **Salzburg** or **Salzburg** gefällt **mir.** *Salzburg is pleasing to me,* i.e. *I like Salzburg.*
Mir gefällt **es hier.** *I like it here.*

For more than one thing, you use **mir** gefallen *are pleasing to me*:
Mir gefallen **die alten Gebäude.** *I like the old buildings.*
Tätowierungen gefallen **mir nicht.** *I don't like tattoos.*

Mir *to me* is the dative case of **ich** *I* (see page 180). To talk about what other people like, all you do is replace **mir**.
Die Landschaft gefällt uns **sehr gut.** *We really like the scenery.*
Uns **gefallen die kleinen Gassen der Altstadt.** *We like the little lanes of the Old Town.*
Ihm **gefallen diese Fotos.** *He likes these photos.*
Gefällt es dir **hier?** *Do you like it here?* (**du**)
Die Architektur gefällt ihr. *She likes the architecture.*
Wie gefällt es euch **in Österreich?** *How do you like it in Austria?* (**ihr**)
Wie gefällt Ihnen **unser Weihnachtsmarkt?** *How do you* (**Sie**) *like our Christmas market?*
Ich glaube, ihnen **gefallen die Bilder.** *They like the pictures.*

You also need the dative case when using a noun.
Meinem Vater/Meiner Mutter **gefallen meine Klamotten nicht.** *My father/ mother doesn't like my clothes.*
Gefällt es deinen Eltern **hier?** *Do your* (**du**) *parents like it here?*

Es gefällt mir, or **mir gefällt es**, can be followed by zu plus an infinitive or dass to mean *to like, to enjoy doing, to be pleased or glad (about).*
Mir gefällt es an der frischen Luft zu **sein.** *I enjoy being in the fresh air.*
Uns gefällt es, dass **ihr hier seid.** *We're pleased that you're here.*

In German, the *Like* button on Facebook is **Gefällt mir**.

liking food or music

Ich mag from **mögen** *to like* is used when you like the personality of someone, or the inner qualities or characteristics of something: when visual appearance is not the key factor.

Compare **Er gefällt mir** *I like him* = I like the way he looks
Ich mag ihn *I like him* = I like him as a person

Mögen is irregular:

ich mag, du magst, er/sie mag, wir mögen, ihr mögt, sie/Sie mögen

Ich mag starken Kaffee. *I like strong coffee.*
Er mag Tiere mehr als Menschen. *He likes animals more than people.*
Welche Computerspiele magst du? *Which computer games do you like?*
Mögen Sie klassische Musik? *Do you like classical music?*
Mögt ihr türkisches Essen? *Do you like Turkish food?*

To make the sentence negative, use **nicht** or, if there's a noun, **kein(e).**
Das mag ich nicht. *I don't like that.*
Sie mag mich nicht. *She doesn't like me.*
Wir mögen keine klassische Musik. *We don't like classical music.*
Sie mag keine Schokolade. *She doesn't like chocolate.*

Mögen needs an object i.e. the thing or person you like. It can be followed by a clause, in which case **es** *it* is inserted to represent the missing object.

Ich mag es, wenn jemand mir Blumen schenkt. *I like it when someone gives me flowers. I like someone giving me flowers.*
Ich mag es nicht, wenn Leute in der Bahn zu laut am Handy quatschen. *I don't like it when people on the train chatter too loudly on their mobile phones.*

The German title of the film *Some Like It Hot* is **Manche mögen's heiß**, where **es** is shortened to **'s**.

An alternative to **ich mag** is **ich finde ... gut/sehr gut/toll/ fantastisch** *I find ... good/very good/fantastic.*
Findest du diese Anwendung gut? *Do you like this app?*
Ich finde das deutsche Duo 2raumwohnung toll. *I really like the German duo 2raumwohnung.*
Ich finde Mozarts Musik fantastisch. *I really like Mozart's music.*

things you like doing

Gefallen and **mögen** are usually used with nouns or pronouns. When saying you like ***doing*** something, there's a verb in the sentence, and you can simply add **gern** or **gerne** after that verb (they both mean the same).

Ich esse gern Pizza. *I like eating pizza.*
Was macht ihr gerne? *What do you guys like doing?*
Spielst du gern Fußball? *Do you like playing football?*
Hörst du gern Musik? *Do you enjoy listening to music?*
Kochen Sie gern? *Do you like cooking?*
Wir trinken gern deutsches Bier. *We like (drinking) German beer.*
Sie wandern gern in den Bergen.*They like hiking in the mountains.*
Mein Kind geht nicht gern in den Kindergarten. *My child doesn't like going to kindergarten.*

Gern doesn't affect the usual word order or sentence structure. With separable verbs in the present tense, **gern** goes after the main body of the verb or after **nicht,** with the separable prefix at the end of the sentence.
Wir sehen nicht so gern fern. *We don't like watching television all that much.* (**fernsehen** *to watch television*)
Hoffentlich muss ich nicht umsteigen. Ich steige nicht gern um. *Hopefully I don't need to change. I don't like changing trains.*

With compound verbs, i.e. those made up of two elements, like **einkaufen gehen** *to go shopping*, **spazieren gehen** *to go for a walk*, **Rad fahren** *to cycle/ ride a bike*, **Ski laufen** *to ski*, **gern** goes after second element (the verb), with the first element going to the end of the sentence.
Samstags gehe ich gern einkaufen. *I like going shopping on Saturdays.*
Unsere Kinder laufen gern Ski. *Our children like skiing.*
Abends gehen wir gern spazieren. *We like going for a walk in the evening.*
Lauft ihr gern Schlittschuh? *Do you enjoy ice-skating?*
In unserer Freizeit fahren wir gern Rad. *We like cycling in our free time.*

Gern can be combined with **mögen** to strengthen the sense of liking.
Ich mag gern deutsche Literatur. *I like German literature very much.*
Wir mögen Knödel besonders gern. *We particularly like dumplings.*

other ways of liking ... and not liking

Just as in English there are other ways in German of saying you like or enjoy something, and the opposite.

(mir) Spaß machen, lit. *to be fun*

Mir macht der Job sehr viel Spaß. *I really like my job. My job is such fun.*
Schwimmen macht mir Spaß. *I like swimming. I find swimming good fun.*
Die Schule macht uns großen Spaß. *We really enjoy school. School's great fun.*
Das macht mir überhaupt keinen Spaß! *I don't like that at all!*
Mir macht die Arbeit keinen Spaß mehr. *I don't like my job any more. My job's no fun any more.*
Es gibt Aktivitäten, die keinen Spaß machen, aber wir müssen sie trotzdem machen. *There are activities which are no fun/which we don't like doing, but we have to do them regardless.*

mich ansprechen *to appeal to me, to take my fancy*

Das spricht mich sehr an. *That appeals to me very much.*
Diese Bilder sprechen mich nicht an. *These pictures don't appeal to me.*

Der Film war nicht mein Fall. *The film wasn't my cup of tea.*
Das ist nicht mein Ding. *It's not my thing/not my bag.*

(mir) schmecken

You can use **schmecken** to talk about liking the taste of food or drink. It works like **gefallen** and **Spaß machen**, where the *I* of English becomes **mir** *to me* in German. You use **mir schmeckt** to talk about something in the singular, and **mir schmecken** to talk about liking more than one thing.

Wie schmeckt euch das Essen? *How do you like the food?* (**ihr**)
Mir schmeckt deutscher Wein. *I like German wine.*
Semmelknödel schmecken (uns) sehr gut. *We like bread dumplings. Bread dumplings taste really good.*
Welche Gerichte schmecken Ihnen nicht? *Which dishes don't you like?*

Dumplings are a favourite with Germans, and there are dozens of ways to eat them – sweet and savoury. **Knödel** is the name of the dish used in the south of Germany and Austria, while **Klöße** is heard more in the west and north.

what you liked and used to like

To talk about what you liked or used to like in German, you use the perfect tense.

The past participle of **gefallen** is also **gefallen**. **Mögen** has the past participle **gemocht** and the past particle of **schmecken** is **geschmeckt**.

Der Film hat mir sehr gut gefallen. *I enjoyed the film very much.*
Der Ausflug hat uns nicht so gut gefallen. *We didn't particularly enjoy the excursion.*
Unsere Fotos haben ihnen richtig gut gefallen. *They really liked our photos.*
Was hat euch dort gefallen? *What did you like there?*

Hast du die Schule gemocht? *Did you like school?*
Deine Eltern haben wir sehr gemocht. *We liked your parents very much.*

Ich habe gern dort gearbeitet. *I enjoyed working there.*
Was hast du als Kind gern gemacht? *What did you like doing when you were a child?*

Hat (Ihnen) das Essen geschmeckt? *Did you like the food?*
Beide Pizzen haben sehr gut geschmeckt. *Both pizzas were very good.*

Immer is *always* and **nie** is *never.*
Das Hotel hat uns immer gefallen. *We always liked the hotel.*
Früher habe ich ihn immer gemocht. *I always used to like him.*
Hast du immer gern Fußball gespielt? *Did you always like playing football?*
Das hat mir nie gefallen. *I never liked it.*
Rock 'n' Roll hat er nie gemocht. *He never liked rock'n'roll.*
Ich bin nie gern schwimmen gegangen. *I never liked going swimming.*

You may come across the imperfect tenses of **gefallen, mögen** and **schmecken** in written German, so it's useful to be able to recognise them.

Die ersten Computerspiele gefielen uns nicht besonders gut, aber die neuen schon. *We didn't like the early computer games, but we do like the new ones.*
Früher mochte er aufgemotzte Sportwagen. *He liked/used to like souped-up sports cars.*
Der Sekt schmeckte nicht so gut. *The champagne wasn't very nice.*

adding nuance to what you say

Slotting words like **sehr** *a lot, very much,* **so sehr** *so much* or **richtig/wirklich/echt** *really* into a sentence adds nuance or depth to what you're saying. It's simple to do: since they're adverbs there's nothing about them to change. They work in any context and are especially useful when you're talking about what you like, since *I like/I don't like* can sound rather stark.

Ich mag Diane Kruger sehr gern. *I like Diane Kruger very much.*
Diese gefallen mir sehr. *I like these a lot.*
Die Show hat uns wirklich gut gefallen. *We really liked the show.*
Gefällt es dir wirklich, oder sagst du's nur so? *Do you like it really, or are you just saying it?*
Uns hat der Aufenthalt richtig/echt gut gefallen. *We really enjoyed our stay.*
Er steht total gerne früh auf. *He really, really likes getting up early.*
Uns gefällt es ein bisschen ... aber nicht so gut. *We quite like it ... but not a lot.*
Ich finde die Farben echt toll. *I just love the colours.*

You add emphasis to phrases about things you don't like with words like **gar nicht/überhaupt nicht/gar kein(e)** *not at all,* **nicht besonders** *not particularly,* or **nicht so sehr/nicht so gut/eher nicht** *not that much.*

Ich mag es überhaupt nicht. *I can't stand it. I don't like it at all.*
Ich wasche gar nicht gerne ab. *I don't like doing the washing-up at all.*
Ich mag gar keine Krimis. *I don't like crime novels at all.*
Das Restaurant mag ich eher nicht. *I'm not very keen on that restaurant.*
Ich mag diesen Stil nicht besonders. *I don't particularly like this style.*
Was hat Ihnen nicht so gut gefallen? *What weren't you so keen on?*

The German verbs **lieben** *to love* and **hassen** *to hate* are stronger in meaning than their English counterparts, and are not used so often. It's better to use one of the *like* phrases above.
Ich liebe dich. *I love you.*
Ich liebe die Sonne. *I absolutely adore the sun.*
Ich hasse Montage. *I really hate Mondays.*
Ich hasse es, früh aufzustehen. *I really hate getting up early.*
A good alternative to **hassen** is **leiden können**, usually used with **nicht** to mean *I can't stand.* **Ich kann Bügeln nicht leiden**. *I can't stand ironing.*

what interests you

The verb **interessieren** means *to interest*, and the reflexive verb **sich interessieren (für)** means *to be interested (in)*.

Ich interessiere mich für die Wissenschaft. *I'm interested in science.*
Wissenschaft interessiert mich. *Science interests me.*
Wir interessieren uns für Ausflüge in die Berge. *We're interested in excursions to the mountains.*
Die Festung Hohensalzburg interessiert uns. *Hohensalzburg Fortress interests us.*
Ich interessiere mich für seine/ihre/Ihre Theorien. *I'm interested in his/her/ your theories.*
Er interessiert sich mehr für die Zukunft als für die Vergangenheit. *He's more interested in the future than the past.*
Katja interessiert sich für Mode. *Katja's interested in fashion.*

Interessierst du dich für Frauenfußball? *Are you interested in women's football?*
Interessieren Sie sich für unser Deutsch-Sprachtraining? *Are you interested in our German language courses?*

Nicht makes the verb negative:
Sophie interessiert sich nicht für Mode. *Sohie isn't interested in fashion.*
Das Thema interessiert mich nicht.*The topic doesn't interest me.*
Wir interessieren uns nicht für Politik. *We're not interested in politics.*

You can also use the verb **finden** with **interessant**, *I find .... interesting.*
Kreuzworträtzel finde ich interessant; Sudokus finde ich nicht interessant. *I find crosswords interesting; I don't find sudokus interesting. Crosswords interest me; sudokus don't interest me.*
Ich finde Ihren Standpunkt interessant. *Your point interests me.*

I was interested is: **Ich habe mich für ... interessiert.**
In der Schule habe ich mich für die Wissenschaft interessiert. *At school I was interested in science.*
Haben Sie sich immer für Technik interessiert? *Were you always interested in technology?*
Er hat sich nie für Sportwetten interessiert. *He was never interested in gambling.*

wordbank

der Sport *sport*
- **das Fallschirmspringen** *parachuting*
- **der Fußball** (**7-a-side**) *football (seven a side)*
- **das Kitesurfen** *kitesurfing*
- **das Klettern/das Bergsteigen** *climbing, mountaineering*
- **das Laufen, der Laufsport** *running*
- **das Rollschuhlaufen** *roller-skating*
- **das Schlittschuhlaufen** *ice-skating*
- **das Schwimmen** *swimming*
- **das Segeln** *sailing,* **das Skifahren** *skiing*
- **das Wandern (mit dem Rucksack)** *walking (backpacking)*
- **das Windsurfen** *windsurfing*

The words ending **-n** or **-en** above are nouns made from the infinitive. The infinitive is written with a small letter, and the noun with a capital letter. You can use either to convey English *-ing* words, although the sentence structure will differ.
Wir mögen Schwimmen. *We like swimming.* (the noun)
Wir schwimmen gern. *We like swimming.* (the verb)

Many sports use the English word, e.g. **das Badminton, der Basketball, das Golf, das Judo, das Rugby, das Squash, das Tennis, der Volleyball, der** or **das Yoga**. And note **das Kricket** or **das Cricket.**
Der Sport has no plural. Instead, use **Sportarten: Wintersportarten, Kampfsportarten** *combat sports,* **Wassersportarten** *water sports.*

in der freien Natur sein *to be in the great outdoors*
- **die frische Luft** *fresh air*
- **das Fitnesstraining** *exercise*
- **ein Gefühl des Wohlbefindens** *a sense of wellbeing*
- **eine bessere Fitness** *improved fitness*
- **der niedrigere Blutdruck** *lower blood pressure*
- **weniger Stress** *reduced stress*
- **der Schlamm** *mud,* **die Ameisen** *ants*
- **die Bienen** *bees,* **die Fliegen** *flies*
- **der Hundehaufen** *dog poo,* **die Mücken** *mosquitoes*
- **die Nesseln** *nettles,* **die Spinne** *spider*
- **die Wespen** *wasps*

Ich mag keine Spinnen. *I don't like spiders.*
Ich mag (die) frische Luft. *I like (the) fresh air.*

die Künste *the arts*

die klassische/sinfonische Musik *classical/symphonic music*
die Popmusik *pop music*
die Chormusik *choral music*, **die Kammermusik** *chamber music*
die (große) Oper *(grand) opera*
die Alternative/die alternative Musik *alternative music*

die heutige/zeitgenössische Musik *modern music*, most of which adapts the English words, e.g. **die Rockmusik, der Hardrock, der Jazz, der Punk-Rock, der Blues, der Rock 'n' Roll, der Hip-Hop, der Rap, der Techno, der Heavy Metal**

die abstrakte Kunst *abstract art*, **die Konzeptkunst** *conceptual art*
die Performance-Kunst *performance art*
die Galerie *gallery*, **das Museum** *museum*
die Ausstellung *exhibition*
das Kino *cinema*, **das Theater** *theatre*
die Show *show*, **die Vorstellung, der Auftritt** *performance*
der Live-Auftritt *live performance*
das Konzert *concert, gig*
die Rollenbesetzung *the cast*
der Schauspieler/die Schauspielerin *the actor/actress*
der Star *leading actor/actress, star;* **die Hauptrolle** *main role*
der moderne Tanz/der Gesellschaftstanz *modern/ballroom dance*

die Haushaltsarbeiten *household jobs*

die Hausarbeit *housework*
im Garten arbeiten *to garden*
Heimwerkerarbeiten machen *to do DIY*
den Lebensmitteleinkauf machen *to do the food shopping*
mit dem Hund spazierengehen/mit dem Hund Gassi gehen *to walk the dog*
abstauben, den Staub abwischen *to dust*
sauber machen *to do the cleaning*
waschen *to wash;* **das Auto waschen** *to wash the car*
abwaschen *to wash the dishes*
kochen *to cook*, **bügeln** *to iron*
den Müll rausbringen *to take out the rubbish*

Use the words on these two pages to practise talking about what you like/don't like, what does and doesn't interest you. If your interests or pet hates aren't included, look them up in a dictionary. There are tips on using a dictionary on pages 117–120.

expressing a preference

The easiest way to express a preference in German is by putting **lieber** after the relevant verb, following the same pattern as for **gern** (page 90).

Ich fahre lieber Kajak. *I prefer canoeing.*
Wir fahren lieber mit dem Auto. *We prefer travelling by car.*
Ich höre lieber Musik. *I prefer listening to music.*
Wir fahren lieber im Frühling dorthin. *We prefer to go there in spring.*
Sie läuft lieber Ski. *She prefers skiing.*

Colloquially, you'll hear **lieber** combined with **mögen**.
Obst mag ich lieber. *I prefer fruit.*
Was magst du lieber? *What do you prefer?*

To is **als**:
Ich trinke lieber Tee als Kaffee. *I prefer tea to coffee.*
Ich sehe Filme lieber zu Hause als im Kino. *I prefer watching films at home to watching them in the cinema.*
Ich habe Rudern lieber als Kajak. *I prefer rowing to canoeing.*
Wir gehen lieber spazieren als zu Hause zu bleiben. *We prefer going out for walks to/than staying at home.*

For *I'd prefer* or *I'd rather*, use **Ich möchte lieber, Ich würde lieber** or **Ich hätte lieber**.
Ich möchte mich lieber ausruhen. *I'd rather rest.*
Ich möchte lieber nicht allein gehen. *I'd rather not go on my own.*
Ich möchte lieber nicht wissen. *I'd prefer not to know.*
Ich würde lieber in ein italienisches Restaurant gehen. *I'd prefer to go to an Italian restaurant.*
Ich hätte lieber mehr Wahlmöglichkeiten. *I'd prefer to have more options.*

There are verbs that mean *to prefer*: the inseparable **bevorzugen** and the separable **vorziehen**, but they're not as common in conversation as **lieber**.
Wir bevorzugen kleine Hotels ohne Animation. *We prefer small hotels that have no entertainment.*
Was ziehst du vor – Theater oder Kino? *What do you prefer – theatre or cinema?*

better and best

Better and *best* in English are both adjectives and adverbs – but not in German. The German adjectives are **besser** and **best...**, and when they're before the noun, these take adjective endings (page 178).
Ich habe ein besseres Angebot bekommen. *I've received a better offer.*
Das Restaurant hat einen besseren Ruf als das Hotel selbst. *The restaurant has a better reputation than the hotel itself.*
Bayern-München ist der beste Fußball-Club Deutschlands. *Bayern Munich is the best football club in Germany.*
***Toni Erdmann* ist einer der besten deutschen Filme seit Jahren.** *Toni Erdmann is one of the best German films in years.*

The adverbs **besser** *better* or **am besten** *best (of all)* never change.
Deutsches Bier schmeckt besser (als englisches). *German beer tastes better (than English beer).*
Heute fühle ich mich besser; es ist nicht so heiß. *I feel better today – it's not as hot.*
Die Kinder fühlen sich auch besser. *The children are/feel better too.*
Welches arbeitet besser/am besten? *Which one works better/best?*
Eine dickflüssige Soße passt am besten zu Nudeln. *A thick sauce goes best with noodles.*

To say something or someone is your favourite, add **Lieblings-** to the beginning of the word:
Mozart ist mein Lieblingskomponist. *Mozart is my favourite composer.*
Berlin ist meine Lieblingsstadt. *Berlin is my favourite city.*
Hier sind meine Lieblingsrezepte. *Here are my favourite recipes.*
Welche ist deine Lieblingsfarbe? *What's your favourite colour?*

With other verbs, **am liebsten** *most of all* can be used:
Das mag ich am liebsten. *I like it best. It's my favourite.*
Ich höre jede Musik gern, aber am liebsten höre ich Hip-Hop und Reggae. *I like all music, but most of all I like hip-hop and reggae/but my favourites are hip-hop and reggae.*
Was machen die Kinder am liebsten? *What do the children like doing best?*

To say what you like least, use **am wenigsten.**
Am wenigsten mag ich Horrorfilme. *I like horror films least.*
Am wenigsten gefällt mir diese Farbe. *I like this colour least. This is my least favourite colour.*

talking the talk

Volker	Läufst du gern Ski?
Sophie	Ja, natürlich. Ich bin in den Bergen geboren! Ich laufe auch sehr gern Schlittschuh. Eigentlich mag ich alle Wintersportarten. Und du? Machst du gern Sport?
Volker	Ja, ich mag viele Sportarten, besonders Segeln und Kajak. Und Schwimmen macht mir Spaß. Und ich spiele gern Tennis und Fußball. Ich spiele aber nicht besonders gut.
Sophie	Also, du magst Wassersportarten, und ich mache lieber Wintersportarten.
Volker	Haargenau! Du hast Recht.
Sophie	Ich mag gern in den Bergen in der freien Natur sein. Ich nehme gern meinen Rucksack und wandere den ganzen Tag. Dort hat man ein Gefühl des Wohlbefindens, und in den Bergen gibt es keine Mücken! Es ist zu kalt!

Volker	Reist du gern?
Sophie	Ja, ich interessiere mich für Architektur und reise gern zu alten Städten und interessanten Orten. Mir gefallen alte Gebäude sehr. Mir gefällt besonders Rothenburg ob der Tauber in Bayern.
Volker	Ja, Rothenburg ist sehr schön, aber die Altstadt von Offenburg gefällt mir besser. Es gibt weniger Touristen. Was für Musik hörst du gern?
Sophie	Ich höre jede Musik gern. Am liebsten mag ich klassische Musik. Mozart ist mein Lieblingskomponist. Aber ich mag auch Popmusik, zum Beispiel manchmal höre ich gern Susanne Lambert. Und du, hörst du gern Musik?
Volker	Ja, ich höre klassische Musik zu Hause, wenn ich Hausarbeit mache.
Sophie	Machst du viel Hausarbeit?
Volker	Nein, aber ich wohne allein. Ich bin geschieden.
Sophie	Ich auch, ich wohne allein. Nein, nicht allein – ich habe einen Hund; ich gehe gern mit ihm spazieren.
Volker	Was für einen Hund hast du?
Sophie	Einen Dackel.*
Volker	Wie süß!

* Although *dachshund* sounds German, the German word for *dachshund* is actually **der Dackel**.

checkpoint 6

1 Which is the odd one out and why? **Bienen, Fliegen, Menschen, Mücken, Wespen**

2 Would you use **gefallen** or **schmecken** in the sentence *I like these photos*?

3 If **Köln gefällt mir** means *I like Cologne*, what's the German for *she likes Cologne* and *he likes Cologne*?

4 How do you tell somebody in German that you like hiking?

5 Which word would you add to **Ich mag Computerspiele** to mean *I don't like any computer games* and where would you put it?

6 What are two ways of saying *I'm interested in politics*, i) using the verb **interessieren** and ii) using **sich interessieren**?

7 What can you add in front of a noun to mean *favourite*?

8 What are two ways, using **mögen** and **gern hören**, of asking a close friend if he or she likes pop music?

9 **Abstauben** *to dust* and **abwaschen** *to wash up* are separable verbs. If **ich staube nicht gern ab** means *I don't like dusting*, how do you say *I don't like washing up*?

10 Which of the following is not a water sport: **Rudern, Schlittschuhlaufen, Segeln, Windsurfen?**

11 How do you say, in three words, *I prefer to cook*?

12 What would you add to .... **mag ich Kriegsfilme** to mean *I like war films least*?

13 If **Die Suppe schmeckt** means *the soup tastes good*, what is *the soup tasted good*?

14 Put the sentence **Das Zimmer gefällt uns sehr** *We like the room very much* in the past tense.

15 Does **ich möchte lieber fernsehen** mean *I like watching television* or *I'd rather watch television*?

16 Which word is missing in this sentence meaning *I prefer fruit to vegetables*: **ich esse lieber Obst .... Gemüse**?

17 What could you say before **nicht** to make two ways of saying *not at all*?

sieben
making plans

Germany gave us our Christmas tree tradition, and it was an Austrian who wrote the carol *Silent Night*, so we have many traditions and celebrations in common with German-speaking Europe. But there are other holidays and celebrations apart from Christmas. The different **Länder** *states* of Germany have different public holidays, with Catholic Bavaria, for instance, celebrating **Epiphanie** or **Dreikönigsfest**, *the Feast of the Three Kings*, while most states don't mark this day.

Munich's **Oktoberfest** – which begins in September – is the largest beer and folk festival in the world, but Germans, Austrians and Swiss Germans love to party at other times of the year, too. The equivalent of Mardi Gras is **Karneval, Fasching** or **Fastnacht** – the name depends on the region – with the main action taking place on **Rosenmontag**, *Rose Monday*, the day before **Fastnachtsdienstag**, *Shrove Tuesday*. **Heiligabend**, *Christmas Eve*, is a family occasion, but larger and noisier celebrations, often including fireworks, take place on **Silvester**, *New Year's Eve*.

Feast days are celebrated in style, with family, food and drink playing a central role. If you're lucky enough to be invited to a traditional celebration, it's worth making sure you know how to accept or to decline graciously, and how to make your thanks sound sincere. It's also crucial to get the date and time right.

offering good wishes

Alles Gute *All the best, Good wishes* or **Herzlichen Glückwunsch** *Congratulations, Best wishes* are all-purpose ways of offering your good wishes.
Alles Gute zum Geburtstag; Herzlichen Glückwunsch zum Geburtstag. *Happy birthday.*
Alles Gute zum Hochzeitstag. *Happy Anniversary.*
Alles Gute zum Muttertag. *Happy Mother's Day.*
Alles Gute zum Namenstag. *Happy Name Day.*

Froh *happy* is used with major celebrations.
Frohe Ostern. *Happy Easter.*
Frohe Weihnachten. *Happy Christmas.*
Gutes/Frohes neues Jahr. *Happy New Year.*

There are phrases for every other occasion too.
Gute Besserung. *Get well soon.*
Gute Reise. *Safe journey. Have a good trip.*
Guten Appetit. *Enjoy your meal.*
Guten Flug. *Have a good flight.*
Schöne Ferien. *Enjoy the holidays. Have a good holiday.*
Schönen Abend noch. *Enjoy your evening.*
Schönen Aufenthalt. *Have a pleasant stay.*
Schönen Feiertag. *Happy holiday.* (public holiday)
Schönen Tag noch. *Have a good day.*
Schönes Wochenende noch. *Have a good weekend.*
Viel Erfolg. *Hope things go well. I/We wish you success.*
Viel Glück. *Good luck.*
Viel Spaß! Viel Vergnügen! *Have a good time! Enjoy yourself/yourselves!*

You can also start with **Ich wünsche dir/euch/Ihnen** *I wish you:*
Ich wünsche Ihnen einen guten Flug. *I hope you have a safe flight.*
Ich wünsche dir alles Gute zum Geburtstag. *I wish you a happy birthday.*
Wir wünschen allen frohe Weihnachten. *Our best wishes to everyone for Christmas.*
Danke. Dir/euch/Ihnen auch. *Thank you. And the same to you too.*

... or, if you want to be less formal:
Einen dicken Kuss zum Geburtstag! *A big kiss for your birthday!*

days and dates

The days of the week are all masculine (**der**).

Montag	*Monday*	
Dienstag	*Tuesday*	
Mittwoch	*Wednesday*	
Donnerstag	*Thursday*	
Freitag	*Friday*	
Samstag	*Saturday*	**Sonnabend** is used in eastern Germany.
Sonntag	*Sunday*	

Wir sehen uns am Sonntag. *See you on Sunday.*
Sonntags ist niemand da. *There's nobody there on Sundays.*
Bis Sonntag. *Till Sunday/See you Sunday.*

The months are also all masculine.

Januar *January*	**Juli** *July*
Februar *February*	**August** *August*
März *March*	**September** *September*
April *April*	**Oktober** *October*
Mai *May*	**November** *November*
Juni *June*	**Dezember** *December*

Im August/jeden August fahre ich nach Schottland. *I go to Scotland in/every August.*
Ich bin im Januar geboren. *I was born in January.*
Er ist am zwölften Oktober geboren. *He was born on 12th October.*
Sie ist neunzehnhundertdreiundneunzig/ eintausendneunhundertdreiundneunzig geboren. *She was born in 1993.*
Mein Enkel ist zweitausendfünfzehn geboren. *My grandson was born in 2015.*
Wollen wir uns am Vierzehnten treffen? *Shall we meet on the 14th?*
Am ersten Mai feiern wir den Geburtstag meiner Mutter. Ihr seid alle eingeladen. *We're celebrating my mother's birthday on 1st May. You're all invited.*
Möchten Sie am achten März bei uns zu Mittag essen? *Would you like to have lunch with us on March 8th?*
Können wir eine Besprechung auf den zweiundzwanzigsten/ auf Dienstag festlegen? *Can we arrange a meeting for the 22nd/for Tuesday?*

suggesting things to do

Like English, German has several ways of making suggestions.
The verb **lassen** means *to let*, and is followed by an infinitive, which goes at the end of the sentence.
Lass/Lasst uns **ein Picknick** machen! *Let's have a picnic!* **(du/ihr)**
Lassen Sie uns **hier** nicht bleiben ! *Let's not stay here.*

Wollen wir *shall we* and **möchtest du/möchtet ihr/möchten Sie** *would you like to* are also used with an infinitive at the end of the sentence.
Wollen wir **an den Strand** gehen? *Shall we go to the beach?*
Wollen wir **essen** gehen? *Shall we go and have something to eat?*
Möchtet ihr **am Wochenende zum Oktoberfest gehen?** *Would you like to go to the Munich Beer Festival at the weekend?*
Möchten Sie **bei uns frühstücken?** *Would you like to have breakfast at our place?*

Lust haben *to fancy, to feel like* can be followed by **zu** + infinitive at the end or by **auf** + noun in the accusative case.
Hast du Lust, **heute Abend ins Fitnesscenter zu gehen?** *Do you feel like going to the gym this evening?*
Hast du Lust **auf ein Bier/auf ein Eis/auf einen Kaffee?** *Do you fancy/feel like going for a beer/an ice cream/a coffee?*

Wie wäre es mit and the more colloquial **wie wär's mit** *How about* can be followed by a noun in the dative case.
Wie wäre es/wär's **mit einem Tennisspiel?** *How about a game of tennis?*
Wie wäre es **mit einem Glas Sekt?** *How about a glass of champagne?*

If you want to say, *Why ... not* or *Why don't we*, you can use **Warum ... nicht** with the verb coming immediately after **warum**.
Warum gehen wir nicht **ein Glas Wein trinken?** *Why don't we go and have a glass of wine?*
Warum gehen wir nicht **ins Theater? Wir müssen allerdings buchen.** *Why don't we go to the theatre? We'll need to book though.*

A statement can serve as an invitation.
Ihr seid alle **zu einer Feier** eingeladen: **am Freitag wird meine Mutter sechzig.** *You're all invited to a party: on Friday my mother will be 60.*

wordbank

These phrases, using verbs, can follow **Lass(t) uns, Möchtest du** etc. and **Wollen wir. Zu** is added before the infinitive when using **Lust haben**.

in die Stadt gehen *go into town;* **Hast du Lust, in die Stadt zu gehen?**
ins (Stadt)Zentrum gehen *go into the (town) centre*
durch die Altstadt bummeln *stroll through the old town*
die Kathedrale/das Schloss/die Sehenswürdigkeiten besichtigen *look round the cathedral/castle/sights*
ins Kaufhaus/Einkaufszentrum gehen *go to the department store/ shopping centre*
ins Kino gehen: heute läuft ... *go to the cinema: ... is on today*
in die Oper/ins Konzert/ins Museum gehen *go to the opera/to a concert/to the museum*
zum Stammtisch gehen *go to the regulars' meet-up at the pub*
eine Pizza essen *go for/have a pizza*

ein Fahrrad mieten *rent a bicycle*
den Regionalzug bis ... nehmen *take the local train as far as ...*
die Dörfer/die Umgebung erkunden *explore the villages/surrounding area*
durch die Weinberge wandern *stroll through the vineyards*
eine Bootsfahrt machen *go on a boat trip*
die besten Weine und Lebensmittel der Gegend probieren *taste the best local wines and products*
die schöne Landschaft bewundern *admire the beautiful countryside*
durch die Insel wandern *walk across the island*

in den Bergen wandern *hike in the mountains*
reiten gehen; in der Nähe gibt es einen Pferdehof *go riding; there are stables nearby*
bergsteigen gehen *go mountain climbing*
kegeln gehen/schwimmen gehen *go and play skittles/go swimming*

Try suggesting doing some of these things, using e.g. warum ... nicht, wollen wir..., lass uns ... , möchtest du ... , hast du Lust ... Then practise using the ihr and Sie forms: Lasst uns eine Pizza essen. **Let's have a pizza.** Habt ihr Lust, ins Museum zu gehen? **Do you fancy going to the museum?** Möchten Sie eine Bootsfahrt machen? **Would you like to go on a boat trip?**

what time?

Wann? Um wie viel Uhr?	*When? At what time?*
mittags	*at midday*
um Mitternacht	*at midnight*
um ein Uhr, um zwei Uhr	*at 1 o'clock, at 2 o'clock*
um Viertel nach acht	*at a quarter past 8*
um Viertel vor drei	*at a quarter to 3*

German doesn't say *half past*, but looks ***ahead*** to the next hour:

um halb elf	*at half past 10*

You can also tell the time using the 24-hour clock.

um dreiundzwanzig Uhr	*at 23.00, at 11 p.m.*
um neun Uhr dreißig	*at 09.30*
um vier Uhr vierzig	*at 04.40*

vor Mitternacht	*before midnight*
vor elf Uhr	*before 11 o'clock*
vor halb acht	*before half past 7*
von neun bis dreizehn Uhr	*from 09.00 to 13.00*
bis zum Mittag	*until middzay*
bis zehn Uhr abends	*until 10 o'clock in the evening*
nach zwei Uhr nachts	*after 2 o'clock in the morning*
um drei Uhr nachmittags	*at 3 o'clock in the afternoon*
um elf Uhr vormittags	*at 11 o'clock in the morning*

You can confirm a time using some of the expressions mentioned earlier:
Wollen wir uns so um halb zehn treffen? *Shall we meet at 9:30 or so?*
Wir werden uns gegen vier Uhr treffen. *See you at about 4 o'clock* (lit. *We'll meet at about 4 o'clock)*
Dann treffen wir uns genau um acht Uhr. *We'll meet at 8 on the dot then.*
Wie wär's mit einem Mojito zur Happy Hour? *How about a mojito at happy hour?*
Möchtest du gegen Mittag kommen? *Would you like to come at about midday/at lunchtime?*
Ich werde pünktlich um neun Uhr da sein. *I'll be there punctually at 9.*

Listen out for interesting expressions involving time of day:
zu Tagesanbruch *at the crack of dawn* **bei Sonnenuntergang** *at sunset*
bei Dämmerung *at twilight* **in den Stoßzeiten** *at rush hour*
um fünf Minuten vor zwölf *at the 11th hour/ last minute*
in den frühen Morgenstunden *in the small hours*

accepting and declining graciously

Vielen Dank, dass Sie mich/uns eingeladen haben. *Thank you so much for inviting me/us.*
Wie nett von dir/euch/Ihnen. *How kind of you.* **(du/ihr/Sie)**
Danke für die Einladung. *Thank you for the invitation.*

yes please

Gern/Ich möchte sehr gern. *Gladly, willingly, I'd love to.*
Mit (dem größten) Vergnügen. *With (the greatest) pleasure.*
Ich nehme Ihre Einladung dankend an. *I gratefully accept your invitation.*
Jawohl, sicher. *Certainly, definitely.*
Was für eine gute/schöne Idee! *What a good/lovely idea!*
Ich werde da sein! *I'll be there!*
Ich freue mich schon. *I can't wait.*

no thank you

Schön wär's! *If only! I wish!*
Es tut mir leid, aber ... *I'm sorry but ...*
Leider geht das nicht. *I'm afraid that's not possible.*
Ich kann nicht/Wir können nicht ... *I/we can't ...*
Leider. *Unfortunately.*
Leider kann ich nicht ... *Unfortunately/I'm afraid I can't ...*

Ich weiß nicht, ob ich kommen kann. *I don't know if I can come.*
Ich bin nicht sicher, ob ich hingehen kann. *I'm not sure if I can go.*

Wirklich schade, aber ... *It's a real shame but ...*
Ich hoffe, dass ich kommen kann, aber ... *I hope to be there but ...*
Ich werde mein Bestes tun, aber ... *I'll do my best but ...*
... ich werde nicht in der Stadt sein. *... I'll be out of town.*
... ich muss arbeiten. *... I've got to work.*
... ich habe schon was vor. *... I've already got something on.*
... wir haben schon was vor. *... we're already committed.*

Jedenfalls danke. *Thank you anyway.*
Vielleicht an einem anderen Tag. *Maybe another day.*

saying thank you

Danke. *Thank you. Thanks.*
Danke schön. *Thanks very much, thanks a lot.*
Vielen Dank/Schönen Dank. *Many thanks.*
Herzlichen Dank. *Thank you so much.*
Tausend Dank. *Thanks a million.*
Recht herzlichen Dank. *Thank you very much indeed.*
Vielen Dank für alles. *Thanks a lot for everything.*
Danke nochmal. *Thanks again.*
Ich bedanke mich bei Ihnen. *Thank you kindly.* **(Sie)**
Ich möchte mich bei Ihnen herzlichst bedanken. *I'd like to express my heartfelt thanks.*

Danke für Ihren Rat. *Thanks for your advice.* **(Sie)**
Danke für eure Geduld. *Thanks for your patience.* **(ihr)**
Danke für die Rückmeldung. *Thanks very much for the feedback.*
Vielen Dank für deine Hilfe. *Thanks a lot for your help.* **(du)**
Vielen Dank für Ihre Antwort. *Thank you for your reply.* **(Sie)**

Ich wollte Ihnen danken, aber ich habe keine Worte dafür. *I wanted to thank you, but I don't have the words.* **(Sie)**
Ich weiß nicht, wie ich mich bei Ihnen bedanken kann. *I don't know how I can thank you.* **(Sie)**

Du bist ein Engel/ein Schatz! *You're an angel/a gem!*
Das ist sehr freundlich/nett von dir. *That's so kind of you.* **(du)**
Das ist sehr großzügig von Ihnen. *That is really generous of you.* **(Sie)**
Ich schulde dir was. *I owe you one.* **(du)**

Es war eine sehr gute Party. *It's been a wonderful party.*
Es war ein sehr guter Tag/Abend. *It's been a great day/evening.*
Ich habe mich sehr amüsiert. *I've really enjoyed myself.*
Ich habe/Wir haben eine sehr gute Zeit gehabt. *I've had a great time/a ball.*
Vielen Dank, dass ihr mich/uns eingeladen habt.*Thank you so much for inviting me/us.*

Bitte. *You're welcome.*
Nichts zu danken. *Think nothing of it, don't mention it.*
Gern geschehen. *Not at all. My pleasure.*

talking about the future

If the future meaning is clear, you use the present tense in German to say what will happen or what's going to happen:
Ich bin gleich fertig. *I'll be ready in a minute.*
Der Flug kommt um acht Uhr an. *The flight will arrive at 8 o'clock.*
Morgen sind wir in Oberammergau. *We'll be in Oberammergau tomorrow.*
Wir treffen uns um zehn Uhr am Alexanderplatz. *We'll meet at 10 o'clock in Alexander Square.*
Am Wochenende besuchen wir unsere Freunde. *We'll be visiting our friends at the weekend.*
Wir machen morgen eine Weinprobe. *We're going to have a wine-tasting session tomorrow.*
Die Besprechung dauert anderthalb Stunden. *The meeting will last an hour and a half.*

However, if there's no certainty that the action is actually going to happen when you say it will, you use the present tense of **werden** plus the infinitive of the verb, which goes to the end of the sentence or clause. This is the German equivalent of the future tense.

ich werde	wir werden
du wirst	ihr werdet
er/sie/es wird	sie/Sie werden

Ich werde dich so um zehn Uhr abholen. *I'll pick you up at about ten.*
Der Zug wird zwanzig Minuten Verspätung haben. *The train will be 20 minutes late.*
In etwa zehn Jahren werde ich Rentner sein. *In about ten years' time I'll be retired.*
Ich werde es mir überlegen. *I'll think about it. I'll think it over.*
Sie werden sich bald an den Rechtsverkehr gewöhnen. *You'll soon get used to driving on the right.*

If German word order rules require that **werden** goes to the end, it goes right to the end, after the infinitive.
Weißt du schon, wo du nach der Schule studieren wirst? *Do you know where you're going to study after school yet?*
Ich weiß nicht, ob der Flug Verspätung haben wird. *I don't know whether the flight will be delayed.*
Meinst du, dass es morgen schneien wird? *Do you think it's going to snow tomorrow?*

weather permitting

Activities such as sailing, windsurfing, mountaineering or skiing require thinking ahead and an understanding of **die Wettervorhersage** *the weather forecast.*

Wie ist das Wetter morgen? *What's the weather going to be like tomorrow?*
Wie ist die Wettervorhersage für die nächsten Tage? *What's the weather forecast for the next few days?*
Das Wetter verspricht gut zu werden. *The weather looks promising.*
Das Wetter wird morgen besser werden. *The weather will improve tomorrow.*
Er/Sie meldet Sonne/Regen. *Sun/Rain is forecast.* lit. *He/She, (i.e. the weather presenter), is announcing sun/rain.*
Laut Wettervorhersage soll es am Sonntag sonnig sein. *The forecast is for sun on Sunday.* lit. *According to the weather forecast it should be sunny on Sunday.*
Laut Wettervorhersage soll es Regen und starken Wind geben. *Rain and strong winds are forecast.*
Wenn das Wetter schön ist, wollen wir im Garten grillen? *If it's fine shall we have a barbecue in the garden?*
Wenn genug Schnee ist/liegt, können wir snowboarden gehen. *If there's enough snow we can go snowboarding.*
Wenn die Wettervorhersage gut ist, dann fahren wir in die Berge. *If the forecast is good, then we'll go into the mountains.*

If you prefer a less scientific forecast: **Abendrot – Gutwetterbot. Morgenrot – Schlechtwetterbot.** *Red (sky at) night, a sign of good weather. Red (sky in the) morning, a sign of bad weather.*

Otherwise the weather tends to be either commented on or described.
Was für ein schönes Wetter! *What good weather!*
Was für ein wunderschönes Wetter! *What glorious weather!*
Schlechtes Wetter, nicht wahr? *Miserable weather, isn't it?*
Es ist heute sehr warm. *It's very warm today.*
Es ist so kalt! *It's so cold!*
Es ist so windig; draußen stürmt es. *It's so windy, it's blowing a gale!*
Was für eine frische Brise. *What a refreshing breeze.*
Es ist schwül heute, oder? *Really muggy today, isn't it?*
Der endlose Regen geht mir auf die Nerven. *This non-stop rain is getting on my nerves.*
Dieser Nebel gefällt mir gar nicht. *I hate this fog.*

Wie ist das Wetter heute? *What's the weather like today?*

Wie ist das Wetter bei Ihnen? *What's the weather like where you are?*
Heute ist schönes/scheußliches Wetter. *It's a lovely/terrible day.*
Es ist so heiß: viel zu heiß! *It's so hot: it's way too hot!*
Es ist fünfunddreißig Grad im Schatten. *It's 35 degrees in the shade.*
Es ist ein bisschen kühl. *It's a bit chilly.*
Es ist saukalt. *It's bitterly cold.* (lit. *it's swinishly cold)*

Es ist ein bisschen bewölkt. *It's a bit cloudy.*
Es ist mild. *It's mild.* **Es ist sehr feucht.** *It's very humid.*
Es ist windig. *It's windy.*
Es regnet: es gießt in Strömen. *It's raining: it's pouring down.*
Es schneit/hagelt. *It's snowing/hailing.*
Laut Wettervorhersage soll ein starker Wind wehen. *The forecast is for strong winds this evening.*
Es nieselt leicht. *There's a fine drizzle.*
Es liegt Schnee auf den Bergen. *There's snow on the mountains.*
Es gibt wenig Schnee in diesem Jahr. *There's not much snow this year.*

In Germany good weather is emperor's weather, and bad weather is dog's weather:

> **Es ist Kaiserwetter.** *It's a glorious day.*
> **Es ist Hundewetter.** *It's a beastly day.*

Wie war das Wetter? *What was the weather like?*

The reply can use the imperfect or perfect tense (pages 76–77):
Es war sehr warm. *It was hot.*
Es war sehr sonnig auf dem Lande. *It was very sunny in the country.*
Der Himmel war bedeckt. *The sky was overcast.*
Gestern hat es geregnet/geschneit/gehagelt. *It was raining/snowing/hailing yesterday.*
In dieser Nacht hat es gedonnert und geblitzt. *There was thunder and lightning during the night.*
Mittags gab es einen Platzregen. *There was a downpour at lunchtime.*
In der Nacht ist viel Schnee gefallen. *A lot of snow fell during the night.*

saying what you would do

To say *I would do something/I'd do something* you use **würde** + infinitive. **Würde** is the subjunctive of **werden**.

ich würde	**wir würden**
du würdest	**ihr würdet**
er/sie/es würde	**sie/Sie würden**

Was würde sie sagen? *What would she say?*
Ich würde jeden Tag Weißwurst essen. *I'd eat German white sausage every day.*

Some common verbs are used in their own subjunctive form rather than with **würde** + infinitive:
ich wäre = ich würde sein *I would be*
ich hätte = ich würde haben *I would have*
ich möchte = ich würde mögen *I would like*
ich könnte = ich würde können *I would be able to, I could*

Das wäre leider unmöglich. *That would be impossible, I'm afraid.*
Wir könnten kegeln gehen, wenn du möchtest. *We could go and play skittles, if you'd like.*
Möchten Sie eine Rheinschifffahrt machen? *Would you like to go for a boat tour on the Rhine?*
Das wäre toll. *That would be great.*

To say what you'd like in restaurants and shops, you can use **ich hätte gern** instead of **ich möchte**.
Ich möchte/Ich hätte gern einen Milchkaffee. *I'd like a milky coffee.*
Wir hätten gern ein Stück Käsekuchen und ein Stück Apfelstrudel. *We'd like a slice of cheesecake and a slice of apple strudel.*

Would in English isn't necessarily translated by **würde.**
Das wagst du nicht! *You wouldn't dare!*
Keine Ahnung! *I wouldn't know.* lit. *No idea.*
Als ich Kind war, sind wir jedes Jahr nach Blackpool gefahren. *When I was a child we would go to Blackpool every year.*

if

In a conditional sentence, i.e. where there's a condition involved, **wenn** means *if*.

When talking about events that you think have a good likelihood of happening, you use the present or future tense.
Ich werde dir helfen, wenn ich kann. *I'll help you if I can.*
Wenn die Sonne scheint, wird alles perfekt sein. *If the sun shines, everything will be perfect.*
Wenn wir im Lotto gewinnen, freuen wir uns sehr. *If we win the lottery, we'll be very happy.*

When talking more tentatively about events that you think are unlikely to happen, you use **würde** + infinitive, or **hätte, wäre** or **könnte.**
Ich würde dir helfen, wenn ich könnte. *I'd help you if I could.*
Wenn ich im Lotto gewinnen würde, würde ich eine Jacht kaufen. *If I won the lottery, I'd buy a yacht.*
Wenn ich reicher/jünger/fitter wäre ... *If I were richer/younger/fitter ...*
Wenn ich nur mehr Zeit hätte. *If only I had more time.*
Wenn ich an deiner Stelle wäre ... *If I were you ...* **(du)**

When talking about events in the past that you cannot change, you use **hätte/wäre** + past participle.
Wenn du mitgekommen wärest, wäre alles perfekt gewesen. *If you had come too, everything would have been perfect.*
Wenn ich es nur gewusst/verstanden/bemerkt hätte! *If I had only known/understood/noticed!*

Wenn is **ein falscher Freund** *a false friend*. It translates the English *when* only when referring to the present or future. Otherwise, **wenn** translates *if*.
Wenn ich ein Wort nicht kenne, schlage ich im Wörterbuch nach. *When/If I don't know a word, I look it up in a dictionary.*
Ich freue mich, wenn wir uns morgen sehen. *I'd like to meet tomorrow.* lit. *I'll be happy if/when we see each other tomorrow.*
For *when* in the past, you use **als.**
Als ich ein Kind war ... *When I was a child ...*
Als wir im Urlaub waren, haben wir ein amerikanisches Ehepaar kennengelernt. *When we were on holiday, we met an American couple.*
Wenn and **als** both send the verb to the end.
When in questions is **Wann?**
Wann kommst du zurück? *When are you coming back?*

talking the talk

Volker	Trinkst du gern Bockbier?
Sophie	Bockbier? Ja. Warum?
Volker	Am Sonntag ist ein Bockbierfest in Kippenheim. Hast du Lust hinzugehen?
Sophie	Ja, gern. Das wäre toll. Laut Wettervorhersage soll es am Sonntag warm und sonnig sein. Warst du schon mal auf dem Bierfest?
Volker	Ja, einmal. Aber es hat viel Spaß gemacht. Das Kippenheimer Bier schmeckt gut und auf den Straßen gibt es viel Musik.
Sophie	Ich freue mich schon! Was für eine schöne Idee! Um wie viel Uhr treffen wir uns?
Volker	Ich werde so um halb zehn bei dir sein. Wir fahren mit meinem Auto.
Sophie	Cool! Bis Sonntag.

Volker	Nun, wie war es? Hast du Spaß gehabt?
Sophie	Ja, es war ein sehr schöner Tag. Ich habe sehr viel Spaß gehabt. Vielen Dank.
Volker	Am Samstag hat meine Mutter Geburtstag. Sie wird sechzig. Wir machen ein Picknick im Wald. Möchtest du mitkommen?
Sophie	Es tut mir leid, aber am Samstag habe ich schon was vor.
Volker	Schade! Möchtest du nächsten Sonntag bei mir zu Mittag essen? Ich mache eine kleine Geburtstagsfeier. Natürlich wird meine Mutter da sein, und mein Vater, mein Bruder Jan und seine Tochter Mia.
Sophie	Mit Vergnügen. Um wie viel Uhr?
Volker	Gegen zwölf Uhr.
Sophie	Also, bis nächsten Sonntag. Vielen Dank für die Einladung. Eine schöne Woche noch!

verb practice 4

1 Write the future forms of these verbs and say what they mean.

a	**kaufen**	**du** ....
b	**fahren**	**sie** *(they)* ....
c	**haben**	**Sie** ....
d	**regnen**	**es** ....
e	**sich treffen**	**wir** ....
f	**vergessen**	**ihr** ....
g	**anrufen**	**ich** ....
h	**machen**	**er** ....

2 Put these sentences into the future tense, and say what they mean.

a **Wann besuchst du uns?**
b **Der Zug hat zehn Minuten Verspätung.**
c **Mit dieser App lernst du neue Leute kennen.**
d **Wir kommen nächstes Jahr zurück.**
e **Hoffentlich gefällt es dir.**

3 Rewrite these sentences, so that they all begin **Ich meine, dass** ... *I think that* ... Remember that **dass** sends the verb to the end.

a **Sie wird nächstes Jahr an der Uni studieren.** *She'll be studying at the university next year.*
b **Es wird in achtzig Jahren kein Rohöl geben.** *In eighty years there won't be any oil.*
c **Wir werden ein gutes Restaurant finden.** *We'll find a good restaurant.*
d **Ich werde vielleicht nächste Woche gehen.** *Perhaps I'll go next week.*

4 Match the two halves to make sentences

a	**Wenn ich Zeit hätte,**	i	**kannst du ein Stück Pizza essen.**
b	**Wenn du ein Tor geschossen hättest,**	ii	**würde ich einen Ferrari kaufen.**
c	**Wenn die Sonne scheint,**	iii	**würde ich mehr lesen.**
d	**Wenn ich Millionär wäre,**	iv	**hätten wir gewonnen.**
e	**Wenn du Hunger hast,**	v	**gehen wir zum Strand.**

checkpoint 7

1 What is an alternative word for **Sonnabend**?

2 What are the two months before **April** and the two months after?

3 What do you add to **Alles Gute zum** to wish someone a *happy birthday*? And what do you add to wish them a *happy anniversary*?

4 What's the difference between **um elf Uhr** and **gegen elf Uhr**? And what time is **halb sechs**?

5 Using **möchtet ihr**, how would you invite two friends to go and play skittles?

6 Which of these are you unlikely to use when accepting an invitation? **es tut mir leid, ich nehme Ihre Einladung dankend an, mit Vergnügen.**

7 What are **die Stoßzeiten**? And what can you add to **um vier Uhr** so that it means *punctually at four*?

8 In reply to good wishes from one person whom you call **Sie**, how do you say *the same to you*?

9 What are **ein Schloss, ein Strand** and **die Sehenswürdigkeiten**?

10 If **es ist kalt; es gibt viel Schnee** means *it's cold; there's a lot of snow*, how do you say *it was cold; there was a lot of snow*?

11 How would you say to a group of friends *Let's go to the cinema*, and *Shall we go to the cinema?*

12 What are shorter ways of saying **ich würde sein** and **ich würde haben**?

13 Which refers to stronger rain: **es gießt in Strömen** or **es nieselt leicht**?

14 Using the phrase **hast du Lust,** how would you ask someone if they feel like going on a boat trip?

15 Is your flight more likely to be delayed because of **eine Brise** or due to **Nebel**?

16 How do you say *the flight lasts an hour and a half*?

17 How do you thank someone for an invitation and say that unfortunately you're already committed?

18 **Wollen wir Tennis spielen? Wie wär's mit Samstag?** Text a reply saying *Sorry, I can't, I've got to work*, then say *perhaps on Sunday at two o'clock?*

how to use a dictionary

A dictionary is an essential tool for language learning, allowing you to personalise phrases and talk about exactly what you choose.

There are a number of dictionaries in print and online. Some of them are much better presented, more detailed and more user-friendly than others, and it's a case of trying a few and seeing which suits you.

grammatical terms and abbreviations

As with most tools, there's a skill to using a dictionary effectively. And, because of differences between the languages, using a German > English dictionary raises different issues from using the English > German version.

Each dictionary entry is defined by its grammatical category such as adjective, adverb, verb (pages 172–175), so you need to understand these basic terms. These are very often given in English in dictionaries designed for English-speaking learners, but the German equivalents are mostly very similar words. The category is generally abbreviated.

Art **Artikel** *art article*
Adj **Adjektiv** *adj adjective*
Adv **Adverb** *adv adverb*
Akk **Akkusativ** *accusative*
Dat **Dativ** *dative*
Gen **Genitiv** *genitive*
itr/tr **intransitiv/transitiv** *intransitive/transitive (verb)*
Nom **Nominativ** *nominative*
Part Perf **Partizip Perfekt** *pp past participle*
Pers **Person** *person*
Pl **Plural** *pl plural*
Präp **Präposition** *prep preposition*
Pron **Pronomen** *pron pronoun*
Sg **Singular** *sing singular*
Subst **Substantiv** *n noun*
umg **umgangssprachlich** *coll colloquial*
unr **unregelmäßig** *irregular*
V **Verb** *v verb*
vulg **vulgär** *vulg vulgar*

Most dictionaries include a comprehensive list of the abbreviations used.

Dictionaries do differ in their approach, however, with most indicating a noun and its gender by writing **der**, **die**, **das** or m (masculine), f (feminine), n (neuter) after it. The fact that a word begins with a capital letter is also an indication that it is a noun. The dictionary might indicate a verb by giving its different forms.

Deutsch → Englisch

German nouns are listed with their gender (**der/die/das**) and plural form, as these are not always guessable. Larger dictionaries give the genitive form too.

Hund ***der***; **~es**, **~e** *dog*: genitive singular is **Hundes**, and plural is **Hunde**
Hotel ***das***; **~s**, **~s** *hotel*: genitive singular is **Hotels**, and plural is **Hotels**
Buch ***das***; **~[e]s**, **Bücher** *book*: genitive singular is **Buchs** or **Buches**, and the plural is **Bücher**
Stadt ***die***; **~**, **Städte** *town*: genitive singular is **Stadt**, and plural is **Städte**

Irregular comparative and superlative forms of adjectives may also be given:
klein: *small, little*
groß, größer, größt...: *big, large*

Verbs that don't follow regular patterns list their different forms. Those that form their perfect tense with **sein**, and separable verbs, are also indicated.

arbeiten, *V*: *work*
kommen, *V* **kam**, **gekommen**; mit **sein**; *come*
lesen, *V* **liest**, **las**, **gelesen**; *read*
an|rufen, *V* **rief an**, **angerufen**; *call, telephone*

Some words belong in more than one grammatical category, but because nouns begin with capital letters and verbs usually end -**en**, it's clear which is which. A few nouns look identical but have a different gender and meaning.

reich ***Adj***: *rich*
Reich ***das;*** **~[e]s, ~e:** *empire*
reichen ***V:*** *be enough*

See[1] ***der;*** ***~s,*** **~n** *lake*
See[2] ***die;*** ***~,*** **~n** *sea*

Most German > English dictionaries list nouns in the singular, adjectives without any endings and verbs in the infinitive. This means that a word you're looking for may not appear exactly as you came across it. For example:

- Words beginning **ge-** are often past participles, so you'll need to take off **ge-** before you can search for the verb in the dictionary. That said, **ge-** is also an inseparable prefix, which you cannot remove; **gefallen** could be the past participle of **fallen** *to fall* or a form of **gefallen** *to please*.
- A verb you are seeking, e.g. **holt, kommen** might be only part of a separable verb; there might be a separable prefix **ab, zurück** elsewhere.
- Some parts of the verb look nothing like their infinitive e.g. **ging** (from **gehen** *to go*), **gezogen** (from **ziehen** *to pull*). A good dictionary will direct you to the infinitive.

English → German

Many English words belong in a single grammatical category, e.g. *terrain* is a noun, *write* can only be a verb, *genuine* can only be an adjective. But there are also many that belong in two or more categories, e.g. *sock* can be something you wear on your foot (noun) or can mean to hit somebody (verb); *snipe* can be a bird (noun), to shoot or to jeer (verbs); *back* can be the rear part (noun), to support (verb) or the opposite of front (adjective).

content I *n* 1 *in pl* Inhalt *der*; **2** *(amount contained)* Gehalt *der*. **II *adj*** zufrieden (**with** mit).

lock I *n* 1 Schloss *das:* combination ~ Kombinationsschloss *das*; **2** (*hair*) [Haar]Büschel *das*; **3** (*wrestling*) Fesselgriff *der*; **4** (*canal*) Schleuse *die*; **5** *(rugby)* Gedrängespieler in der zweiten Reihe *der*. **II *v*** zuschließen.

pitch I *n* 1 (*music*) Tonhöhe *die*; **2** (*sales*) Verkaufsargumentation *die*; **3** (*sports*) Platz *der*; **4** (*substance*) Pech *das*; **5** ~ and putt Minigolf *das*. **II adj** ~ dark pechfinster. **III v 1** (*throw*) werfen; **2** ~ (*tent/camp*) aufschlagen.

table I *n* 1 (*furniture*) Tisch *der*; bedside ~ Nachttisch *der*; dressing ~ Friesierkommode *die;* ~ wine Tischwein *der*. **2** (*chart*) Tabelle *die*; **3** (*chem*) periodic ~ Periodensystem *das*. **4** (*math*) ~s Einmaleins *das*; **5** (sport) ~ tennis Tischtennis *das*. **II *v*** ~ a motion einen Antrag einbringen.

Spelling is, of course, critical. While *hangar* and *hanger* might sound the same in English, they have no connection whatsoever in meaning: *hangar* is **die Flugzeughalle** while *hanger* is **der Bügel**.

Beware of getting carried away and translating word for word from English. One reason why this is a recipe for disaster is owing to English phrasal verbs, which are made up of two parts: a verb followed by a preposition or adverb.

ask in, ask out, ask around
break down, break in, break out, break up
get about, get away, get by, get in, get off, get on, get over
give away, give back, give in, give up

Each has a specific meaning and so has to be treated as an individual item, not as two words. The German equivalent is sometimes a single word.

look v 1 sehen, schauen; 2 ~ at **ansehen**; 3 ~ after (*attend* to) **sich kümmern um**; (*care for*) **sorgen für**; 4 ~ into **untersuchen**; 5 ~ for **suchen nach**; 6 ~ out **aufpassen**; 7 ~ over (*inspect*) **inspizieren**, (*overlook*) **übersehen**; 8 ~ up (*seek info*) **nachschlagen**.

put v 1 stellen; 2 ~ away **wegräumen**; 3 ~ down (*disparage*) **herabsetzen**, (*kill*) **töten**; 4 ~ off (*deter*) **abstoßen, abschrecken**; (*postpone*) **absagen**; 5 ~ out (*extinguish*) **löschen**, (*inconvenience*) **in Verlegenheit bringen**; 6 ~ up (*accommodate*) **unterbringen**, (*raise*) **[he]raufsetzen, anheben**; 7 ~ up with **sich mit jemandem/etwas abfinden**.

take v 1 nehmen; 2 ~ after **jemandem ähnlich sein**; 3 ~ apart **zerlegen**; 4 ~ away, (*math*) **abziehen**, (*food*) **mitnehmen**; 5 ~ off **ausziehen**, (*imitate*) **nachmachen**, (*aero*) **starten**; 5 ~ out **herausnehmen, ziehen**.

If ever you're not sure which option to use, look it up in the other direction. It's always best to do a cross-check in the German > English section, anyway, whatever you look up, since the English > German half of the dictionary doesn't tell you which verbs are separable, nor does it give irregular forms.

Above all, never attempt a literal translation of idiomatic phrases such as *the elephant in the room, the dog's dinner, I could eat a horse, to go cold turkey, you're pulling my leg, to spit with rain*, which don't have the idiomatic meaning in German. German has many interesting idioms of its own:
Ein Haar in der Suppe finden *to be very critical, to find fault in everything*, lit. *to find a piece of hair in the soup*
Jemanden auf den Arm nehmen *to pull someone's leg, lit. to take somebody on your arm*
Sich etwas hinter die Ohren schreiben *to make sure to remember something*, lit. *to write something behind your ears.*

1 Which of these fit into more than one grammatical category?
clear, drive, duck, jam, moral, online, permit, port, present, press, rock, sand, sardine, square, squash, state

2 Work out what you'd need to look up to find the meaning of these words, then look them up in a dictionary.
nouns: **Mütter, Bänder, Herzen, Tieres, Wälder**
adjectives: **ärmste, dunkler, höher, weiße**
verbs: **gebrochen, kannte, pass auf, wart**
(See page 197 for answers.)

acht
needs must

Some verbs are more essential than others. If you were to analyse what you say in English over a day or two, you'd probably be amazed at how often the words *must, want, can, may, need, have to, should, could, might, ought to* crop up. These not words you can easily look up in a dictionary. They are called modal verbs and they're indispensable. They allow you to voice your wishes, desires and needs as well as your most mundane obligations.

In German, the modal verbs are **müssen** *to have to*, **dürfen** *to be allowed to*, **können** *to be able to*, **sollen** *to be supposed to*, **wollen** *to want*, and **mögen** *to like*. They all follow similar patterns and they all send the infinitive of the accompanying verb to the end of the sentence.
Ich muss jetzt gehen. *I must go now.*
Ich sollte jetzt gehen. *I ought to go now.*
Er darf nicht kommen. *He can't come, he's not allowed to come.*
Er kann nicht kommen. *He can't come, he's not able to come.*

Modal verbs are so powerful in themselves that the infinitive can be omitted if it's obvious:
Sie muss zum Zahnarzt (gehen)**.** *She needs to go to the dentist.*
Was soll das (bedeuten)**?** *What's that supposed to mean?*
Kannst du Schach (spielen)**?** *Can you play chess?*

want

The German for *to want* is **wollen**:

ich will, du willst, er/sie will, wir wollen, ihr wollt, sie/Sie wollen

Ich will **dir/euch/Ihnen etwas zeigen.** *I want to show you something.*
Ich will **noch hinzufügen, dass ...** *I just want to add that ...*
Ich will **dich** nicht **stören, aber ...** *I don't wish to bother you but ...*
Ich will **Sie** nicht **länger aufhalten.** *I don't want to keep you.*

Willst du **mitkommen?** *Do you want to come with us?*
Er will **ein Gruppenfoto machen.** *He wants to take a group photo.*
Sie will **fit bleiben.** *She wants to keep fit.*
Wir wollen **dir/euch danken.** *We want to thank you.*
Wir wollen **keine Zeit verschwenden.** *We don't want to waste time.*

Was wollen Sie **damit sagen?** *What do you mean by that?* (lit. *want to say*)
Warum wollen Sie **bei uns arbeiten?** *Why do you want to work for us?*
Viele Leute wissen nicht, was sie wollen. *A lot of people don't know what they want.*

Wollen wir ... ? means *Shall we ... ?*
Wollen wir **ein Glas Wein trinken?** *Shall we have a glass of wine?*
Wollen wir **bergsteigen gehen?** *Shall we go mountain climbing?*
Wollen wir **uns duzen?** *Shall we call each other du?*

I wanted is **ich wollte** (imperfect, pages 184–185).
Ich wollte **den Ort nie verlassen.** *I never wanted to leave the place.*
Es ist hier, wo wir **zu Mittag essen** wollten. *This is where we wanted to have lunch.*
Was wollten Sie **als Kind werden?** *What did you want to be when you were a child?*
Er wollte **nie Präsident werden.** *He never wanted to be president.*
Sie wollte **eigentlich Industriedesign studieren.** *Actually, she wanted to study industrial design*
Sie wollten **nie Kinder**. *They never wanted children.*

would like

I want can sound rather blunt or demanding, so **ich möchte** *I'd like*, which is a form of the verb **mögen** *to like* (page 89) is often used instead:

Ich möchte **anstoßen auf unseren Gastgeber/das Geburtstagskind.** *I'd like to drink the health of our host/the birthday boy/girl.*
Ich möchte **es wenigstens versuchen.** *I'd like to at least try it.*
Ich möchte **sagen, dass ...** *I'd like to say that ...*
Möchtest du **den Hafen ansehen?** *Would you like to see the harbour?*
Möchtet ihr **mitkommen?** *Would you like to come with us?*
Sie möchte **mehr darüber erfahren.** *She'd like to find out more about that.*
Er möchte **heute Abend zum Spiel gehen.** *He'd like to go to the match tonight.*
Wir möchten **eine Reservierung machen.** *We'd like to make a reservation.*
Wir möchten **euch ein bisschen/etwas über uns erzählen.** *We'd like to tell you a bit about us.* **(ihr)**

to feel like, to fancy

More colloquially, you can use **ich habe (keine) Lust** *I (don't) feel like or fancy doing something.* The infinitive that follows goes to the end of the sentence and is preceded by **zu**. With separable verbs **zu** goes between the separable prefix and the main verb.
Haben Sie Lust, wandern zu **gehen?** *Do you feel like going hiking?*
Wir haben Lust, ans Meer zu **fahren.** *We feel like driving to the coast.*
Ich habe keine Lust mitzu**machen.** *I don't fancy taking part.*
Er hat keine Lust zu **arbeiten.** *He doesn't feel like working.*
Sie hat keine Lust, zu Andreas Party zu **gehen.** *She doesn't feel like/She isn't in the mood for going to Andrea's party.*

The pattern is **Lust haben** + **zu** + infinitive, and most German verbs behave in the same way: **es gibt viel zu tun** *there's lots to do,* **ich habe vergessen, dir zu sagen** *I forgot to tell you.*
But modal verbs are exceptions to this general rule; they follow the pattern: verb + infinitive, without **zu**.
Ich habe Lust, spazieren zu gehen. *I feel like/quite fancy going for a walk.*
Ich möchte spazieren gehen. *I'd like to go for a walk.*
Hast du Lust mitzukommen? *Do you feel like coming with us?*
Willst du mitkommen? *Do you want to come with us?*

must, have to, need to

The verb **müssen** translates *must, have to, have got to* and *need to.* It conveys a sense of necessity or obligation:

ich muss, du musst, er/sie/es muss, wir müssen, ihr müsst, sie/Sie müssen

Ich muss dir/Ihnen gratulieren. *I must congratulate you.* **(du/Sie)**
Ich muss darüber nachdenken. *I'll have to think about it.*
Ich muss Jakob eine Nachricht hinterlassen. *I must leave a message for Jakob.*
Er muss jetzt gehen. *He has to go now.*
Wir müssen ein bisschen Sport treiben. *We need to do some exercise.*
Wir müssen ein gutes Restaurant auswählen. *We must choose a good restaurant.*
Müsst ihr jetzt wirklich gehen? *Do you really have to leave now?*
Sie müssen sich beeilen. *You must hurry.*
Sie müssen das Datum bestätigen. *You need to confirm the date.*

I had to is **ich musste** (imperfect, pages 184–185).
Ich musste sehr früh aufstehen. *I had to get up very early.*
Die Hotline mussten wir mehrere Male anrufen. *We had to phone the hotline several times.*
Warum mussten Sie umsteigen? *Why did you have to change (trains)?*

In the negative, **müssen** doesn't mean *you must not do* something in the sense that something is not allowed (for this see **dürfen** page 129); it means that *you needn't* or *don't have to* do something.
Ich muss noch nicht gehen. *I don't have to go yet.*
Sie müssen nicht im Voraus bezahlen. *You don't need to pay in advance.*
Wir müssen nicht gleich auswählen. *We don't need to choose straightaway.*

The verb **brauchen** *to need* is used with a noun: **wir brauchen ein bisschen Hilfe** *we need a bit of help,* or in a negative sentence to convey *don't need to.* The following three sentences are all equivalent to *I don't need to remind you.*
Ich brauche dich nicht zu erinnern.
Ich muss dich nicht erinnern.
Es ist nicht nötig, dich zu erinnern. **(nötig** *necessary)*

should, ought to, be supposed to

Sollen conveys the idea that someone else wants you to do something. It's translated into English in various ways, such as *to be supposed to* or *should.*

ich soll, du sollst, er/sie/es soll, wir sollen, ihr sollt, sie/Sie sollen

Wir sollen **hier bleiben.** *We're supposed to/We have to **wait here.***
Der Arzt hat mir gesagt, ich soll **mehr Sport treiben.** ***The doctor told me** I should **get more exercise.***
Er soll **keine Milchprodukte essen.** *He's not supposed to/He mustn't **eat any dairy products.***
Was sollen wir **jetzt machen?** ***What** are we (supposed) to **do now?***
Sie sollen **im Voraus anrufen.** *You're (meant) to **ring in advance.***
Ich weiß nicht, was ich **machen** soll. ***I don't know what** I'm supposed to **do.***

The Ten Commandments (**die Zehn Gebote**) all begin **du sollst**:
Du sollst nicht stehlen. *Thou shalt not steal.*
Du sollst nicht die Ehe brechen. *Thou shalt not commit adultery.*

Ich sollte *I ought to, I should* conveys the idea of a moral obligation. It is a subjunctive form of **sollen.**

Ich sollte **meine Tante besuchen; sie ist krank.** *I ought to **visit my aunt; she's ill.***
Ich sollte **wohl gehen.** ***I suppose** I ought to **leave.***
Ich glaube, wir sollten **Jasmin anrufen.** ***I think** we **perhaps really** ought to **call Jasmin.***
Du solltest nicht **so viel Kuchen essen.** *You shouldn't **eat so much cake.***
Wir sollten nicht **jammern.** *We shouldn't **moan.***
Ihr solltet nicht **zögern.** *You shouldn't **hesitate.***
Das sollten alle **wissen.** *Everyone should **know that.***
Er sollte **sich was schämen.** *He ought to **be ashamed of himself.***

wish lists

There are different kinds of lists in most people's lives. For the list of things that you want to do in the short to medium term, you use **ich will** *I want to*, which has a decisive feel about it.

Ich will ...

den Job wechseln *change job*
zehn Kilo abnehmen *lose 10 kilos*
fit werden *get fit*
den Führerschein machen *get a driving licence*
einen Marathon unter vier Stunden laufen *run a marathon in under four hours*
Venedig besuchen *visit Venice*
in die Vereinigten Staaten fahren *go to the States*

List five things you want to do in the next 12 months. If they involve going to places, **to** *is nach with neuter destinations: nach Australien, nach Europa, nach Deutschland* **Germany**, *nach Österreich* **Austria**, *nach Bayern* **Bavaria**, *nach Cornwall, nach Helgoland* **Heligoland**.
For the few countries and continents that are not neuter, you need in plus the article in the accusative case: in die Schweiz **to Switzerland**, *in die Türkei* **to Turkey**, *in die USA/in die Vereinigten Staaten* **to the USA**, *in den Libanon* **to Lebanon**, *in die Antarktis* **to Antarctica**.

Are any of the following on your *bucket list* **(die) Wunschliste der Lebensträume** lit. *wish list of life dreams*? To say you want to do these, you use ich möchte ...

mit Delphinen schwimmen *swim with dolphins*
um Kap Hoorn segeln *sail around Cape Horn*
das Nordlicht sehen *see the Northern Lights*
Kilimandscharo besteigen *climb Kilimanjaro*
in der Masai Mara auf Safari gehen *go on safari in the Masai Mara*
eine Trekkingtour in der Mongolei machen *go trekking in Mongolia*
im Großen Barriereriff tauchen *go diving in the Great Barrier Reef*
mit der Transsibirischen Eisenbahn fahren *go on the Trans-Siberian Railway*

Ceate your bucket list in German, looking up any words you need, and say out loud what's on it.

... and to-do lists

Müssen and **sollen** bring you back down to earth, to your to-do list. Whether you choose **ich muss, ich soll** or **ich sollte** depends on your attitude.

Use **ich muss** *I must, I need to* for the things ***you*** think you really have to do, or need to do, such as:

meine Sportschuhe finden *find my trainers*
Milch kaufen *buy some milk*
tanken *put petrol in the car*
mein Handy aufladen *charge my mobile*
Geld aus dem Automaten ziehen *get some money from the cashpoint*
die Rechnungen bezahlen *pay the bills*
die Autoversicherung erneuern *renew the car insurance*
meine Schwester anrufen *phone my sister*
den Schuppen aufräumen *tidy the shed*
den Gefrierschrank abtauen *defrost the freezer*
einen Zahnarzttermin machen *make a dental appointment*

Use **ich soll** if someone else has told you what you need to do:

einige Kilo abnehmen *lose a few kilos*
weniger Kohlenhydrate essen *eat fewer carbohydrates*
Peter sagen, dass wir morgen Training haben *tell Peter that there's training tomorrow*
das Modul/die Aufgabe bis Freitag beenden *finish the module/assignment by Friday*

Use **ich sollte** for the things you ought to do, or feel morally obliged to do:

Annika kontaktieren *get in touch with Annika*
geduldiger sein *be more patient*
Goethe und Schiller lesen *read Goethe and Schiller*
Oma eine Geburtstagskarte schicken *send Granny a birthday card*

Most of us conduct a running commentary in our heads, reminding ourselves of what we need to do, who we need to get in touch with, what we might like to do at the weekend and so on. If you regularly use German for this inner monologue, you'll find that it becomes a habit, one which results in a step-change in your progress. Try adding simple comments and questions: ***How interesting; When's Will's birthday? What a good idea.*** *It goes without saying that when you're on your own it's more effective to do this out loud.*

can, may

Where *can* or *may* refer to ability or possibility, you use **können:**

ich kann, du kannst, er/sie kann, wir können, ihr könnt, sie/Sie können

Kann ich **bitte mit Frau Beuth sprechen?** *Can I please speak to Mrs Beuth?*
Kann ich **etwas vorschlagen, das euch bestimmt interessiert?** *Can I suggest something that I'm sure will interest you guys?* **(ihr)**
Du kannst **uns helfen, wenn du willst.** *You can help us if you want.*
Das kann **sein.** *That may be.*
Man kann **immer nein sagen.** *You/One can always say no.*
Können wir **Ihnen helfen?** *Can we help you?* **(Sie)**
Können wir **die Rechnung haben, bitte?** *Can we have the bill, please?*
Können wir **Ihnen ein Glas Sekt anbieten?** *Can we offer you a glass of champagne?*
Ihr könnt **bei uns übernachten.** *You can stay (overnight) with us.*
Leider können sie nicht **kommen.** *They can't come unfortunately.*

You also use **können** to ask other people to do something.
Kannst du **uns später anrufen?** *Can you call us later?*
Können Sie **uns vorher Bescheid sagen**? *Can you let us know beforehand?*
Können Sie **uns ein gutes Restaurant empfehlen**? *Can you recommend a good restaurant?*
Können Sie **ihr etwas ausrichten?** *Can you pass on a message to her?*

Können is also used to mean *can* in the sense of *know because you've learned.*
Ich kann ein bisschen Deutsch. *I can speak German.* The verb **sprechen** *to speak* is implied.
Ursula kann Klavier spielen. *Ursula can play the piano.*

Look out for *could*, which has more than one meaning. It can be the past tense of *can*, meaning *was able to*. German uses **konnte**, the imperfect tense, for this (pages 184-185).
Leider konnte ich **sie nicht besuchen.** *Unfortunately I couldn't/wasn't able to visit her/them.*
Ich konnte **lange nicht einschlafen.** *I couldn't get to sleep for a long time.*
Wir konnten **das Haus nicht finden.** *We couldn't find the house.*

Could in English also means *would be able to*, and for this meaning you use **könnte**, a subjunctive form of **können**. In questions, it's a very polite form.

Ich könnte hier für immer bleiben. *I could stay here for ever.*
Wir könnten doch auch die U-Bahn nehmen. *We could always take the Underground.*
Wir könnten die anderen einladen. *We could invite the others.*
Könnte ich vielleicht dein Fahrrad ausleihen? *Could I by any chance borrow your bike?*
Könnten wir vielleicht zusammen zu Abend essen? *Could we maybe have dinner together?*
Könntest du uns zum Flughafen mitnehmen? *Could you take us to the airport?*
Könntet ihr uns einen Gefallen tun? *Could you do us a favour?*
Könnten Sie mir sagen, wo die Jugendherberge ist? *Could you tell me where the youth hostel is?*

When *can* or *may* has the sense of asking or giving permission, use **dürfen**:

ich darf, du darfst, er/sie darf, wir dürfen, ihr dürft, sie/Sie dürfen

Darf ich Sie mal kurz stören? *Can I disturb you for a moment?*
Darf ich einen Vorschlag machen? *May I make a suggestion?*
Natürlich darf deine Freundin mitkommen. *Of course your friend can come with us.*
Man darf überall zelten. *You/One can camp everywhere.*
Hier dürfen Sie fotografieren. *You can/may take photos here.*
Hier darf man die Straße nicht überqueren. *You must not/You're not allowed to cross the street here.*
Wissen Sie, ob man da drüben parken darf? *Do you know if we can park over there?*
Dürfen wir mal gucken? *Can/May we just have a look?*

You'll often hear **Was darf es sein?** lit. *What may it be?* in shops to mean *Can I help you? What would you like? What can I do for you?*

Können can be used in colloquial speech as an alternative to **dürfen**.
Kann ich reinkommen? Darf ich reinkommen? *Can/May I come in?*
Kann ich mal durch, bitte? Darf ich mal durch, bitte? *Can/May I get past please?*

talking the talk

Volker	Ich möchte dir Offenburg zeigen. Wollen wir am Wochenende dorthin fahren? Du solltest die Altstadt besuchen. Die Gebäude sind sehr schön.
Sophie:	Offenburg? Gerne. Ich war noch nie in Offenburg. Ich habe gehört, dass die Architektur schön ist.
Volker	Gut. Lass uns am Samstag hinfahren. Was würdest du zu einer Radtour sagen? Wir könnten zwei Fahrräder in Offenburg mieten.
Sophie	Schöne Idee! Leider kann ich am Samstag nicht. Ich muss ein paar Stunden arbeiten.
Volker	Wann? Am Vormittag oder am Nachmittag?
Sophie	Am Vormittag.
Volker	Wann bist du fertig?
Sophie	Ich weiß nicht genau. Kann ich dich am Samstag Vormittag anrufen?
Volker	Sicher. Aber wir könnten doch an einem anderen Tag nach Offenburg fahren. Kein Problem! Was machst du jetzt? Darf ich dich zu einem Kaffee einladen?
Sophie	Nein, ich muss gehen. Sammy wartet auf mich.
Volker	Sammy? Wer ist Sammy?
Sophie	Mein Hund! Er ist allein zu Hause. Er hat bestimmt Hunger.

verb practice 5

For the following activities you need to be familiar with the various endings of **müssen, wollen, sollen, können** and **dürfen.**

1 Fill the gaps with the present tense of **müssen, wollen, sollen, können** and **dürfen**. Time yourself – then do this again in a couple of hours' time, again in a day, and again in two days. Come back to it yet again after a week.

a	**müssen**	**du**	**ihr** ....
b	**wollen**	**ich**	**sie** (*they*) ....
c	**dürfen**	**sie** (*she*)	**ich** ....
d	**sollen**	**er**	**wir** ....
e	**müssen**	**er**	**Sie** ....
f	**dürfen**	**wir**	**ihr** ....
g	**wollen**	**du**	**wir** ....
h	**sollen**	**man**	**du** ....

2 What's the difference in meaning between:

a **Ich kann keinen Alkohol trinken** and **Ich soll keinen Alkohol trinken.**

b **Ich muss es nicht sagen** and **Ich darf es nicht sagen.**

c **Was willst du?** and **Was möchtest du?**

d **Wir müssen Deutsch lernen** and **Wir sollten Deutsch lernen.**

3 Many of the examples on the previous pages focus on using *I*, *we* and *you*. Now it's time to practise talking about other people.

Convert at least ten of the *I/we* ... examples to mean *he/she* ... by changing the verb ending, e.g. **wir wollen euch danken** *we want to thank you* > **er will euch danken** *he wants to thank you*, **ich muss noch nicht gehen** *I don't need to go yet* > **sie müssen noch nicht gehen** *they don't need to go yet*. This will help you to remember the words as well as to learn the verb endings.

4 Put these sentences into the imperfect tense.

a **Ich will mit dir sprechen.**

b **Kannst du nicht schlafen?**

c **Er muss lange warten.**

d **Wir wollen mitkommen, aber wir können nicht.**

checkpoint 8

1 **Das konnte ich machen** and **Das könnte ich machen** both translate the English *I could do it*, but which one would you use to talk about something that hasn't happened yet?

2 How would you explain that Dominik has to go and that he wants to take a group photo?

3 A social media site ad asks **möchtest du neue Leute kennenlernen?** What is it asking?

4 What does **Ich brauche ein neues Handy** mean?

5 Which of these are not in the imperfect tense: **ich konnte, wir wollen, ihr müsst, du möchtest, Sie könnten, er musste, ich wollte**?

6 **Reisen** means *to travel*: what's the German for *I'd like to travel, I'm able to travel, I want to travel, I had to travel*?

7 What does the verb **umsteigen** mean?

8 What's another way of saying **Möchtet ihr an den Strand gehen?** using the verb **Lust haben**?

9 If someone suggests **Wollen wir uns duzen?** what do they want to do in future?

10 Where are you likely to see the phrase **Du sollst neben mir keine anderen Götter haben**, and what do you think it means?

11 If you hear **hier dürfen Sie nicht parken**, what are you being told?

12 What does someone who asks you **Können Sie Deutsch?** want to know?

13 Which of the following places are not preceded by **nach** when you want to say *to*: **Deutschland, Europa, London, Schweiz, Yorkshire, USA**?

14 How would you ask for the bill in a restaurant?

15 What is the infinitive of the verb **möchte**?

16 Where are you most likely to hear the phrase **Was darf es sein?**

17 How would you say i) you'd like to get fit, and ii) you ought to phone your mother?

18 If **Ich habe Lust, ins Kino zu gehen** is *I feel like going to the cinema*, what is *I don't feel like going to the cinema*?

neun
sharing opinions

Whether you're chatting to a neighbour or someone you've met on holiday, socialising with German business contacts, taking part in a cultural exchange or meeting your child's new Austrian mother-in-law, it's very satisfying to be able to exchange views on anything and everything.

As Europe's largest economy, and sharing borders with nine other countries, Germany is an outward-looking nation, and many Germans are interested in world affairs. As a foreign visitor you may well be asked **Was denken Sie über** ... *What do you think about* ... **die politische Lage** *the political situation*, **den Klimawandel** *climate change* or **die Europäische Union** *the European Union*.

Regardless of whether the subject under discussion is a major political or cultural matter, a mutual acquaintance, the amount of traffic on the roads, a nearby **Lokal** or – very likely in Germany – **Fußball**, the basic language structures you need are the same. They help to air your views without sounding blunt or over-assertive, and, of course, to invite other people's views.

A point of view becomes much more convincing when it's supported. There are words that make an opinion sound persuasive and self-evident, such as **sicher** *certainly* and **natürlich** *of course*, but what usually clinches an argument is a solid rationale and/or an impressive statistic or two.

asking someone's opinion

There are different ways of asking other people what they think. You could start by asking them if they agree with you.
... nicht wahr/oder? *... don't you think?*

Er ist fantastisch, nicht wahr? Was für eine Stimme! *He's amazing, don't you think? What a voice!*
Sie haben gestern gut gespielt, oder? *They played well yesterday, don't you think?*

The verbs to use for asking someone's opinion are **meinen** *to think*, **glauben** *to believe, think*, **finden** *to find, think*, and **denken** *to think*.

Was meinst/denkst du? Was meint/denkt ihr? Was meinen/denken Sie? *What do you think? What's your view?*
Was meinst/denkst du dazu? *What do you think about it?*
Und ihr zwei, was meint ihr? Was ist die beste Lösung? *What do you two think is the best solution?*
Die Lage ist unerträglich; was meinen Sie dazu? *The situation's intolerable; what do you think about it?*
Ich finde die Frage kompliziert. Was meinst du? *I think it's a complex question. What do you think?*
Ist das fertig, glaubst du? *Is this ready, do you think?*
Glaubt ihr, wir schaffen es? *Do you think we'll do/make it?*
Findest du das eine gute Idee? *Do you think it's a good idea?*
Findest du es hier nicht ein bisschen zu warm? *Do you not think it's a bit too warm here?*

You can also use the nouns **die Ansicht** *view* and **die Meinung** *opinion*.
Was ist deine/Ihre Ansicht dazu? *What's your view about that?*
Was ist deine/Ihre Meinung dazu? *What's your opinion about that?*
Deiner/Eurer/Ihrer Ansicht nach ... *In your view ...*
Deiner/Eurer/Ihrer Meinung nach ... *In your opinion ...*

Ihrer Meinung nach, ist das möglich? *In your opinion is it possible?*
Deiner Meinung nach, spielt Dortmund besser als Bayern? *In your opinion, is Borussia Dortmund better than Bayern Munich?*

saying what you think

There are several ways of offering your opinion in German, using **meiner Meinung nach/meiner Ansicht nach** *in my opinion/view*, **ich meine** *I think*, **ich finde** *I find, I think* or **ich glaube** *I believe/think*.

Meiner Meinung nach ist Chelsea der beste Fußballverein. *Chelsea is the best football club in my opinion.*
Meiner Meinung nach verdient es mehr als vier Sterne. *I think it deserves more than four stars.*
Meiner Ansicht nach ist Atomkraft moralisch unvertretbar. *In my view nuclear power is morally indefensible.*
Ich meine, das passt nicht. *I don't think it's suitable.*
Ich meine, eine vegetarische Ernährung ist gesund. *I think a vegetarian diet is healthy.*
Ich finde solche Geräte so praktisch. *I think such gadgets are so handy*, lit. *I find such gadgets so handy.*
Ich glaube, er/sie liebt mich nicht mehr. *I don't think he/she loves me any more.*

If you include **dass** *that*, which is usually optional, the verb goes to the end.
Ich glaube, Onlinedating kann gefährlich sein. *I believe online dating can be dangerous.*
OR: **Ich glaube, dass Onlinedating gefährlich sein kann.**
Noch dazu meine ich, dass das ein entscheidendes Spiel ist. *What's more, I think that this is a crucial match.*
Ich glaube fest daran, dass ihr nicht enttäuscht sein werdet. *I strongly believe that you won't be disappointed.*

More formally, there's **Ich bin der Meinung, dass ...** *I'm of the opinion that ...*
Ich bin der Meinung, dass der Euro unterbewertet ist. *I'm of the opinion that the euro is undervalued.*
Ich bin nicht der Meinung, dass die Regierung unbedingt den Steinkohlebergbau subventionieren muss. *I don't think that the government should subsidise the coal mining industry.*

You can also use **glauben an** *to believe in:*
Ich glaube nicht an Geister. *I don't believe in ghosts.*
Ich glaube fest ans Karma. *I believe strongly in karma.*
Ich glaube voll und ganz an Redefreiheit. *I believe wholeheartedly in free speech.*

agreeing and disagreeing

How you agree and disagree with someone has all to do with the context of the discussion. There's a world of difference between friendly banter about football in the bar, an exchange of views on immigration at a reception and a dialogue on quality issues in the boardroom.

agreeing

Bravo! *Well said! Hear, hear!*
Eben/Genau. *Exactly. Precisely.* **Ja, durchaus!** *Yes, absolutely!*
Natürlich/Selbstverständlich. *Of course.*
Das kann man wohl sagen! *I'll say; indeed.*
Sicher *Certainly, indeed.* **Jawohl** *Yes, indeed.*
Das ist wahr. Das ist ja so wahr! *It's true. So true!*
Du hast/ihr habt/Sie haben (völlig) Recht. *You're (absolutely) right*
Ich bin deiner/eurer/Ihrer Meinung. *I agree with you.*
Genau! Ich bin völlig dieser Meinung. *Exactly! I couldn't agree more.*
Wir sind uns ganz/völlig einig. *We're in complete agreement.*
Ich teile Ihre Meinung. *I share your opinion.*
Wir haben dieselbe Wellenlänge. *We're on the same wavelength.*
Das finde ich auch. *I think so too.*
Zweifellos. *Undoubtedly.*
Ich habe keine Zweifel/Daran gibt es keine Zweifel. *There's no doubt in my mind.*
Ohne den geringsten Zweifel. *Without a shadow of a doubt.*
Du bist ein Genie! *You're a genius!*
Du hast's erfasst! *You've got it!*

disagreeing

Da muss ich widersprechen. *I have to disagree/contradict.*
Nein, Entschuldigung, aber ich bin nicht dieser Meinung. *No, I'm sorry but I don't agree.*
Unsere Ansichten stehen im Widerspruch zueinander. *We have conflicting views.*
Es scheint ein (großes) Missverständnis gegeben zu haben. *There seems to have been a (big) misunderstanding.*
Das ist nicht richtig. Im Gegenteil, du hast Unrecht. *That's not correct. Indeed/On the contrary, you're mistaken*
Das stimmt nicht. *That's not correct.*
Das ist einfach nicht so. *That's simply not so.*
Ich glaube, dass du dich irrst. *I think you're wrong.*

Entschuldigen Sie mich, aber Sie irren sich meiner Meinung nach. *Excuse me but you're mistaken in my view.*
Das ist vielleicht Ansichtssache. *It's perhaps a matter of opinion.*
Das kann sein, aber ... *That may be so, but ...*

Ganz und gar nicht! *Nothing of the sort!*
Um Gottes willen! Von wegen! *For goodness' sake! You're joking!*
Ach, komm ... du redest Unsinn! *Oh, come on ... you're talking nonsense!*
Was für ein Quatsch! *Utter twaddle! What rubbish!*

You use **doch** instead of **ja** *yes* to contradict what has just been said.
A. **Das ist nicht wahr**. *That's not true.* B. **Doch!** *Yes, it is!*
A. **Deutsch ist nicht besonders schwierig.** *German isn't particularly difficult.* B. **Doch! Es ist sehr schwierig.** *On the contrary, it* **is** *difficult.*

being non-committal

Es kommt darauf an. Es hängt davon ab. *It depends.*
Ich habe dazu keine Meinung. *I've no opinion on the matter.*
Ich habe dazu nicht viel zu sagen. *I haven't got much to say on the matter.*
Das ist mir egal. *I don't mind.*
Das macht mir nichts aus. *I couldn't care one way or the other.*

In very colloquial speech you might hear **Jein** in answer to a question.
Jein is a word coined only in the last ten years or so and is a mixture of **ja** and **nein**. It's used where in English we might answer *well, both yes and no* or *I suppose*, because neither **ja** or **nein** answers the question fully.
Warst du schon in Frankfurt? Jein, ich war nur zwei Stunden im Flughafen. *Have you ever been to Frankfurt? Well, yes and no, I only spent two hours in the airport.*
Hast du den neuen Michael Fassbender film gesehen? Jein, ich habe nur den Trailer gesehen. *Have you seen the new Michael Fassbender film? Yes and no, I've only seen the trailer.*

making the case

To back up your opinion, you'll need **weil** *because* and **da** *as, since*, both of which send the verb to the end. **Weil** is the more common in spoken German. A **da** clause usually comes first.

Da wir keine genauen Zahlen haben, ist es schwierig das zu wissen. *As we don't have precise figures, it's hard to know.*

Meiner Ansicht nach verdienen sie massenhaft Geld, weil sie wirklich talentiert sind. *In my view, they earn loads because they're really talented.*

Ich finde es nicht richtig, weil sie keine Steuer zahlen. *I don't think it's right because they don't pay taxes.*

Ich glaube, es ist akzeptabel, da es ökologische Vorteile gibt. *I believe it's acceptable as there are ecological advantages.*

Ich sage das, weil ich persönliche Erfahrung in diesem Bereich habe. *I say this as I have personal experience of the sector.*

Weil and **da** are not, of course, restricted to discussing major issues:

Ich will dorthin gehen, weil ich gelesen habe, dass es wirklich wunderbar ist. *I want to go there because I've read that it's really wonderful.*

Wir müssen zu Fuß gehen, weil ich nicht getankt habe. *We'll have to walk because I haven't put petrol in the car.*

Da es so heiß ist, brauchen wir einen Platz im Schatten. *As it's so hot, we need a place in the shade.*

Da ich das Passwort vergessen habe, kann ich die Adresse nicht finden. *Since I've forgotten the password, I can't find the address.*

Separable verbs in the present tense join up again at the end of the clause:

Da er weggeht, bin ich traurig. *As he's going away, I'm sad.*

Ich halte den Mund, weil ich mich nicht auskenne. *I'm keeping quiet because I don't know anything about the issue.*

Think of how you might complete these sentences using weil or da.
Ich bleibe heute zu Hause, ... **I'm going to stay at home today ...**
Ich möchte Deutsch lernen, ... **I'd like to learn German ...**
Ich suche eine neue Arbeitsstelle, ... **I'm looking for a new job ...**
It might be to do with the weather: es regnet **it's raining**, die Sonne scheint **the sun's shining**, or to do with you: ich bin müde **I'm tired**, ich reise gern **I like travelling**, meine Arbeit macht mir keinen Spaß mehr **I'm not enjoying my job any more** – or you could make up your own reasons.

Think of other sentences you could make. Remember the position of the verb.

what do *you* think?

Meiner Meinung nach ... *In my opinion ...*
sollte die Regierung ... *the government ought to ...*
könnte jeder Mensch ... *every individual could ...*
müssen Gemeinden ... *communities must/should ...*
müssen die Behörden ... *the authorities must/should ...*

Give your opinion on some major issues, mixing and matching the above cues with the verbs and topics below. The infinitive goes at the end and the nouns in the left-hand column are in the accusative case.

Meiner Meinung nach sollte die Regierung die Internetkriminalität beenden. In my opinion, the government should put a stop to cybercrime.
Meiner Meinung nach könnte jeder Mensch Tierrechte unterstützen. In my opinion, every person could support animal rights.
Meiner Meinung nach sollten Gemeinden Einwanderern helfen. In my opinion, communities ought to help immigrants.

den Kampf um/gegen *the fight for/against*
die Sicherheit *security*
Ruhe und Ordnung *law and order*
den Extremismus *extremism*
die Internetkriminalität *cybercrime*
den Identitätsdiebstahl *identity theft*
den Drogenhandel *drug trafficking*
Drogensüchtige *drug addicts*
die Umwelt *environment*
den Abfall *waste (refuse)*
die Erderwärmung *global warming*
erneuerbare Energien *renewable energies*
die Wirtschaft *economy*
Steuern *taxes*
die Steuerumgehung *tax avoidance*
den Mindestlohn *minimum wage*
die Sozialleistungen *(state) benefits*
Menschenrechte *human rights*
die (legale/illegale) Migration *(legal/illegal) migration*
die Einwanderung/Immigration *immigration*
Tierrechte *animal rights*

angehen *to tackle*
beseitigen *to eradicate*
beenden *to put a stop to*
berichten *to report*
besiegen *to defeat*
entwickeln *to develop*
erhöhen *to increase*
senken *to decrease*
fördern *to boost, encourage*
helfen *to help* + dative
ignorieren *to ignore*
legalisieren *to legalise*
recyceln *to recycle*
reduzieren *to reduce*
schützen *to protect*
unterstützen *to support*
verbessern *to improve*
verbieten *to ban*
verhängen *to impose*

wordbank

Try combining these words, too, with the verbs on the previous page, and look up any words for issues you feel strongly about. Vary the sentences by beginning Ich finde or Ich meine **I think**. *Expand on a couple of points using weil* **because** *or da* **since**.

Ich finde, viele Leute ignorieren Rassismus und Diskriminierung. **I think many people ignore racism and discrimination.**
Ich meine, wir müssen alle die Umwelt schützen, weil der Klimawandel ein großes Problem ist. **I think we should all protect the environment, because climate change is a big problem.**

der/die Abgeordnete *MP*
der/die Arbeitslose *unemployed person*
die Arbeitslosigkeit *unemployment*
die Armut *poverty*
der/die Asylsuchende *asylum seeker*
die Außenpolitik *foreign policy*
der Bundeskanzler/die Bundeskanzlerin *Chancellor* (in Germany)
die Chancengleichheit *equal opportunities*
die Demokratie *democracy*
die Diskriminierung *discrimination*
die ethnische Minderheit *ethnic minority*
die Erziehung *education*
der Flüchtling *refugee*
fossile Brennstoffe *fossil fuels*
die Gentechnologie *genetic engineering*
das Gesetz *law*
die Gleichstellung der Geschlechter *gender equality*
der karitative Sektor *charity sector*
der Klimawandel *climate change*
der Menschenhandel *people trafficking*
die NRO/NGO (Nichtregierungsorganisation) *non-governmental organisation*
der öffentliche Sektor *public sector*
die Politik *politics*
der Politiker/die Politikerin *politician*
der Premierminister/die Premierministerin *prime minister*
der private Sektor *private sector*
der Terrorakt *terrorist act*
die Verschmutzung *pollution*
die Vielfalt *diversity*
der Wirtschaftsmigrant *economic migrant*
der Weltraum *(outer) space*
die Weltraumforschung *space exploration*

Most words ending *-ism* in English are masculine nouns ending **-ismus** in German: **der Extremismus, Fundamentalismus, Rassismus, Sexismus, Terrorismus.** *Ageism*, however, is **die Altersdiskriminierung**.

using numbers and statistics in conversation

Statistics create the impression that you really know what you're talking about. If you need a reminder of German numbers, go to pages 190–191. For the cases that follow prepositions, and the endings for these cases, go to page 180 and page 177–178.

nach den neuesten Zahlen/laut den neuesten Zahlen ... *according to the latest figures ...* **laut** and **nach** are both followed by the dative case.
die Daten/Tatsachen zeigen, dass ... *the data/facts show that ...*
Tatsache ist, dass .../Fakt ist, dass ... *It's a fact/a given that ...*

Fakt ist, dass zweitausend Jobs in Gefahr sind. *The fact of the matter is that 2,000 jobs are in danger.*
Tatsache ist, dass es mehr als fünfhundertausend Euro kostet. *It's a fact that it's costing more than 500,000 euros.*
Laut Protokoll waren am Donnerstag bei der Besprechung einundzwanzig Leute. *According to the minutes, there were 21 people at Thursday's meeting.*
Die Zahlen zeigen, dass weniger als fünfzig Leute davongekommen sind. *The figures show that fewer than 50 people escaped.*

% is **Prozent** (n): **fünfundzwanzig Prozent** *25%*, **fünfzig Prozent** *50%*
Ich bin mir zu neunzig Prozent sicher. *I'm 90% certain.*
Dieser Käse hat weniger als zehn Prozent Fett. *This cheese has less than 10% fat.*
Schnaps enthält zwischen dreißig und vierzig Prozent Alkohol. *Schnapps contains between 30 and 40% alcohol.*
Er gewährt einen Rabatt von bis zu zwanzig Prozent. *He's offering up to a 20% discount.*
Die Zahlen zeigen einen Zuwachs von fünf Prozent im Vergleich zu letztem Jahr/im Vergleich zu zweitausendfünfzehn. *The figures show an increase of 5% compared to last year/2015.*
Die neuesten Daten zeigen, dass die jährliche Inflationsrate null Komma drei Prozent (0,3%) beträgt. *The latest data shows that annual inflation is 0.3%.*

German uses a space or a full stop where English uses a comma in large numbers, and it uses a comma where English uses a decimal point. The English 64,956 is **vierundsechzigtausendneunhundertsechsundfünfzig** in German, written or 64 956 or 64.956. The English 64.956 is **vierundsechzig Komma neun fünf sechs** in German, written 64,956.

when you're not sure of the exact number

... you can use **ungefähr, etwa, circa/zirka** *approximately, or so*; **fast** *almost, nearly*; **über** *over, more than*; **ein paar** *a few*; **einige, manche** *some*; **mehrere** *several*; **zig** *umpteen*; **zigmal** *umpteen/hundreds of times.*

Ich sehe dich in ungefähr/etwa zwanzig Minuten. *I'll see you in about twenty minutes.*
Ich habe circa zwölf Seiten gelesen. *I've read about twelve pages.*
Das Konzert hat fast zweieinhalb Stunden gedauert. *The concert lasted nearly two and a half hours.*
Meine Tochter hat mehrere Stunden dort verbracht. *My daughter spent several hours there.*
Zigtausende Menschen/Besucher waren auf dem Oktoberfest. *There were hundreds of thousands of people at Munich's Beer Festival.*
Er ist für ein paar Tage nach Leipzig gefahren. *He's gone to Leipzig for a few days.*
Ein paar Dutzend Leute waren da. *There were a few dozen people there.*
Es gab gestern hunderte von Fans in der Stadt. *There were hundreds of fans in the town yesterday.*
Da gab es Millionen von Mücken. Scheußlich! *There were millions of mosquitoes there. Disgusting!*
Er ist vor über neun Monaten gestorben. *He died over nine months ago.*

Ordinals, i.e. *first, second, third*, etc. (page 192) are adjectives so when they're used with a noun the endings have to agree with the noun. If there's a preposition, this will affect the case, and hence the ending.

Während des Zweiten Weltkriegs ... *During the Second World War ...*
Sie ist seine dritte Frau. *She's his third wife.*
Anna ist im achten Monat schwanger. *Anna's eight months pregnant* (lit. *in the eighth month of pregnancy*).
Heute ist sein achtzigster Geburtstag. *It's his 80th birthday today.*
Diese Serie ist die zehnte und die letzte. *This series is the 10th and the last.*
Er war an siebenundzwanzigster Stelle beim London Marathon. *He came 27th in the London marathon.*
Sie hat ihre Brille zum zigsten Mal verloren. *She's lost her glasses for the umpteenth time.*

more or less

Mehr *more* and **weniger** *less, fewer* don't add endings.
Das ist mehr als genug. *It's more than enough.*
Die Karten haben mehr als hundert Euro gekostet. *The tickets cost more than €100.*
Es gibt weniger Mücken hier. *There are fewer mosquitoes here.*
Im Juli gab es zehn Tausend (10.000) weniger Arbeitslose. *In July there were 10,000 fewer unemployed.*

You don't use **mehr** to say e.g. *more beautiful, more interesting*. Instead, you add **-er** to all adjectives. Some short common adjectives spelled with an **a, o** or **u** also add an umlaut: **ä, ö, ü**. Adjectives before a noun take endings.

Dieses Rätsel ist leichter. *This puzzle is easier.* **Das ist ein leichteres Rätsel.** *This is an easier puzzle.*
Rothenburg ist älter und schöner. *Rothenburg is older and more beautiful.*
Rothenburg ist eine ältere und schönere Stadt. *Rothenburg is an older and more beautiful town.*
Elke ist jünger, schlanker und reicher. *Elke's younger, slimmer and richer.*
Mein jüngerer Bruder ist viel größer als ich. *My younger brother is much taller than me.*
Diese Gegend ist interessanter: es gibt mehr zu tun. *This region is more interesting: there's more to do.*
Jetzt haben wir ein besseres Auto. *We've got a better car now.*
Die Wettervorhersage ist schlechter. *The forecast is worse.*
Heute morgen fühlt er sich schlechter. *He's feeling worse this morning.*

German adverbs are identical to adjectives. They never add endings: **laut** means both *loud* and *loudly*, and **lauter** means *louder* and *more loudly*.
Diese Website erklärt besser,was wir tun müssen. *This website explains better what to do.*
Es regnet noch stärker. *It's raining even harder.*

Bad/Worse in a mild sense, meaning *not good* is **schlecht(er)**; but for something very bad with serious consequences you use **schlimm(er)**.
Er hat schlechte Noten bekommen. *He got bad marks.*
Er hat schlechtere Noten bekommen. *He got worse marks.*
Das ist schlimm für ihn. *That's bad/serious for him.*
Das ist schlimmer für ihn. *That's worse/more serious for him.*

the most and the least

For the superlatives of adjectives, e.g. *the smallest, the most annoying*, you add **-st** plus the appropriate adjective ending. In a sentence like *the biggest/ best ... in Germany, in the world, in* is expressed by the genitive case.

Trier ist die älteste Stadt Deutschlands. *Trier is the oldest city in Germany.*
Das ist eine der günstigsten Städte Deutschlands. *It's one of the cheapest/ most reasonable towns in Germany.*
Die Alarmbereitschaft ist auf dem höchsten Niveau. *The terror alert is at the highest level.*
Das ist das größte Einkaufszentrum Europas. *It's the biggest shopping mall in Europe.*
Wo sind die nächsten Toiletten? *Where are the nearest toilets?* (irregular; from **nah** *near*)

The superlative of adverbs is **am ... sten**.
Im Durchschnitt ist es im Dezember am kältesten. *On average it's coldest in December.*
Welcher der Ausflüge dauert am längsten? *Which of the excursions lasts longest?*
Welche Sonnencreme schützt am besten vor Sonnenbrand? *Which sun cream best protects against sunburn?*

Less ... is **weniger ...** and *least* is **am wenigsten**, but Germans tend to use alternatives because these can become rather clumsy and long-winded.
Sie kommen seltener hierher. *They come here more seldom.*
instead of **Sie kommen weniger oft hierher.** *They come here less often.*
Das ist das uninteressanteste Museum. *That's the least interesting museum.* (lit. *the most uninteresting*)

Immer translates *more and more*, and **so ... wie möglich** *as ... as possible.*
Die Lage wird immer komplizierter. *The situation's becoming more and more complicated.*
Ich verbringe immer weniger Zeit im Fitnesszentrum. *I spend less and less time in the gym.*
Wir fahren so oft wie möglich in die Schweiz. *We go to Switzerland as often as possible.*
Man muss so früh wie möglich buchen. *You need to book as early as possible.*

talking the talk

Sophie Komm Sammy, wir gehen Gassi.

Volker Ich finde deinen Hund richtig sympatisch. Er ist freundlich, nicht wahr?

Sophie Das kann man wohl sagen! Vielleicht ein bisschen zu freundlich. Er will immer mit allen spielen.

Volker Im Gegenteil! Ich glaube, er interessiert sich auch für Architektur und alte Gebäude, genau wie du, Sophie. Ich finde, er schaut dieses Gebäude so ernst an! Was meinst du?

Sophie Natürlich interessiert er sich für dieses Gebäude. Hier gibt es Wurst. Und Sammy hat immer Hunger! Magst du Hunde gern? Hast du nie einen Hund gehabt?

Volker Doch, als ich ein Kind war, hatten wir einen Golden Retriever. Er war sehr lieb und ruhig.

Sophie Ja, tatsächlich. Retriever sind wirklich ruhig und geduldig.

Volker Aber jetzt habe ich keinen Hund, weil ich nur eine kleine Wohnung habe. Und ich habe keinen Garten, nur eine kleine Terrasse. Was ist deine Meinung dazu?

Sophie Es kommt darauf an. Ich habe auch eine kleine Wohnung. Aber Sammy selbst ist auch klein! Ich finde, es ist kein Problem für ihn.

Sophie Volker, ich muss dir erklären, wo ich gestern Abend war.

Volker Das ist nicht nötig. Du brauchst mir nichts zu erklären.

Sophie Nein, ich muss dir sagen, warum ich so schnell weggegangen bin.

Volker Wohin bist du gegangen?

Sophie Zu meinem Cousin.

Volker Zu Oskar?

Sophie Ja, er hatte Angst.

Volker Angst? Warum?

Sophie Seine Nachbarin war in Ohnmacht gefallen, und sie ist ziemlich alt. Oskar wusste nicht, was er tun sollte.

checkpoint 9

1. What else could you tag on to a statement, apart from **nicht wahr**, to ask if someone agrees with you? How would you say *It was a good film, wasn't it?*
2. Give three verbs that translate the English *to think.*
3. Which word do you use instead of **ja** to mean *yes* when contradicting what has just been said? Which word would you use if you found it impossible to give a straight *yes* or *no* answer?
4. Which of the following would you not use if you agree wholeheartedly with what has just been said: **das stimmt, natürlich, selbstverständlich, was für ein Quatsch, zweifellos**?
5. How would you say *10%* in German?
6. Which word is missing in **Was meinen Sie .....?** to mean *What do you think about it?*
7. With what other word, in addition to **da**, could you introduce an explanation to support your opinion?
8. What's the difference in meaning between **etwa hundert Leute** and **genau hundert Leute**?
9. Write in figures, both the German way and the English way, the numbers **fünfunddreißigtausendhundertzwölf** and **acht Komma null eins.**
10. If **Obst** is fruit, how would you say *I eat as much fruit as possible*?
11. **Stefan ist jünger als Theo, aber zwei Jahre älter als Max.** Who's the youngest of the three boys? What's *the youngest child* in German?
12. Which two words translate the English *bad?*
13. What is another way of saying *in my opinion*, apart from **Meiner Ansicht nach**?
14. Given that *love at first sight* is **Liebe auf den ersten Blick** in German, how would you ask somebody **(du)** if they believe in love at first sight?
15. When would you say **Das ist mir egal**?
16. How does the word **gut** change if, instead of saying **Die Wettervorhersage ist gut** *the weather forecast is good*, you say *a good weather forecast?*
17. How would you say *Vienna* **(Wien)** *is the largest city in Austria?*
18. Rewrite the sentence, **Ich glaube, der Popsänger ist wirklich talentiert,** by adding **dass** *that*, beginning **Ich glaube, dass ...**

zehn
inside information

There's no better way of finding out about a place than by talking to the locals. They're the ones with inside information about what's available, how to do something, where to buy the best **Bratwurst** *fried sausage* or a replacement charger for your phone, where to go for healthcare, who's who. And they always know the best places to eat.

Tapping into this local knowledge involves asking questions and explaining why you want the information. The language structures you need work in any context: you simply slot in the relevant vocabulary. Don't forget the strategies on pages 58–59 for making sure that people understand you and that you understand their replies.

When others give you instructions or advice in conversation, they're likely to use a form of the verb called the imperative. If you've already come across directions to places, such as **nehmen Sie die erste Straße links** *take the first on the left*, then you're already familiar with the imperative.

There are more Michelin three-starred restaurants in Germany than in Britain or Italy, so Germany takes its cuisine very seriously. It's rich and hearty, and German cakes and pastries are to die for – tough on the waistline, alas! German cuisine can't be summed up in a word – it's as diverse as the country is, with every region having its own gastronomic specialities. You'll find yourself talking about food a lot. As they say in Germany, **Man ist was man isst** *You are what you eat.*

what's available

Es gibt is a very useful phrase that means both *there is* and *there are*. **Gibt es?** *Is/Are there?* is often shortened to **gibt's?** The noun that follows is in the accusative case.

Es gibt in der Nähe einen kleinen Supermarkt. *There's a small supermarket near here.*
Gibt es in dieser Stadt einen Weihnachtsmarkt? *Is there a Christmas market in this town?*
Auf der Balingerstraße gibt es ein Polizeirevier. *There's a police station in Balinger Street.*
Es gibt viele Kirchen in der Altstadt. *There are a lot of churches in the old town.*
Es gibt drei Möglichkeiten. *There are three possibilities.*
Heute gibt es richtig viel Schnee. *There's a fair amount of snow today.*
Gibt es noch Karten? *Are there still tickets available?*
Gibt's andere? *Are there any others/any other kinds?*
Was gibt es zum Nachtisch? *What is there for dessert?*
Was gibt's hier zu tun? *What is there to do here?*
Es gibt viel zu tun. Packen wir's an. *There's loads to do. Let's get started!*

To say *there was/were* use either the imperfect tense **es gab**, which is commonly used, or the perfect **es hat gegeben**.
Es gab ein Problem/Es hat ein Problem gegeben. *There was a problem.*
Es gab sechs Gänge/Es hat sechs Gänge gegeben. *There were six courses.*
Zum Nachtisch gab es Eis/Zum Nachtisch hat es Eis gegeben. *There was ice cream for dessert.*

To say *there isn't* or *there aren't, there wasn't* or *there weren't* you'll need the negative article **kein** with the accusative ending that goes with the noun.
Es gibt kein Problem. *There's no/There isn't any problem.*
Es gibt keine Probleme. *There are no/There aren't any problems.*
Es gab keinen Parkplatz. *There was no parking space.*

... or **nicht** before an adverb.
Es gibt nicht genug Milch. *There's not enough milk.*
Es gab nicht viel zu essen. *There wasn't much to eat.*

When talking about the presence of something at a specific location or a particular time, you simply use the verb *to be:* **es ist/es sind**. **Es** is only needed at the beginning of the sentence, otherwise it's omitted.

Am Samstag ist ein Konzert. *There's a concert on Saturday.*
Es ist eine Katze im Zimmer/Im Zimmer ist eine Katze. *There's a cat in the room.*
Da ist niemand/Es ist niemand da. *There's no one there.*
Es sind viele Leute auf den Straßen. *There are a lot of people on the streets today.*
Es sind fast keine Autos unterwegs. *There are practically no cars on the roads.*
Da waren wenige Leute. *There were few people there.*

The verb **fehlen** *to be missing* can also be used to express a lack of something.
Mir fehlen zehn Euro. *I'm ten euros short.* lit. *To me are missing ten euros.*
Gestern haben mir zehn Euro gefehlt. *I was ten euros short yesterday.*
Hier fehlt ein Glas. *There's a glass missing here.*
An deinem Hemd fehlt ein Knopf. *Your shirt's got a button missing.*

You use **fehlen** to tell someone you're missing them. It agrees with the person you're missing, and the person speaking goes into the dative case.
Du fehlst mir. *I miss you* lit. *You are missing to me.*
Ihr habt uns gefehlt. *We missed you.*
Mein Hund fehlt mir so. *I miss my dog so much.*
Ihr beide fehlt mir/uns. *I/We miss you both.*

Fehlen is often used in conversations about health.
Fehlt Ihnen etwas? *Is there something the matter (with you)?*
Was fehlt Ihnen? *What seems to be the matter?*

finding out how to do something

To ask how something is done or how you do something, use **man** + third person singular of a verb, i.e. the form used with **er/sie/es**. The object of the verb goes into the accusative case (page 177). The English equivalent is usually *How do I ... ? How do you ... ? How does one ... ?*

Wie sagt man ... auf Deutsch? *How do you say ... in German?*
Wie spricht man dieses Wort aus? *How is this word pronounced?*
Wie schreibt man das? *How is it written? How do you spell it?*
Wie gebraucht man dieses Gerät? *How do you use this gadget?*
Wie öffnet man Austern? *How do you open oysters?*
Wie bestellt man etwas online? *How do you order something online?*
Wie isst man eine Mango/Litschis? *How do you eat mango/lychees?*
Wie kommt man hier raus? *How do you get out of here?*
Wie macht man das Licht an? *How do I turn the light on?*
Wie geht man bei einer Online-Buchung vor? *How do you go about booking online?*
Wie kann man sich mit WLAN verbinden? Wie kann man sich ins WLAN einloggen? *How do you connect to the Wi-Fi?*

See how many similar questions you can come up with in just ten minutes. Use a mix of the words in the examples, some of the following words and any other words you know. Don't forget to say the questions out loud.
ausschalten (sep) **to switch off**, laden (man lädt) **to charge**, downloaden, bekommen **to get**, verstecken **to hide**, vorbereiten (sep) **to prepare**, mieten **to hire**, spielen **to play**, vermeiden **to avoid**, behandeln **to treat**, wechseln **to change, swap over.**

der Akku **battery**, das Auto **car**, der Ausweis **pass, ID card**, der Computer, Eishockey, das Fahrrad **bike**, Filme **films**, das Fleisch **meat**, das Gemüse **vegetables**, Handball, die Kaffeemaschine **coffee machine**, Karten **tickets**, der Kater **hangover**, Knödel **dumplings**, Krämpfe **cramp**, Lieder **songs**, die Nummer **number**, der Parkausweis **parking permit**, Schmerzen im Rücken **backache**, Schach **chess**, das Visum **visa**.

To ask what someone or something is called, use the verb **heißen.**
Wie heißt das auf Deutsch? *What's that called in German?*
Wie heißt dein Mann/dieses Lied? *What's your husband/this song called?*
Wie heißen die Lieder? *What are the songs called?*

asking for advice and information

Attract someone's attention with **Entschuldigung, Entschuldigen Sie bitte** *Excuse me please* or **Sagen Sie bitte/Sagen Sie mir bitte** *Tell me please,* followed by a straightforward question:

... **was ist passiert?** ... *what (has) happened?*
... **welche Nummer muss ich anrufen?** ... *what number do I need to call?*
... **wo befindet sich die nächste Apotheke?** ... *where is the nearest chemist?*
... **um wieviel Uhr öffnet sie?** ... *what time does it* (the chemist, f) *open?*
... **wie kommt man am besten zum Stadion?** ... *what's the best way to get to the stadium?*
... **wie steht das Spiel?** ... *what's the score?*
... **was bedeutet das?** ... *what does this mean?*

To sound less abrupt, you can start with:
Kannst du/Können Sie mir sagen ... *Can you tell me ...*
Wer kann mir sagen ... *Who can tell me ...*
Kann mir jemand sagen ... *Can anyone tell me ...*
These send the verb in your question to the end – just as happens in English. So, you can say either:
Entschuldigen Sie bitte, wo ist der Ausgang? *Tell me please, where's the exit?*
Or **Können Sie mir sagen, wo der Ausgang ist?** *Can you tell me where the exit is?*
Sagen Sie mir bitte, wie lange dauert es? *Tell me please, how long does it take/last?*
Or **Kann mir jemand sagen, wie lange es dauert?** *Can anyone tell me how long it takes/lasts?*
You'll need **ob** *if/whether* for questions without a question word.
Kannst du mir sagen, ob es Handtücher gibt? *Can you tell me whether there are any towels?*
Wer kann mir sagen, ob es etwas Neues gibt? *Who can tell me if there's any news?*

Use one of the three phrases above to make a less abrupt-sounding question. Remember, they send the verb to the end.
Warum ist Marius nicht gekommen? Why didn't Marius come?
Wo kann ich einen Ausweis bekommen? Where can I get a pass?
Wie ist seine/ihre Adresse? What is his/her address?
Gibt es warmes Wasser? Is there any hot water?
War der Arzt/die Ärztin dort? Was the doctor (m/f) there?

giving advice and instructions

When you're giving instructions, you use a form of the verb called the imperative, which has **du, ihr** and **Sie** forms. Separable verbs separate, with the prefix going to the end.

For most verbs, the du imperative is the stem of the infinitive. An added **-e** is optional unless the stem ends in **-d**, **-t** or **-n**:
kommen *to come* → Komm! Komme! *Come!*
warten *to wait* → Warte! *Wait!*
sich beruhigen *to calm down* → Beruhige dich! *Calm down!*
sagen *to say, to tell* → Sage **nichts.** *Don't say anything. Say nothing.*
Sag **mir, was ich machen muss!** *Tell me what to do!*
Schlaf **gut.** *Sleep well.*
Stehe **nicht zu früh** auf. *Don't get up too early.*
Lass **mich dir helfen.** *Let me help you.*
Mach dir **keine Sorgen darüber!** *Don't worry about it!*
Beeile dich! *Hurry up!*

For verbs with a change of vowel in the **du** form, the imperative is simply the **du** stem, without an ending:
nehmen *to take* → **du nimmst** *you take* → nimm! *Take!*
sprechen *to speak* → **du sprichst** *you speak* → sprich! *Speak!*
helfen *to help* → **du hilfst** → Hilf mir! *Help me!*
vergessen *to forget* → **du vergisst** *you forget* → Vergiss nicht **einen Ausweis mitzubringen.** *Don't forget to bring ID with you.*

The **du** imperative of **sein** *to be* is **sei!** *Be!*
Sei **ernsthaft!** *Be serious!*; Sei **ruhig!** *Be quiet!*
Sei **doch realistisch!** *Be realistic!*; Sei **doch geduldig!** *Be patient now!*

The **ihr** imperative has the same form as the **ihr** present tense:
ihr geht *you go, you are going* → Geht! *Go!*
ihr seid *you are* → **Seid!** *Be!* Seid **glücklich!** *Be happy!*
Habt keine **Angst!** *Don't be afraid!*
Arbeitet **nicht zu viel!** *Don't work too hard!*
Kommt **gut nach Hause!** *Have a safe journey home!*
Beeilt euch! *Hurry up!*
Macht euch **keine Sorgen darüber!** *Don't worry about it!*

The **Sie** imperative has the same form as **Sie** present tense questions.
Gehen Sie? *Do you go? Are you going?* **Gehen Sie!** *Go!*

The only verb that doesn't follow this pattern is **sein** *to be*. The question form is **sind Sie?** *are you?* but the imperative is **Seien Sie!** *Be!*
Seien Sie so nett und geben Sie mir eine Kopie davon. *Would you be kind enough to give me a copy of it?*

Sagen Sie bitte .... *Tell me please ...*
Befolgen Sie die Anweisungen. *Follow the instructions.*
Trinken Sie am besten keinen Alkohol, wenn Sie diese Medikamente einnehmen. *Ideally, don't drink alcohol while taking this medication.*
Erwarten Sie keine Wunder! *Don't expect miracles!*
Rufen Sie den Notdienst an. *Call the emergency services.*
Amüsieren Sie sich. *Enjoy yourself/yourselves.*

being even more imperative

Mal after an imperative is used colloquially for emphasis. It often can't be translated, although sometimes the English *just* or *please* does the same job.
Warte mal! *Wait, please!*
Sieh das mal an! *Just take a look at that!*
Probiert mal diesen Nachtisch: ich habe ihn selbst gemacht. *Try this dessert: I made it myself.*

You'll come across the imperative in many common phrases:
Komm! Fass Mut! *Come on! Cheer up!*
Nutze den Tag! *Seize the moment! Carpe diem.*
Gib dein Bestes. *Do your best.*
Gib alles! *Give it everything!*
Kümmere dich um deine eigenen Angelegenheiten. *Mind your own business.*
Nimm keine Notiz. Vergiss es. *Take no notice. Forget it.*
Stör mich nicht. *Don't disturb me. Don't bug me.*
Bleib dort! *Stay there!*
Bitte pass auf! *Please be careful! Look out!*
Beiß die Zähne zusammen. *Grit your teeth.*
Halt die Augen offen. *Keep your eyes peeled.*
Halt dich tapfer. *Have courage. Be strong.*

official signs and instructions

The imperative is used mostly when giving verbal instructions. In written German you're more likely to see the infinitive, which comes at the end of the phrase. You'll see it in street signs:

Ziehen *Pull* **Drücken** *Push* **Warten** *Wait*
Bitte nicht eintreten *Do not enter*
Bitte nicht stören *Do not disturb*
Tür bitte freihalten! *Keep the doorway clear*
Links gehen, rechts stehen *Walk on the left, stand on the right* (escalator)
Bitte die Tauben nicht füttern *Please do not feed the pigeons*

... on a computer when it tells you what to do:

Drucken *Print* **Klicken** *Click* **Mehr zeigen** *Show more*
Schließen *Close* **Senden** *Send* **Speichern** *Save*

... and in recipes:
Zwiebel und Knoblauch schälen und klein schneiden. *Peel the onion and garlic and chop finely.*
Mit einer Prise Salz, Pfeffer und Basilikum würzen. *Season with a pinch of salt, pepper and basil.*
Den Kuchen aus den Ofen nehmen und abkühlen lassen. *Remove the cake from the oven and allow to cool.*
Eigelb und Eiweiß trennen. Das Eiweiß zu festem Eischnee schlagen. *Separate the egg yolks from the whites. Whisk the egg white to stiff peaks* lit. egg snow.

To say what you mustn't do, a past participle is used: **verboten** *forbidden* (from **verbieten** *to forbid*), **nicht gestattet** *not permitted* (from **gestatten** *to allow, permit*), **verweigert** *denied, refused* (from **verweigern** *to refuse*). These past participles go to the end.

Rauchen verboten. *Smoking is not allowed. No smoking.*
Einfahrt verboten. *No entry.*
Parken verboten. *No parking.*
Fotografieren verboten. *No photography.*
Übernachten nicht gestattet. *No overnight parking.*
Anlehnen von Fahrrädern nicht gestattet. *Do not leave bicycles here.*
Zugriff verweigert *Access denied.* (computer)

talking about food

Food and drink play an important role in German life, so it's well worth having a stock of expressions relating to them.

Hast du Hunger? Haben Sie Hunger? *Are you hungry?*
Ich habe (großen) Hunger/Durst. *I'm (very) hungry/thirsty.*
Ich sterbe vor Hunger/Durst. *I'm absolutely famished.* (lit. *I'm dying of hunger/I'm dying of thirst.*)
Ich habe einen Bärenhunger. *I could eat a horse.* (lit. *I have a bear's hunger.*)
Ich habe keinen Appetit. *I don't feel like eating.*
Danke, aber ich kann wirklich nicht mehr. *Thanks, but I really can't manage any more.*

Wie schmeckt es dir/Ihnen? *How do you like it? Does it taste good?*
Es schmeckt sehr gut/lecker. *It's very good/delicious.*
Sie schmecken echt gut. *They taste really good.*
Es ist sehr schmackhaft. *It's full of flavour.*
Ich bin schon satt. *I'm full.*
Ich habe schon drei gegessen. *I've already eaten three.*
Das ist ein bisschen stark/scharf. *It's a bit too strong/hot and spicy.*
Sie sind nicht süß /salzig genug. *They're not sweet/salty enough.*

Die Rechnung, bitte. *The bill please.*
Ich lade dich/euch ein. *My treat.* lit. *I invite you.* **(du/ihr)**
Wir laden Sie ein. *Our treat.*
Diese Runde geht auf mich. *I'm paying for this round.*
Jetzt bin ich dran. *It's my turn to pay.*
Jeder zahlt für sich selbst. *Let's go Dutch. Let's share the cost.*
Lasst uns die Rechnung aufteilen. *Let's split the bill.*

With **Wurst** *sausage* being so popular in Germany, it's not surprising that it's had an effect on the language, too.
Du armes Würstchen! *You poor soul!* lit. *You poor sausage.*
Es geht um die Wurst. *It's crunch time.* lit. *It's all about the sausage.*
Das ist mir Wurst. *I couldn't care less.* lit. *It's sausage to me.*
Er spielt die beleidigte Leberwurst. *He's sulking/in a huff.* lit. *He's playing the offended liver sausage.*
Er lässt sich die Wurst nicht vom Brot nehmen. *He doesn't let himself be pushed around.* lit. *He doesn't let the sausage be taken from the bread.*
Alles hat ein Ende, nur die Wurst hat zwei. *Everything must come to an end.* lit. *Everything has an end, only the sausage has two.*

wordbank

das Essen *food*
die Mahlzeit *meal*

- **das Frühstück** *breakfast*
- **das zweite Frühstück** *elevenses*
- **das Mittagessen** *lunch*
- **Kaffee und Kuchen** *afternoon snack of coffee and cake*
- **das Abendessen/Abendbrot** *evening meal*
- **die Zwischenmahlzeit, der Imbiss** *snack*
- **die Brotzeit** *savoury snack* (in Bavaria)

Germans traditionally eat their main meal of the day, generally something hot, at lunchtime. One word for *evening meal* **Abendbrot** literally *evening bread*, reflects the fact that this is a lighter meal, often of bread and cold cuts. *Bon appétit* in German is **Guten Appetit!** or **Mahlzeit!** The latter also serves as a word of greeting to colleagues, said around midday.

- **eine ausgewogene Mahlzeit/Ernährung** *a balanced meal/diet*
- **ein Gourmet-Gericht** *a gourmet dish*
- **die Vorspeisen** *appetisers, hors d'œuvres*

There are two words for *diet*. A restrictive diet that you follow for health reasons is **die Diät**, while *diet* meaning a typical way of eating is **die Ernährung.**
eine strenge Diät *a strict diet*
eine Kohlenhydratarme Diät *a low-carb diet*
eine Eiweißreiche Diät *a high-protein diet*
eine vegetarische Ernährung *a vegetarian diet*
die mediterrane Ernährung *the Mediterranean diet*

essen und fressen

Humans **essen**, but the verb that refers to animals eating is **fressen: Mein Kind isst nicht viel** *My child doesn't eat a lot*, **mein Hund frisst nicht viel** *my dog doesn't eat a lot*. When **fressen** is used to refer to people, it suggests they're being greedy: **sich vollfressen** *to stuff oneself, pig out*. *Glutton* is **der Vielfraß**.
Gierig means *greedy, and* **gierig verschlingen** is *to wolf down*.
Feudal essen *to have a slap-up meal*, literally means *to eat feudal-style:* **ein feudales Essen** *a slap-up meal*.
Zu viel essen/trinken *is to eat/drink too much;* **das Besäufnis** means *booze-up* while *to binge on chocolate* is **sich mit Schokolade vollstopfen**.

health matters

Talking about how you're feeling physically isn't confined to medical discussions; there are times, for example, when it's tactful to explain why you can't eat something.

Iss! Essen Sie! Schmeckt's nicht? *Do eat! Don't you like it?*
Ich bin ... *I'm ...*
- **... Diabetiker(in)** (m/f)/**zuckerkrank** ... *diabetic*
- **... Vegetarier(in)** (m/f) ... *vegetarian*
- **... Veganer(in)** (m/f) ... *vegan*
- **... Zöliakie-Betroffener/Betroffene** (m/f) ... *coeliac*
- **... allergisch gegen Weizen/Milchprodukte/Nüsse.** *I'm allergic to wheat/dairy produce/nuts.*

Ich muss beim Essen aufpassen. *I have to watch what I eat.*
Ich mache eine Diät. *I'm on a diet.*
Ich muss sechs Kilo abnehmen. *I need to lose six kilos.*
Enthält das Erdnüsse? *Does it contain peanuts?*

Du hast nichts gegessen. Was ist mit dir los? *You haven't eaten a thing. What's the matter?*
Mir geht es nicht gut. *I'm not well*
Mir ist übel/fürchterlich schlecht. *I feel sick/terrible.*
Ich fühle mich krank/scheußlich. *I feel ill/dreadful.*
Ich habe ... *I have ...*
- **... Zahnschmerzen** ... *toothache*
- **... Halschmerzen** ... *a sore throat*
- **... Magenschmerzen** ... *tummy ache*
- **... Fieber** ... *a temperature*
- **... einen Kater** ... *a hangover*
- **... eine Magenverstimmung** ... *an upset stomach*

Möchten Sie diesen Wein probieren? *Would you like to try this wine?*
Nur ein bisschen/ein kleines Gläschen, bitte. *Just a small amount/a tiny glass, please.*
Ich trinke keinen Alkohol. *I don't drink alcohol.*
Ich nehme Medikamente gegen .... ein. *I take medication for ...*
- **... hohen Blutdruck** ... *high blood pressure.*
- **... Diabetes/Zuckerkrankheit** ... *diabetes.*
- **... ein Herzleiden** ... *a heart condition.*

Ich bin (im fünften Monat) schwanger. *I'm (five months) pregnant.*

Similarly, you might need to explain why you aren't keen or able to join in.

Wollen wir eine Wanderung in den Bergen machen? *Shall we go hiking in the mountains?*
Ich habe Arthritis/Schmerzen im Rücken/Schnupfen/Heuschnupfen. *I've got arthritis/backache/a head cold/hay fever.*
Ich habe eine entzündete Sehne. *I've got an inflamed tendon.*
Ich glaube, ich bin dehydriert. *I think I'm dehydrated.*
Mein Bein tut mir weh. *My leg hurts.*
Meine Knie/Füße tun mir weh. *My knees/feet hurt.*
Wir sind gestern zu weit gegangen. *We walked too far yesterday.*

The verb *to hurt* is **wehtun**. The person in pain goes into the dative case. **Mein Kopf tut mir weh.** *My head hurts.*
Ihr Zahn tut ihr weh. *Her tooth hurts.*
Ihre Schultern tun ihr weh. *Her shoulders hurt.*
Seine Beine tun ihm weh. *His legs hurt.*

Kommst du ins Fitnesszentrum nicht mit? Was ist los? *Aren't you coming with us to the gym? What's up?*
Ich habe mir einen Muskel ... gezerrt. *I've pulled a muscle ...*
...**in der Wade/in der Leiste** ... *in my calf/in my groin.*
Ich kann mein Knie nicht beugen. *I can't bend my knee.*
Ich bin völlig kaputt. *I'm shattered.*

Wo ist Theo? Was ist mit ihm los? *Where's Theo? What's happened to him?*
Er ist krank. *He's ill.*
Er liegt im Krankenhaus. *He's in hospital.*
Ich weiß nicht, was ihm fehlt. *I don't know what's wrong with him.*
Heute morgen ist er hingefallen. *He fell over this morning.*
Er hat einen Unfall gehabt. *He's had an accident.*
Es hat einen Unfall gegeben. *There's been an accident.*

Wir gehen heute an den Strand. Willst du mitkommen? *We're going to the beach today. Do you want to join us?*
Ich bin erkältet. *I've got a cold.*
Ich fühle mich so müde. *I feel so tired.*
Mir ist ein bisschen schwindlig. *I feel a bit dizzy.*
Ich habe Kopfschmerzen. *I've got a headache.*
Ich habe Sonnenbrand. Guckt mal! *I'm sunburnt. Look!*

talking the talk

Volker Sophie, wo bist du? Ich warte auf dich.

Sophie Entschuldigung, Volker. Ich habe vergessen, dich anzurufen. Ich bin bei Oskar. Wir mussten den Notdienst anrufen.

Volker Mein Gott! Was ist passiert? Hat es einen Unfall gegeben?

Sophie Beruhige dich! Nein, es hat keinen Unfall gegeben. Die Nachbarin von Oskar liegt im Krankenhaus.

Volker Die alte Frau?

Sophie Ja, genau. Es scheint, dass sie ein Herzleiden hat. Heute hat sie vergessen, ihre Medikamente einzunehmen, und ihr ist schlecht geworden. Oskar hat mich angerufen, und ich bin sofort zu ihm nach Hause gefahren. Wir haben den Notdienst angerufen, und wir sind zusammen mit Frau Scholz ins Krankenhaus gefahren. Wir sind gerade nach Hause zurückgekommen.

Volker Und wie geht es ihr jetzt? Und wie geht es euch beiden?

Sophie Frau Scholz wird noch einige Tage im Krankenhaus bleiben, aber ihr geht es schon besser. Und Oskar und ich sind völlig kaputt. Wir gehen jetzt in die Wohnung von Frau Scholz, um zu sehen, ob alles in Ordnung ist.

Volker Ja, natürlich. Geh sofort hin, und ruf mich später an.

Volker Naja, wie geht's? War alles in Ordnung?

Sophie Ja, kein Problem. Wir haben ihre Medikamente gefunden. Sie nimmt so viele Tabletten ein. Jetzt fühle ich mich so müde, und ich habe Kopfschmerzen. Außerdem sterbe ich vor Hunger.

Volker Komm doch zu mir. Oskar auch – lade ihn doch auch ein. Ich bestelle eine große Pizza.

Sophie Das ist nett von dir. Danke. Hast du auch Aspirin zu Hause?

Volker Nein, aber es gibt eine Apotheke unter meiner Wohnung. Sie ist noch offen. Ich gehe sofort und kaufe Aspirin für dich. Beeilt euch! Bis gleich.

Sophie Ja, wir kommen gleich. Bis dann.

checkpoint 10

1. If a German friend asks you **Wie heißt das auf Englisch?** what do they want to know?
2. **Vorsichtig** means careful, so how would you say *be careful* in the **du, ihr** and **Sie** forms?
3. How would you ask if there's a pharmacy near here?
4. What does the sign on a door **Bitte nicht eintreten** mean?
5. What little word can you add to an imperative to show you really mean it?
6. What's another way of saying **Niemand war zu Hause** *There's no one at home*, beginning **Es**?
7. What do **pass auf** and **beeile dich** mean? How do they change when used with someone you call **Sie** and with two friends?
8. *Cake* in German is **(der) Kuchen**, and its plural is the same. How would you say *This cake tastes good* and *These cakes taste good*?
9. How do you tell someone that you're on a diet and need to lose five kilos?
10. At the end of a meal, how might you say that you're full?
11. What do you change in **mir geht es nicht gut** to say *she's not well* and *he's not well.*
12. How do you say *forbidden* in German?
13. What words do you need to add to these two sentences to make them negative, remembering that **Wein** is masculine – **der Wein: es gibt .... Wein** and **es gibt .... genug Wein**?
14. **Ich lade dich ein** *my treat* is literally *I invite you.* What's the infinitive of the verb *to invite?*
15. How would you write to your family members that you're missing them all?
16. How do you start a question to someone you call **Sie** with *Can you tell me*? Using this, ask what's happened, how to get to the airport, if there's any news, how you can order a pizza.
17. How do you say i) *My foot hurts*, ii) *I've got a head cold*, iii) *I feel tired*?

elf

keeping in touch

Whether you're keeping in touch with people or with what's going on in the world, the chances are that you'll be doing it via the internet. To access it on your tablet or smartphone in Germany, Austria or German-speaking Switzerland, you might need **Haben Sie gratis WLAN?** *Do you have free Wi-Fi?* and **Wie ist das Passwort?** *What's the password?* **WLAN** stands for the English *wireless local area network*. It's pronounced *Veh-lan*.

Even if you're no technophile, the influence of technology on everyday life is such that it's worth understanding key terminology in German. This isn't a major hurdle, as English words are widely used.

What's interesting for someone learning German is the way the adopted words are used. Their origin might be English but they're governed by the rules of German grammar: nouns are written with a capital letter **das Training, die Performance**, and you'll hear **gegoogelt** and **getweetet**. The words are usually pronounced the English way, although **w** is pronounced *v*: *getveetet*.

As in other languages, shortcuts are increasingly prevalent on the internet, particularly on social networking sites. It can be a bit disconcerting when you first come across **n8** or what you think is the single word **div**, but these just mean **Nacht**, because **8** is **acht**, and **div** is actually an acronym of **danke im Voraus**, *thanks in advance*.

Denglisch

The number of English words used in German has grown hugely in recent years. The phenomenon is called **Denglisch**; **Denglish** in English.

It's very noticeable in the world of business, although the word for *business* itself in German is home-grown: **das Geschäft**.
Morgen haben wir ein Meeting mit unseren Consultants, um den neuen Slogan zu diskutieren. *We've a meeting tomorrow with our consultants to discuss the new slogan.*
Ich organisiere einen Workshop für das ganze Team. *I'm organising a workshop for the whole team.*

Der Sport often involves English words:
Spielst du Golf/Baseball? *Do you play golf/baseball?*
Ich möchte mit dem Bodybuilding anfangen. *I'd like to begin with bodybuilding.*
Wir freuen uns auf das Lokalderby. *We're looking forward to the derby.*

Germany has its own **klassische Musik** tradition and, like English, uses Italian words for this, but English words have been adopted for other genres.
Er ist verrückt nach Rap. *He's crazy about rap music.*
Er spielt in einer Boyband. *He plays in a boyband.*
Am liebsten mag ich Jazz. *I like jazz best.*

Some words are unexpected to native English speakers: **der Streetworker** *a social worker who works in deprived neighbourhoods*, **das Bodybag** *backpack*, **das Basecap** *baseball cap*, **das Happy End** *happy ending.*

Sometimes a word has a different meaning or usage in German: **chatten** has the specific meaning of *to chat online in a chatroom*; *to have a chat* is **reden, plaudern, schwatzen** or **sich unterhalten.**

Words are generally pronounced the English way: **der Computer** has the un-German ***pyu*** sound in the middle, just like the English word, and the **poste** of **poste es auf Facebook** *post it on Facebook* has a rounded **o** as in the English *post*; the **o** of the German **Post** *post-office*, on the other hand, is like the *o* in *lost*. However, German **a** sounds more like *e*: **das Backup** is pronounced *beck-up*. The ***w*** of **das Workshop** and other words is pronounced *v*.

Denglisch is most in evidence in the world of IT. English words predominate on the internet, particularly among the computer savvy and on social media. Like other loan words, they generally follow the rules of German grammar.

Nouns have a gender. Sometimes the gender is the same as for the equivalent German word: **die Wolke** is *cloud* in German, **die Seite** is *page* and it's **die App** because of **die Applikation**, but more often than not the choice of gender seems arbitrary. Often, the Germans can't decide:
der/das Blog/Vlog, der Browser, der Chat, die Cloud, der Cyberspace, der Desktop, die E-Mail, das Emoticon, das Forum, die Homepage, der Hotspot, das Icon, das Internet, der Laptop, der Link, der Scanner, die Slideshow, das Smiley, die Software/Hardware, das Streaming, das Tablet, der USB Stick.

Plurals add **s**, unlike home-grown German words. If the English word has what looks like a typically German ending, e.g. **-er**, then the plural follows German rules.

So, it's **der Bodybuilder/die Bodybuilder**, just as it's **der Lehrer/die Lehrer** *teacher/teachers*. A female bodybuilder is **die Bodybuilderin**, and its plural is **die Bodybuilderinnen**.

Diese Blogs sind sehr interessant. *These blogs are very interesting.*
Liest du Tweets von Politikern? *Do you read politicians' tweets?*
Heute habe ich vier E-Mails von meiner Mutter erhalten. *I've received four emails from my mother today.*
Welche Rapper magst du gerne? *Which rappers do you like?*
Die deutschen Snowboarder und Snowboarderinnen haben gewonnen. *The German snowboarders (male and female) won.*

Infinitives of verbs end in **-en** as you'd expect, with consonants often doubling up, as happens with parts of English verbs, too (*stop/stopping*).
booten, scannen, streamen, taggen, zippen.

Many modern German verbs based on English end in **-ieren**:
formatieren, kopieren, programmieren, sortieren.
They will be separable if they begin with a separable prefix e.g. **ein**, the equivalent of the English *in*, or **aus** *out*:
ausloggen, einloggen; **ich logge mich ein** *I log in*
There is still uncertainty among Germans as to whether **downloaden** is a separable verb or not; you will hear both **gedownloadet** and **downgeloadet**.

saying thank you and goodbye

Finally come the goodbyes and the thanks.

Auf Wiedersehen, or **Auf Wiederschauen** in Austria and southern Germany, means *Until we see each other again*. More final is **Leb wohl/Leben Sie wohl** *farewell*, which literally means *Live well*.

A simple *thanks* or *thank you* is **danke** but when someone's really gone out of their way for you, you might want to add to it.

Danke schön/sehr/vielmals. *Thanks very much/a lot.*
Vielen/Tausend/Herzlichen Dank. *Thanks a lot/a million/warmly.*
Danke nochmal. *Thanks again.*

... or you could use the verbs **danken** and **sich bedanken** *to thank*.

Ich danke dir/euch. *I thank you.* **(du/ihr)**
Ich danke Ihnen herzlich. *I thank you so much.* **(Sie)**
Ich bedanke mich bei Ihnen. *I thank you.* **(Sie)**

For after thank you expressions is **für**, and it's followed by the accusative.
Danke für einen Super-Urlaub. *Thanks for a super holiday.*
Vielen Dank für deine/eure/Ihre Hilfe. *Thanks for your help.*
Vielen Dank für deine/eure/Ihre Gastfreundschaft. *Thank you for your hospitality, Thanks for having me/us.* **(du/ihr/Sie)**
Tausend Dank für alles. *Thanks a million for everything.*
Ich danke Ihnen für alles, was Sie für uns getan haben. *Thank you for everything (you've done for us).*

There are other ways of expressing your appreciation:
Ich kann dir nicht genug danken. *I can't thank you enough.*
Ich weiß nicht, wie ich euch danken kann. *I don't know how to thank you.*
Du bist ein Engel/ein Schatz! *You're an angel/a treasure!*
Du bist sehr nett. So-o-o nett. *You're very kind. Too kind.*
Sie sind sehr großzügig. *You're really generous.*
Ich schulde dir was. *I owe you big time.*
Ich habe mich wirklich amüsiert. *I've had a great time/a ball.*
Wir haben eine wunderschöne Zeit gehabt. *We've had a wonderful time.*

The answer to **danke** can be a simple **bitte** *no worries, you're welcome* or:

Gern geschehen. *You're welcome, my pleasure*
Nichts zu danken. *Think nothing of it, don't mention it.*
Es war mir/uns ein Vergnügen. *It's been a pleasure.*

keeping in touch

After the goodbyes and thanks, talk usually turns to staying in touch, perhaps by phone, social media or email.

Es war mir ein Vergnügen, Sie kennenzulernen. *It's been a pleasure meeting you.*
Wir werden bestimmt nochmal kommen. *We'll definitely come again.*
Du wirst mir fehlen. *I'll miss you.*
Ihr werdet mir alle fehlen. *I'll miss you all.*
Wir bleiben in Verbindung. *We'll stay in touch.*
Wir melden uns bald (bei euch). *We'll be in touch soon (with you).*

You've already come across the language structures you need.

asking questions: chapter 2

Wie ist deine E-Mail-Adresse? *What's your email address?*
Wie ist Ihre Telefonnummer? *What's your phone number?*
Bist du bei WhatsApp? *Are you on WhatsApp?*
Wann installierst du WhatsApp? *When are you going to install WhatsApp?*
Welche Fotos hat sie auf Instagram gepostet? *What photos did she post on Instagram?*

modal verbs: chapter 8

Wir müssen in Verbindung bleiben. *We must keep in touch.*
Wollen wir Adressen austauschen? *Shall we exchange addresses?*
Wir könnten eine Skype Gruppe einrichten. *We could set up a Skype group.*
Florian kann die besten Fotos schicken. *Florian can send the best photos.*

talking about the future: chapter 7

Ich rufe dich am Sonntag an. *I'll call you on Sunday.*
Ich finde dich dann auf Facebook. *I'll find you on Facebook.*
Ich sende dir die Informationen per SMS. *I'll text you the details.*
Wir laden das Video am besten in die Cloud hoch. *We'll upload the video to the cloud.*

imperative: chapter 10

Sende mir eine SMS oder eine E-Mail. *Send me a text or an email.*
Stell's mal auf Facebook? *Put it on Facebook, OK?*
Vergiss/Vergesst/Vergessen Sie nicht ... *Don't forget to ...* **(du/ihr/Sie)**
   ... die Fotos in der Cloud zu teilen. *... share the photos on iCloud.*
   ... mir eine E-Mail zu senden. *... send me an email.*

phone calls

If you're planning to phone someone, it's worth knowing the following.
Hallo. *Hello.* **Hallo, Hans Beck.** *Hello, Hans Beck speaking.*
Wer spricht, bitte?/Wie ist Ihr Name? *Who's calling?*
Mit wem spreche ich? *Who am I speaking to?*
Spreche ich mit Frau Müller? *Am I speaking to Mrs Muller?*
Am Apparat. *Speaking.*
Hallo, hier ist Simon Barnes. *Hello, this is Simon Barnes.*

To answer with **Hallo** is fairly casual. Many Germans will answer with their name followed by a greeting: **Stefan Kaufmann, guten Tag**, or simply their surname: **Kaufmann.**
When answering their work direct line, Germans will tend to first give the company name, then their own name, then maybe a greeting: **Bilfinger, Kaufmann, guten Tag.**

Hast du/Haben Sie die Nummer von Anka? *Do you have Anka's number?*
Entschuldigung, ich habe mich verwählt. *Sorry, wrong number.*
Auf Wiederhören. *Goodbye.* (on the phone only)

Ich höre dich/Sie schlecht. *I can't hear you very well.* lit. *I hear you badly.*
Wir haben eine schlechte Verbindung. *It's a bad line/connection.*
Das Signal ist schwach. *The signal's weak.*
Der Akku ist schwach/gleich leer. *The battery's low/almost flat.*
Ich habe (fast) kein Guthaben mehr. *I've (almost) no more credit.*
Ich kann Sie nicht verstehen. *I can't understand you.*

A sentence you'll hear often is **Bitte hinterlassen Sie eine Nachricht nach dem Signalton.** *Please leave a message after the tone.*

Germans often break their phone number into smaller 'chunks', e.g. 0175 3926841 would be 0175 3 92 68 41 **nullhundertfünfundsiebzig drei-zweiundneunzig achtundsechzig-einundvierzig**. To avoid confusion, you can check your comprehension by repeating back each number individually: **null eins sieben fünf drei neun zwo sechs acht vier eins.**
Zwo is often used instead of **zwei** on the phone, because of possible confusion with **drei**.

The general word for *telephone* is **das Telefon**. *Mobile phone* is **das Handy**, pronounced *hendy.* **Anrufen** *to telephone* is a separable verb: **Ich rufe später noch einmal an.** *I'll phone back later.*

emails

When giving someone your email address or a website address, you do so with the verb **lauten**, which is used when saying a sequence of characters; **es lautet** is similar to the English *it reads.*

Meine E-Mail-Adresse lautet ... *My email address is ...*
Das Passwort lautet ... *The password is ...*
Die URL lautet ... *The URL is ...*
Die Website heißt ... *The website is called ...*

URL is pronounced as one syllable *oorrl.* It's usually **die URL** because of the association with **die Internetadresse**, but you will also see **der URL** in technical contexts, because it's **der Locator.**

You'll need to know how to spell out words (page 19) and punctuation:

* **das Sternchen**
@ **das At-Zeichen**
/ **der Schrägstrich, Slash**
& **das Und-Zeichen**
\ **der umgekehrte Schrägstrich**
, **das Komma**
. **der Punkt**
! **das Ausrufezeichen**
? **das Fragezeichen**
- **der (Binde-)Strich**
_ **der Unterstrich**
das Doppelkreuz
(in brackets) **in Klammern**
space **das Leerzeichen**

The way to say **www.** is *veh-veh-veh Punkt.*
Upper case letter is **der Großbuchstabe** (plural **die Großbuchstaben**).
Lower case letter **der Kleinbuchstabe** (plural **die Kleinbuchstaben**).

An email to a close friend starts with **Lieber/Liebe** (m/f) followed by the name, or **Hallo** *Hi*: **Lieber Jörg; Liebe Sabine; Hallo Jörg; Hallo Sabine.**

A more formal email, to someone you address as **Sie**, begins **Sehr geehrter/ Sehr geehrte:**
Sehr geehrter Herr Lehnhardt; Sehr geehrte Frau Wagner.

Best wishes at the end of a friendly email is: **Viele Grüße** or **Liebe Grüße.** Or, for very close friends, you can say: **Alles Liebe** *Love.*
Best wishes at the end a formal email is: **Mit freundlichen Grüßen.**

wordbank

IT is **EDV (die elektronische Datenverarbeitung)**, and computer is **der Computer**, pronounced the English way.

der Bildschirm *screen*
der Bildschirmschoner *screensaver*
das Kabel *cable, wire*
der Akku *battery*
das Ladegerät *charger*

die Tastatur *keyboard*
die Taste *key*
die Maus *mouse*
der Drucker *printer*
die Sprecher *speakers* (sing. **der**)
der Kopfhörer *headphones* (singular in German)

das Betriebssystem *operating system*
der Arbeitsspeicher *memory*
das Programm *program*
der Benutzername *user name*
das Passwort *password*

das Menü *menu*
der Cursor/Mauszeiger *cursor*
der Pfeil *arrow*
die Werkzeugleiste *toolbar*
die Datei *file*
der Ordner *folder*

die Suchmaschine *search engine*
das Bookmark/Lesezeichen *bookmark*
der Favorit *favourite*

verbinden *to connect*
online sein *to be online*
die Website *website*
die Webseite *web page*
abgestürzt *frozen, crashed*

anschalten *to switch on*
booten *to boot up*
neu booten *to restart, reboot*
abschalten *to shut down*
suchen *to search (for)*
surfen *to browse/surf*

downloaden *to download*
aktualisieren *to update*
sichern *to back up*
entfernen *to delete*
zurücknehmen *to undo*

*Create ten sentences in German using these verbs and nouns and others that you know, beginning wie ... man or wie kann man ..., e.g. **How do I/you switch the computer on? How do I download videos? How do I back up my emails?***

*Or use other verbs you know to say **I'd like to read my email, I want/need/ought to send an email, find/update/delete a file or photo, search for a website.** Try asking if there's a password and what it is.*

shortcuts

Abkürzungen *shortcuts* are now an online phenomenon in German as they are in English, especially on social media sites and in chatrooms.

The aim is to be as brief as possible while still comprehensible.
akla? **alles klar?** *is everything clear?*
mamima **mail mir mal** *send me an email*
rumian **ruf mich an** *call me*
tabu **tausend Bussis** *lots of love and kisses*
wamaduheu **was machst du heute?** *What are you doing today?*
we **Wochenende** *weekend*

English transcribes the sound *ate/eight* as 8: *great* → *gr8*, but in German 8 is **acht**, so 8ung is **Achtung** *Watch out* and gn8 is **gute Nacht** *good night*. Other numbers generally don't feature.

Acronyms abound, including:
bis **bin im Stress** *I'm madly busy*
bs **bis später** *see you later, till later*
dad **denke an dich** *thinking of you*
div **danke im Voraus** *thanks in advance*
ka **keine Ahnung** *no idea*
lg **liebe Grüße** *all the best, lots of love*

Germans use some of the more ubiquitous English abbreviations:
lol *laughing out loud*. The German would be **laut auflachen.**
btw *by the way*. In German *by the way* is **übrigens.**
sry *sorry*. The German for *sorry* is **Entschuldigung.**

Shortening words isn't confined to internet jargon in Germany. Germans abbreviate many common words and expressions as a matter of routine.

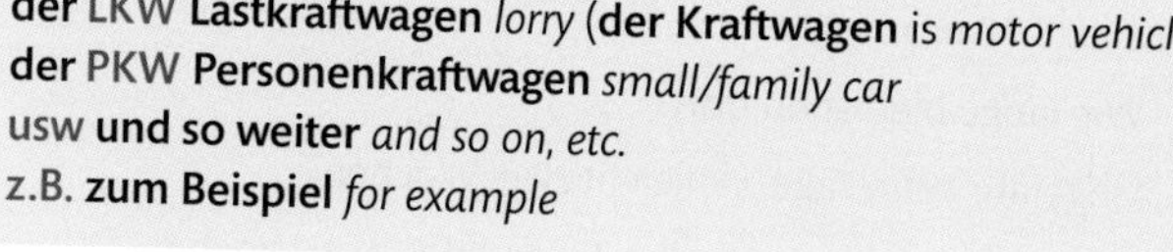

bzw. **beziehungsweise** *respectively, or rather*
der LKW **Lastkraftwagen** *lorry* (**der Kraftwagen** is *motor vehicle*)
der PKW **Personenkraftwagen** *small/family car*
usw **und so weiter** *and so on, etc.*
z.B. **zum Beispiel** *for example*

talking the talk

Volker Was nimmst du?

Sophie Einen Kaffee und einen Nudelsalat mit Parmaschinken.

Volker Wollen wir draußen sitzen?

Sophie Ja, warum nicht? Das Wetter ist schön und mir gefällt der Garten hier.

Volker Hier gibt es gratis WLAN. Ich will dir was im Internet zeigen. Guck mal! Da gibt's einen Tisch.

Volker Also, unser Projekt ist fast zu Ende. Was machst du nach diesem Projekt?

Sophie Ich glaube, ich fahre zu meinen Eltern in die Alpen. Ich habe sie seit mehreren Monaten nicht gesehen. Heute habe ich schon zwei E-Mails von meiner Mutter erhalten, und gestern habe ich drei von ihr bekommen. Wahrscheinlich werde ich morgen früh hinfahren.

Volker Also, vielen Dank für deine Hilfe und alles, was du für uns getan hast. Es war sehr nett, dass wir an diesem Projekt zusammengearbeitet haben.

Sophie Es war mir ein Vergnügen. Ihr werdet mir alle fehlen.

Volker Und du wirst mir fehlen, Sophie. Und Sammy wird mir fehlen. Ich mag ihn sehr gern.

Sophie Und er hat dich auch sehr gern. Du hast aber meine Handynummer, oder?

Volker Ja. Du hast aber nur meine berufliche E-Mail-Adresse, glaube ich. Ich gebe dir meine private Adresse; das wäre besser.

Sophie Ja, wir bleiben in Verbindung. Ich sende dir morgen Abend eine E-Mail aus Bayern.

Volker Wie lange bleibst du dort?

Sophie Ungefähr zehn Tage, vielleicht zwei Wochen.

Volker Dann sehen wir uns in zehn Tagen oder zwei Wochen. Du wirst mir fehlen, Sophie. Lass uns jetzt ein Glas Sekt auf das Wiedersehen trinken.

Sophie Gern, danke.

checkpoint 11

Most of the vocabulary is from this chapter but some of the language structures assume knowledge from the rest of the book.

1. What's the German for *We'll be in touch soon*?
2. What is *a mobile phone* in German?
3. **Ein Showmaster** is *a male host of a TV show*. What do you think the *female host of a TV show* is, and what are the plurals of both words?
4. When would you say **Auf Wiederhören**?
5. What are **ein Doppelkreuz, ein Fragezeichen, ein Punkt, Klammern** and **Kleinbuchstaben**?
6. If you're told **Es tut mir leid, Sie haben sich verwählt**, what have you done?
7. What single word is missing from **Danke .... den schönen Tag** for it to mean *Thank you for a lovely day*?
8. What's the difference between **anschalten** and **abschalten**?
9. How do you ask in a café if they have free Wi-Fi?
10. What are **z.B., usw** and **LKW** short for?
11. Given that **hochladen**, a strong, separable verb, means *to upload*, how do you say in German *I need to/We ought to/We want to upload the photos*, and *Jakob has uploaded the file*?
12. How do you tell someone not to forget to do something **(du, ihr, Sie)**?
13. Using knowledge from this and previous chapters, how would you say *I have lost my USB stick* and *We need to buy a charger*?
14. Imagine your German friend's phone number is 0151 4 84 30 56. How would your friend say the number?
15. What is the German for *mouse* and *keyboard*?
16. How would you begin an email to your friend Kathi?
17. How would you put the sentence **ich rufe dich am Samstag an** into the past (i.e. perfect) tense?
18. You'd say **Ich danke Ihnen** *I thank you* to someone you address as **Sie**. How does **Ihnen** change when talking to one close friend, and to a group of friends?
19. *It's been a pleasure* – how does a couple say this in German?

grammar terminology

The **accusative case** is used for the direct object of a sentence: *the boy is reading a book.*

Adjectives are words that describe nouns and pronouns: *good idea, strong red wine, my fault, she's tall, it was weird.*

Adverbs add information to verbs, adjectives, other adverbs and whole sentences: *a very good idea, he's acting weirdly, luckily he's not here.*

Agreement: A German article or adjective has to **agree** with, i.e. match, the noun/pronoun it relates to, in terms of gender (masculine, feminine or neuter), number (singular or plural) and case (nominative, accusative, dative or genitive).

Articles are **definite:** *the house, the houses*, or **indefinite:** *a house, an area.*

Case refers to the function that a noun/pronoun performs in a sentence. There are four cases in German: **nominative**, **accusative**, **dative** and **genitive**.

A **clause** is a group of words with a subject and a verb that forms part of a sentence. A **main clause** makes sense on its own, but a **subordinate clause** does not: *He arrived home on time although the train was delayed.* The main clause *he arrived home on time* makes sense on its own, but the subordinate clause *although the train was delayed* does not.

Comparative is *more ..., or ....er* when comparing two things: *bigger, more interesting, more slowly.*

A **conjunction** links words, phrases and clauses, e.g. *and, but, although, despite, because.* Most conjunctions in German are **subordinating conjunctions**, which means that they send the verb to the end.

Consonants and vowels make up the alphabet: the vowels are **a, ä, e, i, o, ö, u, ü, y**; the rest are consonants. **Y** is very occasionally a consonant, but only in foreign words e.g. **das Yo-Yo, die Yucca**.

The **dative case** is used for the indirect object of a sentence: *she's reading a book to the boy.*

A word's **endings** are its final letter(s). In English, a noun ending in *-s* is often plural, a verb ending in *-ed* tells you it happened in the past. In German, the endings of nouns, adjectives, articles and verbs change for a variety of reasons.

Feminine: See Gender.

Gender: In German, every noun is masculine, feminine or neuter. This is its gender, and you need to know a noun's gender because words used with the noun, such as articles and adjectives, have corresponding masculine, feminine and neuter forms in German.

The **genitive case** is used to indicate possession, the equivalent of *'s* in English: *the boy's book*.

The **imperative** is the verb form used to give instructions or commands: ***Wait** for me*, ***Don't say** that*, ***Take** the first left*.

The **imperfect tense** of a verb is used mostly in written German to talk about things that happened or have happened in the past.

Infinitive: German verbs are listed in a dictionary in their infinitive form, ending in **-en** or just **-n.** The English equivalent uses *to*: **essen** *to eat*, **wandern** *to hike*, **tun** *to do*.

Inseparable verbs begin with certain prefixes, e.g. **entgehen** *to escape*, **missverstehen** *to misunderstand*, **verschlafen** *to oversleep*. These prefixes never separate off as they do in **separable verbs**.

Masculine: See Gender.

Modal verbs usually accompany another verb. German has six modal verbs: **dürfen** *to be allowed to*, **können** *to be able to*, **mögen** *to like*, **müssen** *to have to*, **sollen** *to be (supposed) to*, **wollen** *to want to*. They behave differently from other German verbs.

Negatives are words like *not*, *never*, *nothing*, *nobody* and *not ... ever*, *not ... anybody*, *not ... anything*. The negative **kein** *no*, *not any*, has different endings depending on gender, case and number.

Neuter: See Gender.

The **nominative case** is used for the subject of a sentence: *the boy is reading a book*.

Nouns are the words for living beings, things, places and abstract concepts: *father*, *analyst*, *Siân*, *giraffe*, *chair*, *village*, *Berlin*, *time*, *courage*.

Number refers to the difference between **singular** (one) and **plural** (more than one).

The **object** of a verb is at the receiving end. An object can be **direct**: *He bought a ticket*; or **indirect**, in which case it's often preceded by *to* or *for*: *He bought a ticket for me*, *He gave a ticket to me*.

Ordinal numbers are *first*, *second*, *third*, *fourth*, etc.

The passive is used when the object becomes the subject of the verb – because you want to highlight the action rather than the person doing the action: *my bag was stolen*.

The past participle of a verb is used with *have* when talking about the past: *I have finished, he has eaten, they had gone*. It's used with *be* when a verb is in the passive form or when used as an adjective: *my passport was stolen, the museum is closed.*

The perfect tense of a verb is used in spoken German to talk about the past; it expresses the English *I worked, I have worked, I was working, I used to work.*

The person of a verb indicates who or what is doing something:
1st person = the speaker: *I* (singular), *we* (plural)
2nd person = the person(s) being addressed: *you*
3rd person = who/what is being talked about: *he/she/it/they*

Personal pronouns are words like *I, you, we, she, her, them.*

The pluperfect tense translates *had done something.*

Plural means more than one.

Prefixes are letters attached to the beginning of a word to form another word, e.g. *re-, over-, dis-*.

Prepositions are words like *by, in, on, with, for, through, next to.*

The present tense of a verb is used to talk about things being done now or done often or regularly: *I'm working, I work.* It's also used to talk about the future if the context is clear: *I'm going to Cardiff tomorrow.*

Reflexive pronouns are mich/mir, dich/dir, sich, uns, euch, used as an integral part of reflexive verbs.

Reflexive verbs in German have sich before the infinitive: sich **beeilen** *to hurry up*.

Regular nouns, adjectives, verbs etc. conform to a pattern and are entirely predictable. The ones that don't conform are irregular.

Separable verbs start with a prefix, e.g. aus**gehen** *to go out*, um**sehen** *to look around*, zurück**kommen** *to come back*. In certain circumstances the prefix breaks off from the main part of the verb and goes to the end of the sentence/main clause.

Singular means **one**, while plural means **more than one**.

The stem of a German verb is what's left when you remove the -**en**, or -**n** ending of the infinitive.

Strong verbs undergo a vowel change in at least one of their verb forms and their past participle ends in -**en**: **sprechen, spricht, sprach, gesprochen** *to speak, speaks, spoke, spoken;* **verstehen, verstand, verstanden** *to understand, understood, understood.*

The **subject** of a sentence is whoever or whatever is carrying out the verb: *They have two children, Anna reads the paper, This house cost a lot of money, Peace is possible.*

Subject pronouns are *I, we, you, he, she, it, they.*

The **subjunctive** is a form of a verb that's rarely used in English, other than in phrases like *if I were you*, but is more frequently used in German with certain verbs and in defined grammatical circumstances.

A **subordinate clause** is a clause that is dependent on a main clause and does not make sense on its own. Subordinate clauses are frequently introduced by a subordinating conjunction such as **weil** *because*, **dass** *that*, **wenn** *if*. The verb comes at the end of a subordinate clause.

Superlative is *the most ..., ...est* when comparing several things: *the most interesting, the biggest.*

A **syllable** is a unit that contains a vowel and consists of a single sound: *can* has one syllable, *can·ter* has two, while *Can·ter·bu·ry* has four.

Tense refers to when the verb is happening: in the past, present or future. Tenses have names, e.g. present, perfect, imperfect.

Verbs relate to doing and being, identifiable in English because you can put *to* in front of them: *to live, to be, to speak, to play, to think, to have, to need.* German verbs divide into two main groups: strong and weak.

Vowels and consonants make up the alphabet: the vowels are a, ä, e, i, o, ö, u, ü, y; the rest are consonants. **Y** is very occasionally a consonant, but only in foreign words e.g. **das Yo-Yo, die Yucca**.

Weak verbs never undergo a vowel change in any verb form, and their past tenses, both imperfect and perfect, are formed with -**t**: **kaufen/ kaufte, gekauft** *to buy/ bought*; **machen/ machte, gemacht** *to make/ made.*

grammar summary

nouns

Nouns are written with a capital letter in German: **der Tisch** *table*, **die Milch** *milk*.

Nouns have a **gender** (masculine, feminine or neuter), which is indicated by the definite article that accompanies the noun: **der Wein** *wine* (masculine), **die Limonade** *lemonade* (feminine), **das Bier** *beer* (neuter). Gender can appear arbitrary, even illogical – it's **das Kind** *child*, **das Mädchen** *girl* and **das Pferd** *horse*, even though all are living things – and the best way to learn each noun's gender is to learn the article as well as the noun when you are learning vocabulary.

Sometimes a noun's gender can be determined from its ending or meaning:

- Masculine nouns (**der**): end in **-ant, -ich, -ig, -ismus, -ling, -or, -us** + days of the week, months, seasons (but **das Jahr**, **die Woche**), points of the compass, makes of cars, rivers outside Germany.
- Feminine nouns (**die**): end in **-age, -ei, -enz, -heit, -ie, -keit, -schaft, -tion, -tät, -ung, -ur** + German rivers (except **der Rhein**).
- Neuter nouns (**das**): end in **-chen, -lein** + metals and chemical elements, letters of the alphabet, verbs used as nouns, towns, provinces and most countries.

Compound nouns take the gender of the last element: **der Bahnhof (die Bahn, der Hof)**.

There are several ways of forming the **plural** of nouns and it is hard to guess. For this reason, German > English dictionaries and dictionaries targeted at native German speakers usually give the plural of each noun.

Nouns don't change much according to case. The only exceptions are the genitive singular of masculine and neuter nouns, which add an **-s** (two-syllable words or longer) or **-es** (one-syllable words), and the dative plural of all genders, where an **-n** is added, if there isn't one already:
Der Name meines Vaters/meiner Mutter/meines Kindes *The name of my father/mother/child.*
Ich war mit meinen Kindern. *I was with my children.* (nominative plural is **Kinder**)
Ich war mit meinen Eltern. *I was with my parents.* (nominative plural is **Eltern**)

It used to be that some masculine and neuter nouns added **-e** in the dative singular. This rule is mostly ignored in modern German, except for a few words: **zu Hause** *at home*, **nach Hause** *(to) home* (nominative is **das Haus**), **auf dem Lande** *in the country(side)* (nominative is **das Land**).

case

There are four grammatical cases in German, and they exist in the singular and plural. The choice of which case to use depends on the function that a noun or pronoun, and any accompanying adjectives and articles, is performing in a sentence. Case affects pronouns, adjectives, articles, possessive adjectives and, to a lesser extent, nouns.

Nominative: used to indicate the subject of a sentence, the person or thing carrying out the action of the verb. Nouns are given in the dictionary in the nominative singular.

Accusative: used to indicate the direct object of a sentence, the person or thing receiving the action of the verb.

Dative: used to indicate the indirect object of a sentence, the person or thing affected indirectly by the action of the verb. It is often indicated by *to* or *for* in English.

Genitive: used when referring to possession. It is the equivalent of *'s* in English.

The accusative, dative and genitive cases are used after prepositions.

articles

German has:

- definite articles (*the*): **der, die, das**. The plural of all three forms is **die**.
- indefinite articles (*a/an*): **ein, eine**. There is no plural of **ein**, but there is a plural of its negative, **kein, keine** *no, not a*, which is **keine**.

	masculine	feminine	neuter	plural
nominative	**der** **[k]ein**	**die** **[k]eine**	**das** **[k]ein**	**die** **keine**
accusative	**den** **[k]einen**	**die** **[k]eine**	**das** **[k]ein**	**die** **keine**
dative	**dem** **[k]einem**	**der** **[k]einer**	**dem** **[k]einem**	**den** **keinen**
genitive	**des** **[k]eines**	**der** **[k]einer**	**des** **[k]eines**	**der** **keiner**

Dieser *this*, **jeder** *every* and **welcher** *which* follow the **der** pattern.

Possessive adjectives (mein, dein, sein, ihr, unser, euer, Ihr) follow the **ein** pattern.

Ich nehme dieses Buch/jedes Buch/dein Buch. *I'll take this book/every book/ your book.*

adjectives

When an adjective comes after a noun, it doesn't have any endings, and is always in the same form as in the dictionary. When it comes before a noun it takes endings; these depend on the gender, case and number (singular or plural) of that noun, and also on what, if anything, precedes the adjective.

adjective endings after the definite article (**der, die, das**), also after **dieser** *this*, **jeder** *every*, and **welcher** *which*

	masculine	feminine	neuter	plural
nominative	**-e**	**-e**	**-e**	**-en**
accusative	**-en**	**-e**	**-e**	**-en**
dative	**-en**	**-en**	**-en**	**-en**
genitive	**-en**	**-en**	**-en**	**-en**

adjective endings after the indefinite article (**ein, eine**), also after **kein** *no, not a*, all possessive adjectives (**mein, dein, sein, ihr, unser, euer, Ihr**)

	masculine	feminine	neuter	plural
nominative	**-er**	**-e**	**-es**	**-en**
accusative	**-en**	**-e**	**-es**	**-en**
dative	**-en**	**-en**	**-en**	**-en**
genitive	**-en**	**-en**	**-en**	**-en**

adjective endings when there is no preceding article or possessive

	masculine	feminine	neuter	plural
nominative	**-er**	**-e**	**-es**	**-e**
accusative	**-en**	**-e**	**-es**	**-e**
dative	**-em**	**-er**	**-em**	**-en**
genitive	**-en**	**-er**	**-en**	**-er**

Mein kleiner Bruder heißt Markus. *My little brother is called Markus.*
Wie heißt deine neue Freundin? *What is your new (girl)friend called?*
Wir haben ein kleines Auto. *We've got a small car.*
Ich wohne in einer schönen Stadt. *I live in a beautiful town.*
Sie wohnt in einem schönen Dorf. *She lives in a beautiful village.*
Deutscher Wein ist sehr gut. *German wine is very good.*
Ich trinke französischen Wein mit deutschem Käse. *I drink French wine with German cheese*
vor kurzer Zeit *a short time ago*

adverbs

In German most adjectives double up as adverbs. Adverbs don't have endings – they never change:
Ich kann laute Musik nicht leiden. *I can't stand loud music.*
Die Kinder singen laut. *The children are singing loudly.*

comparatives and superlatives

Adjectives and adverbs form their comparatives by adding **-er**, regardless of the length of the word. Most one-syllable adjectives and adverbs containing an **a**, **o** or **u** add an umlaut to that vowel. Adjectives have endings if they are before a noun. *Than* is **als**.
Quedlinburg ist kleiner/älter/interessanter als Leipzig. *Quedlinburg is smaller/older/more interesting than Leipzig.*
Quedlinburg ist eine kleinere/ältere/interessantere Stadt als Leipzig. *Quedlinburg is a smaller/older/more interesting town than Leipzig.*
Maria singt schön, aber Laura singt schöner. *Maria sings beautifully, but Laura sings more beautifully.*

Adjectives form their superlatives by adding **-(e)st** plus the appropriate adjective ending. ... *in* (Germany, the world etc) is expressed by the genitive case.
Quedlinburg ist die schönste Stadt Deutschlands. *Quedlinburg is the most beautiful town in Germany.*
Du hast den größten Kuchen gegessen! *You've eaten the biggest cake!*

The superlative of an adverb is made up of two words: **am** + the adverb with the ending **-(e)sten**:
Helga singt am schönsten. *Helga sings the most beautifully.*

personal pronouns

These exist in the nominative, accusative and dative cases.

nominative (subject pronoun)	accusative (object pronoun)	dative (indirect object pronoun)
ich *I*	**mich** *me*	**mir** *(to) me*
du *you*	**dich** *you*	**dir** *(to) you*
er *he, it*	**ihn** *him, it*	**ihm** *(to) him*
sie *she, it*	**sie** *her, it*	**ihr** *(to) her*
es *it*	**es** *it*	**ihm** *(to) it*
wir *we*	**uns** *us*	**uns** *(to) us*
ihr *you*	**euch** *you*	**euch** *(to) you*
sie *they*	**sie** *them*	**ihnen** *(to) them*
Sie *you*	**Sie** *you*	**Ihnen** *(to) you*

Gib mir/ihm das Buch. *Give (to) me/him the book.*
Ich war mit euch/ihnen. *I was with you/them.*
Kennen Sie ihn/sie? *Do you know him/her/them?*
Das hat er uns/dir schon gesagt. *He's already told us/you that.*

prepositions

Prepositions followed by the accusative: **bis** *until*, **durch** *through*, **entlang** *along*, **für** *for*, **gegen** *against*, **ohne** *without*, **um** *around, at* (time)

Entlang comes after the noun: **Er geht den Fluss entlang.** *He's walking along the river.*

Prepositions followed by the dative: **aus** *from, out of*; **bei** *at the house of, for* (a company); **gegenüber** *opposite*; **laut** *according to*; **mit** *with*; **nach** *after, to*; **seit** *since, for*; **von** *from*, **zu** *to*

Laut can also be followed by the genitive.

Prepositions followed by the genitive: **während** *during*, **wegen** *because of*

Some prepositions are followed by the accusative case when movement is involved, and by the dative case when the focus is on location: **an** *on, at*; **auf** *on, onto*; **in** *in, into*; **hinter** *behind*; **neben** *next to*; **über** *over, above*; **unter** *under, among*; **vor** *in front of, before*; **zwischen** *between*.

Some short prepositions usually combine with a shortened definite article in the accusative or dative, although it's not wrong to use the two words:

an + dem → am; an + das → ans
bei + dem → beim
in + dem → im; in + das → ins
für + das → fürs
um + das → ums
von + dem → vom
zu + dem → zum; zu + der → zur

Gestern waren wir im Theater. *Yesterday we were at the theatre.*
Gestern sind wir ins Theater gegangen. *Yesterday we went to the theatre.*
Wie komme ich am besten zum Stadion/zur Post? *What's the best way for me to get to the stadium/post office?*
Ich wohne in der Nähe vom Bahnhof. *I live near the station.*

verbs

In a dictionary, German verbs are listed in the **infinitive**, the equivalent of *to eat*. Nearly all German infinitives end in **-en**; a handful end in **-n**: **kommen** *to come*, **lächeln** *to smile*, **wandern** *to hike*, **tun** *to do*, **sein** *to be*. When you take off the **-en**, or **-n** you are left with the stem.

Broadly speaking, German verbs divide into two groups: weak and strong. **Weak verbs** don't change their main vowel in any tense. Their past tenses, both imperfect and perfect, are formed with a **t**: **kaufen, kaufte, gekauft** *to buy/bought*. Weak verbs are the biggest group of verbs in German and they are always regular, so they all behave in this way.

Strong verbs change their vowel in at least one of their verb forms and their past participle ends in **-en**: **sprechen, spricht, sprach, gesprochen** *to speak/speaks/spoke/spoken*.

There is something very similar in English with the past tense of some verbs ending *-t* or *-d*: *dreamt, played*, and the past tense of others verbs, ending *-en*: *taken, spoken*.

present tense

Almost all verbs have the same set of endings in the present tense. These endings are added to the stem.

ich	**-e**	**wir**	**-en**
du	**-st**	**ihr**	**-t**
er/sie/es	**-t**	**sie/Sie**	**-en**

An extra **e** is sometimes added in the **du**, **er/sie/es** and **ihr** forms to ease pronunciation.

	machen	arbeiten	gehen	wandern	tun
ich	mache	arbeite	gehe	wand(e)re	tue
du	machst	arbeitest	gehst	wanderst	tust
er/sie/es	macht	arbeitet	geht	wandert	tut
wir	machen	arbeiten	gehen	wandern	tun
ihr	macht	arbeitet	geht	wandert	tut
sie/Sie	machen	arbeiten	gehen	wandern	tun

Ich wandere and **ich wandre** are both in use.

In the present tense, some (but not all) strong verbs undergo a stem change in the **du** and **er/sie/es** forms. Here are some common ones:

	fahren	essen	geben	helfen	lassen
ich	fahre	esse	gebe	helfe	lasse
du	fährst	isst	gibst	hilfst	lässt
er/sie/es	fährt	isst	gibt	hilft	lässt
wir	fahren	essen	geben	helfen	lassen
ihr	fahrt	esst	gebt	helft	lasst
sie/Sie	fahren	essen	geben	helfen	lassen

	lesen	nehmen	sehen	sprechen	treffen
ich	lese	nehme	sehe	spreche	treffe
du	liest	nimmst	siehst	sprichst	triffst
er/sie/es	liest	nimmt	sieht	spricht	trifft
wir	lesen	nehmen	sehen	sprechen	treffen
ihr	lest	nehmt	seht	sprecht	trefft
sie/Sie	lesen	nehmen	sehen	sprechen	treffen

The **du** and **er/sie/es** forms of verbs whose stems end **-s** (e.g. **lesen, essen**) are the same. The **du** form adds **-t**, not **-st**.

A handful of verbs don't follow the patterns above. These include all six modal verbs.

	haben	sein	wissen	werden	dürfen
ich	habe	bin	weiß	werde	darf
du	hast	bist	weißt	wirst	darfst
er/sie/es	hat	ist	weiß	wird	darf
wir	haben	sind	wissen	werden	dürfen
ihr	habt	seid	wisst	werdet	dürft
sie/Sie	haben	sind	wissen	werden	dürfen

	können	mögen	müssen	sollen	wollen
ich	kann	mag	muss	soll	will
du	kannst	magst	musst	sollst	willst
er/sie/es	kann	mag	muss	soll	will
wir	können	mögen	müssen	sollen	wollen
ihr	könnt	mögt	müsst	sollt	wollt
sie/Sie	können	mögen	müssen	sollen	wollen

separable verbs

Separable verbs begin with a prefix that separates from the rest of the verb and goes to the end of the sentence. Common separable prefixes are: **ab-, an-, auf-, ein-, mit-, vor-, weg-, zu-, zurück-**:
ich rufe ... an, du stehst ... auf, er kommt ... mit, sie fährt ... weg, wir kommen ... zurück etc.

perfect tense

Most verbs form their perfect tense (*have done, did*) from the present tense of **haben** plus the past participle. Some verbs use **sein** instead of **haben**; these are mostly verbs expressing movement (e.g. **gehen, fahren, kommen**) or a change of state (**sterben, werden**). The verb **sein** itself, and **bleiben**, also take **sein**.

past participle

Weak verbs: take the **-en** off the infinitive, and replace it with **-t** (or **-et** if pronunciation demands). Add **ge-** to the beginning: **machen → gemacht, arbeiten → gearbeitet**.

Strong verbs: the past participle of all strong verbs ends in **-en**. Sometimes the stem undergoes a vowel change. This isn't always easy to guess, so it's best to learn each verb as you come across it: **essen → gegessen** (the extra **g** is to ease pronunciation), **gehen → gegangen, fahren → gefahren, geben → gegeben, helfen → geholfen, lassen → gelassen, lesen → gelesen, nehmen →**

genommen, sehen → gesehen, sein → gewesen, sprechen → gesprochen, treffen → getroffen, trinken → getrunken, werden → geworden

Verbs ending **-ieren** are weak, so their past participle ends **-iert**. They do not add the prefix **ge-**: **studieren → studiert, fotografieren → fotografiert**.

There is a small group of verbs whose past participle ends in **-t**, but the stem changes: **bringen → gebracht, denken → gedacht, kennen → gekannt, wissen → gewusst**. The modal verbs fall into this group, although their past participles are rarely used: **gedürft, gekonnt, gemocht, gemusst, gesollt, gewollt**. In grammar books, these verbs are sometimes called mixed verbs and sometimes irregular weak verbs.

Separable verbs: the **ge-** of the past participle goes between the separable prefix and the main body of the verb: **abholen → abgeholt, anrufen → angerufen, aufstehen → aufgestanden, einladen → eingeladen, mitnehmen → mitgenommen, vorstellen → vorgestellt, wegfahren → weggefahren, zuhören → zugehört, zurückkommen → zurückgekommen**. The prefix is always stressed.

The past participles of inseparable verbs do not add **ge-**: **besuchen → besucht, empfehlen → empfohlen, erinnern → erinnert, gefallen → gefallen, verstehen → verstanden**. Common inseparable prefixes are: **be-, emp-, er-, ge-, ver-**. Inseparable prefixes are never stressed; the stress is on the second syllable. These prefixes never separate from the rest of the verb in any tense.

imperfect tense

The imperfect tense of most verbs is mostly used in writing, but it is useful to be able to recognise it. The imperfect is one of the verb forms given for strong verbs in a dictionary (the second form if there are no vowel changes in the present tense, the third form if there *is* a vowel change): **gehen, <u>ging</u>, gegangen; sehen, sieht, <u>sah</u>, gesehen**.

Weak verbs: take off the **-en** of the infinitive and add **-t-** (or **-et-** if pronunciation requires) plus the following endings:

ich	-te
du	-test
er/sie/es	-te
wir	-ten
ihr	-tet
sie/Sie	-ten

ich machte, du kauftest, er sagte, sie arbeitete, wir fragten, ihr wartetet, sie wanderten.

The imperfect tense of **haben** and all the modal verbs is commonly used in spoken German in preference to the perfect tense. The stem of these verbs changes, but there is always a **-t-** before the endings, which are the same as the weak endings above.

	haben	dürfen	können	mögen	müssen	sollen
ich	hatte	durfte	konnte	mochte	musste	sollte
du	hattest	durftest	konntest	mochtest	musstest	solltest
er/sie/es	hatte	durfte	konnte	mochte	musste	sollte
wir	hatten	durften	konnten	mochten	mussten	sollten
ihr	hattet	durftet	konntet	mochtet	musstet	solltet
sie/Sie	hatten	durften	konnten	mochten	mussten	sollten

Wollen is like **sollen: ich wollte, du wolltest, er wollte, wir wollten**, etc.

Strong verbs: add the following endings to the imperfect tense form given in the dictionary. The vowel, or vowel sound, in the imperfect tense stem is never the same as that in the infinitive:

ich	-
du	-st
er/sie/es	-
wir	-en
ihr	-t
sie/Sie	-en

Here are some strong verbs in the imperfect:

	bleiben	geben	kommen	sein	werden
ich	blieb	gab	kam	war	wurde
du	bliebst	gabst	kamst	warst	wurdest
er/sie/es	blieb	gab	kam	war	wurde
wir	blieben	gaben	kamen	waren	wurden
ihr	bliebt	gabt	kamt	wart	wurdet
sie/Sie	blieben	gaben	kamen	waren	wurden

The imperfect of **geben, sein** and **werden** are commonly used in spoken German. The imperfect of other verbs is heard more frequently in northern Germany. The choice of which past tense to use is often a regional or personal preference.

pluperfect tense

The pluperfect tense (*had done, had been doing*) is formed with the imperfect tense of **haben** or **sein** plus the past participle: **ich hatte ... gemacht, ich war ... gekommen.**

future tense

The future tense is formed using the present tense of **werden** plus the infinitive, which goes to the end of the clause or sentence: **ich werde .... kommen, du wirst ... bleiben, er wird .... sein.**

would

Would is expressed in most cases with **würde**, the subjunctive form of **werden**, plus the infinitive: **ich würde ... sagen** *I would say*, **du würdest ... kommen** *you would come*, **er würde ... machen** *he would do*. For **sein** *to be*, **haben** *to have* and the modal verbs, their subjunctive forms are used instead: **ich wäre** *I would be*, **ich hätte** *I would have*, **ich könnte** *I could/would be able to*, **ich möchte** *I would like*.

reflexive verbs

Reflexive verbs consist of two parts, the extra element being a reflexive pronoun. Reflexive pronouns equate to *myself, yourself, oneself* etc. although this is often not apparent in the English translation.

	sich beeilen *to hurry*
ich	**beeile mich**
du	**beeilst dich**
er/sie	**beeilt sich**
wir	**beeilen uns**
ihr	**beeilt euch**
sie/Sie	**beeilen sich**

Common reflexive verbs are: **sich amüsieren** *to enjoy oneself*, **sich freuen (auf)** *to look forward (to)*, **sich freuen (über)** *to be pleased (about)*, **sich (hin)setzen** *to sit down*, **sich befinden** *to be situated.*

The reflexive pronouns above are all accusative. A few reflexive verbs need a dative pronoun, since they refer to doing something ***to*** or ***for*** oneself. Only the **ich** and **du** forms of the verb are affected by this, with **mir** used instead of **mich**, and **dir** used instead of **dich**. The separable verb **sich vorstellen** *to imagine* (*to oneself* is implied) is a common verb of this type:

	sich vorstellen *to imagine*
ich	**stelle mir vor**
du	**stellst dir vor**
er/sie	**stellt sich vor**
wir	**stellen uns vor**
ihr	**stellt euch vor**
sie/Sie	**stellen sich vor**

imperative

The imperative form of the verb is used to issue commands to others (*turn left, come here*). There are **du, ihr** and **Sie** forms of the imperative.

For the **du** imperative of verbs that do not undergo a vowel change in the present tense, take off the **-st** present tense ending and replace it with **-e**. This **-e** is optional for most verbs: **Mache!/Mach! Komme!/Komm!**

For verbs with a vowel change, the **du** imperative is the **du** form of the present tense without the **-st** ending: **Gib! Nimm!**

The **ihr** imperative is the **ihr** present tense form, but without the pronoun: **Macht! Kommt! Gebt! Nehmt!**

The **Sie** imperative is the **Sie** form of the verb but the words are transposed: **Machen Sie! Kommen Sie! Geben Sie! Nehmen Sie!**

The imperative forms of **sein** are: **Sei! Seid! Seien Sie!** The imperative forms of **haben** are: **Hab! Habt! Haben Sie!**

passive

The passive form of the verb is used when you are more concerned with the action, than with who did the action e.g. *My bag was stolen, English is spoken here*, as opposed to *Someone stole my bag, People speak English here*. The passive in German is formed by **werden** in the appropriate tense, plus the past participle, which goes to the end of the clause.
Englisch wird gesprochen. *English is spoken.*
Meine Tasche wurde gestohlen. *My bag was stolen.*

word order

In main, or independent, clauses and sentences, the verb always comes in second place – not necessarily the second word, but the second element or idea. You can have any element in first place, but the position of the verb never changes.
Meine Eltern fahren jedes Jahr nach Spanien. *My parents go to Spain every year.*
Jedes Jahr fahren meine Eltern nach Spanien.
Nach Spanien fahren meine Eltern jedes Jahr.

In longer sentences containing several elements, the usual word order is time – manner – place:
Meine Eltern fahren jedes Jahr mit dem Auto nach Spanien. *My parents go to Spain every year by car.*
Jedes Jahr fahren meine Eltern mit dem Auto nach Spanien.

If there are two verbs in a clause, the second one, which will be in the infinitive, goes to the end.
Ich möchte nächstes Jahr nach Spanien fahren. *I'd like to go to Spain next year.*
Hoffentlich werde ich dich nächstes Jahr besuchen. *Hopefully I'll visit you next year.*

Apart from after modal verbs, **werden** and a handful of other verbs, **zu** is needed before the infinitive. With separable verbs, **zu** comes between the prefix and the main part of the verb.
Es gibt viel zu tun. *There's a lot to do.*
Ich habe vergessen, die E-Mail zu schreiben. *I forgot to write the email.*
Ich habe vergessen, meine Mutter anzurufen. *I forgot to phone my mother.*

Clauses can be joined by conjunctions. The conjunctions **und** *and*, **oder** *or* or **aber** *but* have no effect on word order at all – it's as if they weren't there. These are called co-ordinating conjunctions and they join clauses which make sense on their own:
Ich wohne in Berlin, aber meine Familie wohnt in Prag. *I live in Berlin, but my family live in Prague.*

Some clauses don't make sense on their own – they are dependent on another clause (e.g. *because I have to work, whether I need to work tomorrow, that he's coming on Monday*). These are called subordinate clauses, and are introduced by subordinating conjunctions such as **als** *when*, **da** *since*, **dass** *that*, **ob** *whether*, **weil** *because*, **wenn** *if, when(ever)*. Subordinating conjunctions send the verb to the end of the clause:

Leider kann ich nicht kommen, weil ich morgen arbeiten muss.
Unfortunately I can't come because I have to work tomorrow.
Ich weiß noch nicht, ob ich morgen arbeiten muss. *I don't know yet whether I need to work tomorrow.*
Er hat mir gesagt, dass er am Dienstag kommt. *He told me that he'd be coming on Tuesday.*

Separable verbs, which are split in main clauses, join up again in subordinate clauses:
Er fährt am Montag weg. *He's leaving on Monday.*
Ich weiß noch nicht, ob er am Montag wegfährt. *I don't yet know whether he's leaving on Monday.*

Question words, when used in indirect question clauses, also send the verb to the end:
Ich weiß noch nicht, was ich tun möchte. *I don't yet know what I'd like to do.*
Weißt du, wo sie im Moment arbeitet? *Do you know where she's working at the moment?*

Relative pronouns send the verb to the end of the clause. Relative pronouns in the nominative and accusative cases are identical to the definite article.
Ich habe einen Freund, der in Spanien wohnt. *I've a friend who lives in Spain.*
Ich habe viele Freunde, die in Spanien wohnen. *I've a lot of friends who live in Spain.*
Markus ist der Freund, den ich letztes Jahr besucht habe. *Markus is the friend whom I visited last year.*

numbers

numbers 1–99

1 eins
2 zwei
3 drei
4 vier
5 fünf
6 sechs
7 sieben
8 acht
9 neun
10 zehn
11 elf
12 zwölf
13 dreizehn
14 vierzehn
15 fünfzehn
16 sechzehn
17 siebzehn
18 achtzehn
19 neunzehn

- Zehn *ten* is added to the numbers 13–19.
- The second s is dropped from sechs in sechzehn.
- Siebzehn is formed without the en used in sieben.
- Zwo is sometimes used instead of zwei, especially on the telephone, to avoid confusion with drei.

20 zwanzig
21 einundzwanzig
22 zweiundzwanzig
23 dreiundzwanzig
24 vierundzwanzig
25 fünfundzwanzig
26 sechsundzwanzig
27 siebenundzwanzig
28 achtundzwanzig
29 neunundzwanzig
30 dreißig
40 vierzig
50 fünfzig
60 sechzig
70 siebzig
80 achtzig
90 neunzig

- 31–99 repeat the pattern 21–29, i.e. the unit + und + the tens: 21 is literally *one-and-twenty*, 22 *two-and-twenty*, etc: vierundfünfzig 54, dreiundachtzig 83, achtundneunzig 98
- Eins drops the s in numbers above 20: einunddreißig 31, einundsiebzig 71
- Dreißig is spelled with ß instead of z: vierunddreißig 34
- The second s in sechs is dropped to form sechzig: einundsechzig 61, zweiundsechzig 62
- The en is dropped in siebzig: fünfundsiebzig 75, neunundsiebzig 79
- % is Prozent; a Komma *comma* is used to indicate a decimal point: fünfzig Prozent 50%; 12,5 Prozent 12.5%, said as zwölf Komma fünf Prozent

numbers 100 +

100 **(ein)hundert**
101 **(ein)hunderteins**
102 **(ein)hundertzwei**
200 **zweihundert**
210 **zweihundertzehn**
250 **zweihundertfünfzig**
500 **fünfhundert**
1 000 000 **eine Million**
2 000 000 **zwei Millionen**
1 000 000 000 **eine Milliarde**

1 000 **(ein)tausend**
1 100 **(ein)tausendeinhundert**
1 500 **(ein)tausendfünfhundert**
2 000 **zweitausend**
10 000 **zehntausend**
100 000 **hunderttausend**
500 000 **fünfhunderttausend**

- **Ein** is often dropped when referring to numbers from 100–199: **hundertzehn** 110, **hundertvierundneunzig** 194
- **Ein**, however, is not dropped with thousands: **zweitausendeinhundertsieben** 2,107, **elftausendeinhundert** 11,100
- **Und** is not normally added after hundreds or thousands: **einhundertzweiundvierzig** 142, **fünftausendvierundsechzig** 5,064
- 100 and 1,000 have a plural only when used in general terms: **hunderte von Menschen** *hundreds of people*; **tausende von Besuchern** *thousands of visitors*. **Eine Million** and **eine Milliarde** are always **Millionen** and **Milliarden** in the plural:
  drei Millionen einhunderttausend 3,100,000
  vier Milliarden 4,000,000,000
- a **Punkt** full stop or a space can be used to separate thousands.
  1.000/1 000 1,000
  10.000/10 000 10,000
  6.000.000/6 000 000 6,000,000

Eins one is used differently from other German numbers. When used before nouns, its endings reflect the gender and case of the noun, just like the indefinite article *a/an* (page 177):
Das Haus kostet eine Million Euro. *The house costs one million euros.*
Sie haben einen Sohn. *They've got one son.*

first, second, third, etc.

Ordinal numbers 1st–19th are formed by adding **-te** to the cardinal numbers. Slightly irregular forms are **erste** *first*, **dritte** *third*, **siebte** *seventh* and **achte** *eighth*.

1st **erste** (1.)
2nd **zweite** (2.)
3rd **dritte** (3.)
4th **vierte** (4.)
5th **fünfte** (5.)
6th **sechste** (6.)
7th **siebte** (7.)
8th **achte** (8.)
9th **neunte** (9.)
10th **zehnte** (10.)
12th **zwölfte** (12.)
15th **fünfzehnte** (15.)
18th **achtzehnte** (18.)
19th **neunzehnte** (19.)

From 20th onwards, ordinal numbers are formed by adding **-ste** to the cardinal number:

20th **zwanzigste**
21st **einundzwanzigste**
22nd **zweiundzwanzigste**
30th **dreißigste**
60th **sechzigste**
100th **hundertste**

Ordinal numbers are used much the same as in English, except that they change their endings as any other adjective:
die erste Nacht *the first night*
am ersten Juni *on the first of June*

When referring to sovereigns or popes, you use **der** for masculine and **die** for feminine names:
Heinrich der Achte *Henry VIII*
Kaiser Wilhelm der Zweite *Kaiser William II*
Königin Elisabeth die Erste *Queen Elizabeth I*
Königin Elisabeth die Zweite *Queen Elizabeth II*
Papst Benedikt der Sechzehnte *Pope Benedict XVI*
König Ludwig der Vierzehnte *King Louis XIV*

Seeing German words on a regular basis helps to embed them in your memory. If you search on the internet for **Jahreskalender** and the relevant year, you'll find downloadable calendars which will provide a daily reminder of the days and the months as well as German public holidays.

answers

answers to checkpoints

checkpoint 1 page 24

1 Guten Abend; *2* Bitte schön; *3* Sie; *4* On the phone; *5* Bitte; *6* Ich heiße ...; *7* Sehr erfreut; *8* Meinen; *9* Schwiegersohn; *10* Hallo, Entschuldigung; *11* Schönen Tag; *12* Commiserate; schlecht means bad; *13* Nicht; *14* ß; *15* Das sind meine Schwestern; *16* Nichts zu danken; *17* More than one; *18* Wo wohnt ihr? *19* Help yourself to food and/or drink; *20* Annas Partner – no apostrophe and capital P

checkpoint 2 page 42

1 oder, or gell; *2* lebt; *3* Kann ich dir helfen? *4* wer, welcher, warum, was, wann, wo, wie, wie viele, wie viel, was für; *5* wie; *6* Das Hotel hat keine Sauna. *7* A bit down (Heimweh haben means to be homesick); *8* To want to, feel like; *9* Er ist Schweizer. *10* Dentist; *11* Frau Müller; *12* die Gartenterrasse; *13* glücklich; *14* one cake; *15* zusammen; *16* alt-neu, kurz-lang, ledig-verheiratet, riesig-winzig, sauber-schmutzig; *17* Wir haben den Zwanzigsten means it's the 20th (= date) and Wir sind zwanzig Jahre alt means we're 20 years old. *18* Ich möchte auf Deutsch sprechen.

checkpoint 3 page 56

1 Arzt-Krankenhaus, Lehrerin- Grundschule, Rechtsanwalt-Kanzlei, Dozent-Universität, Koch- Restaurant. A Klempner is a plumber; *2* als; *3* Ich arbeite hier seit fünfzehn Jahren; *4* Der Meteorologe, die Meteorologin; rheumatologist, archaeologist, psychologist. *5* Was sind Sie von Beruf? *6* Ein Ausbilder is an instructor and ein Auszubildender is a trainee or apprentice. Ausbilden means to instruct, train. *7* Your grandfather; *8* Mein Partner ist selbstständig; *9* In HR, in the public sector, in retail, on a farm; *10* Was ist Ihre Funktion? *11* eine Schauspielerin; *12* bei; *13* Deputy head of department; *14* Meine Schwester arbeitet in einer karitativen Organisation My sister works in a charity. *15* Ich war Lehrer(in). *16* My grandfather was a police officer.

checkpoint 4 page 70

1 Repeat what you've just said. *2* ganz lustig; *3* ausgezeichnet; *4* A term of admiration; *5* Ist alles klar? *6* They agree with you; *7* im Allgemeinen; *8* Ich verstehe nicht is I don't understand and ich habe nicht verstanden is I didn't understand. *9* Zum Beispiel; *10* Positive: wie schön, wie spannend. Negative: wie schrecklich, wie langweilig, wie ärgerlich; *11* Entschuldigen Sie, bitte; *12* As well; *13* Wie heißt das auf Deutsch? *14* ein bisschen; *15* Well-behaved;

16 offen gesagt; 17 Was bedeutet Stammtisch? 18 man; 19 The omelette pan is light and works well. 20 unhöflich

checkpoint 5 page 86

1 Bevorzugt; entdeckt; 2 Ich bin in Manchester geboren. 3 Vorgestern; 4 Ich habe mein Portemonnaie verloren. 5 Those ending -ieren and inseparable verbs. 6 Wir sind letztes Jahr mit dem Zug nach Berlin gefahren or Letztes Jahr sind wir mit dem Zug nach Berlin gefahren. 7 An accident, a (car) breakdown, an asthma attack; 8 Was haben Sie gestern gemacht? 9 umsteigen; 10 vor; it comes before the time expression; 11 Bleiben to stay, sein to be, werden to become, sprechen to speak, verstehen to understand, aufwachsen to grow up; 12 Warst du schon mal in Zürich? 13 Where did you get to know each other? 14 I saw or I have seen/I had seen; he went or he has gone/he had gone. 15 gestern, vorgestern, vor kurzer Zeit, vor zwei Jahren; 16 Was ist passiert? 17 Was ist eine Katastrophe? means What is a catastrophe? and Was für eine Katastrophe! means What a catastrophe! 18 Glücklicherweise-leider, gut-schlecht, langsam-schnell; 19 I had worked as a postman

checkpoint 6 page 100

1 Menschen people; the others are insects; 2 gefallen; 3 Köln gefällt ihr; Köln gefällt ihm; 4 Ich wandere gern; 5 Ich mag keine Computerspiele;
6 i) Politik interessiert mich and ii) Ich interessiere mich für Politik; 7 Lieblings; 8 Magst du Popmusik?/Hörst du gern Popmusik? 9 ich wasche nicht gern ab; 10 Schlittschuhlaufen; 11 Ich koche lieber; 12 Am wenigsten; 13 Die Suppe hat geschmeckt; 14 Das Zimmer hat uns sehr gefallen; 15 I'd rather watch television? 16 als; 17 gar or überhaupt

checkpoint 7 page 116

1 Samstag; 2 Februar, März, Mai, Juni; 3 Geburtstag, Hochzeitstag; 4 Um elf Uhr is at eleven o'clock and gegen elf Uhr is at about eleven o'clock. Halb sechs is half past five. 5 Möchtet ihr kegeln gehen? 6 Es tut mir leid; 7 Rush hour; pünktlich; 8 Ihnen auch; 9 A castle, a beach, the sights; 10 Es war kalt; es gab viel Schnee; 11 Lasst uns ins Kino gehen, Wollen wir ins Kino gehen? 12 Ich wäre, ich hätte; 13 Es gießt in Strömen; 14 Hast du Lust eine Bootsfahrt zu machen; 15 Nebel; 16 Der Flug dauert anderthalb Stunden; 17 Danke für die Einladung. Leider habe ich schon was vor. 18 Es tut mir Leid, ich kann nicht. Ich muss arbeiten. Vielleicht am Sonntag, um zwei Uhr?

checkpoint 8 page 132

1 Das könnte ich machen; 2 Dominik muss gehen; er will ein Gruppenfoto machen; 3 Would you like to meet new people? 4 I need a new mobile phone. 5 wir wollen, ihr müsst, du möchtest, Sie könnten; 6 ich möchte reisen, ich kann reisen, ich will reisen, ich musste reisen; 7 to change (trains, trams or buses); 8 Habt ihr Lust, an den Strand zu gehen? 9 They want you

to address each other du, instead of Sie. *10* In the Bible. Thou shalt have no other gods before me. *11* You're not allowed to park here. *12* Whether you speak German. *13* Schweiz, USA; *14* Kann ich/Können wir die Rechnung haben, bitte? *15* mögen; *16* In a shop; *17* i) ich möchte fit werden, ii) ich sollte meine Mutter anrufen. *18* Ich habe keine Lust, ins Kino zu gehen

checkpoint 9 page 146

1 Oder; Es war ein guter Film, nicht wahr?/Es war ein guter Film, oder? *2* Three of denken, glauben, meinen, finden. *3* Doch; jein; *4* was für ein Quatsch; *5* zehn Prozent; *6* dazu; *7* weil; *8* about a hundred people and exactly a hundred people. *9* 35 112/35.112 (German), 35,112 (English); 8,01 (German), 8.01 (English); *10* Ich esse so viel Obst wie möglich. *11* Max; das jüngste Kind; *12* Schlimm, schlecht; *13* Meiner Meinung nach; *14* Glaubst du an Liebe auf den ersten Blick? *15* When you don't mind or are non-committal. *16* Eine gute Wettervorhersage; *17* Wien ist die größte Stadt Österreichs; *18* Ich glaube, dass der Popsänger wirklich talentiert ist.

checkpoint 10 page 160

1 What something is called in English. *2* Sei/Seid/Seien Sie vorsichtig; *3* Gibt es eine Apotheke in der Nähe? *4* Do not enter; *5* Mal; *6* Es war niemand zu Hause; *7* Look out! Hurry up! Passen Sie auf, passt auf; beeilen Sie sich, beeilt euch; *8* Dieser Kuchen schmeckt gut, and diese Kuchen schmecken gut; *9* Ich mache eine Diät; ich muss fünf Kilo abnehmen; *10* Ich bin schon satt; *11* mir becomes ihr for she's and ihm for he's. *12* verboten; *13* es gibt keinen Wein, es gibt nicht genug Wein; *14* einladen; *15* Ihr alle fehlt mir or Ihr fehlt mir alle; *16* Können Sie mir sagen, ... was passiert ist; wie man am besten zum Flughafen kommt; ob es etwas Neues gibt; wie ich eine Pizza bestellen kann. *17* i) Mein Fuß tut mir weh. ii) Ich habe Schnupfen. iii) Ich fühle mich müde.

checkpoint 11 page 171

1 Wir melden uns bald. *2* Ein Handy; *3* Eine Showmasterin; die Showmaster/Showmasterinnen; *4* When you are saying goodbye on the phone. *5* Hashtag, question mark, full stop, brackets, lower-case letters; *6* Dialled the wrong number; *7* Für ; *8* anschalten is to switch/turn on, and abschalten is to switch/turn off. *9* Haben Sie gratis WLAN? *10* z.B. is zum Beispiel for example, usw is und so weiter and so on, and LKW Lastkraftwagen lorry; *11* Ich muss die Fotos hochladen; Wir sollten die Fotos hochladen; Er will die Fotos hochladen; Jakob hat die Datei hochgeladen. *12* Vergiss nicht, Vergesst nicht, Vergessen Sie nicht; *13* Ich habe meinen USB Stick verloren, wir müssen ein Ladegerät kaufen. *14* Nullhunderteinundfünfzig vier-vierundachtzig dreißig-sechsundfünfzig. *15* Die Maus, die Tastatur; *16* Liebe Kathi or Hallo Kathi; *17* Ich habe dich am Samstag angerufen; *18* dir, euch; *19* Es war uns ein Vergnügen.

answers to verb practice

verb practice 1 page 41

1 *a* ist My brother is divorced; *b* sind We're not English; *c* ist Kati is very stubborn; *d* sind Paul and his brother are twins; *e* Sind Are you Austrian? *f* ist The hotel is clean and comfortable; *g* bin I'm not particularly religious; *h* Seid Are you married? *i* sind How old are your children? *j* bist You're Scottish, aren't you?

2 *a* habe, hat I've got blue eyes, but my brother has brown eyes; *b* hat Ingrid doesn't feel like going to the restaurant; *c* hast How many brothers and sisters do you have? *d* hat My husband's in a bad mood; *e* habt How much luggage do you have? *f* hast You've got two children, haven't you? *g* haben My parents have got a small garden; *h* Haben Are you hungry? Would you like a cake?

3 *a* Ist sie Kanadierin oder Amerikanerin? *b* Sind Nadja und Anja Zwillinge? *c* Hat das Hotel ein Schwimmbad? *d* Markus ist schwul, nicht wahr? *e* Hast du/habt ihr/haben Sie Durst? *f* Gibt es eine Terrasse?

verb practice 2 page 55

1 *a* du bekommst; *b* Sie fahren zurück; *c* wir beeilen uns; *d* ihr versteht; *e* es bietet; *f* ich unterstütze; *g* sie hofft; *h* ich fange an; *i* wir suchen; *j* er hört zu; *k* sie fragen; *l* ich ziehe mich um

2 *a* inseparable; *b* inseparable; *c* separable; *d* separable; *e* inseparable

3 *a* du triffst; *b* du versprichst; *c* du fängst an; *d* du siehst; *e* du gibst aus

4 *a* dich; *b* sich; *c* euch; *d* sich; *e* mich

verb practice 3 page 85

1 *a* ich habe gehofft; *b* wir haben getanzt; *c* sie haben sich geküsst; *d* du hast gesagt; *e* sie hat geglaubt; *f* ihr habt gemacht; *g* Sie haben gelernt; *h* er hat geschickt

2 *a* Warst du schon mal in Österreich? Have you ever been to Austria? *b* Es gab viele Probleme. There were a lot of problems. *c* Ich hatte nicht genug Zeit. I didn't have enough time. *d* Gestern Abend war er müde. He was tired yesterday evening. *e* Ich hoffe, du hattest Spaß. I hope you had fun.

3 klettern to climb; laufen to run; springen to jump

4 Gestern morgen bin ich in die Stadt gefahren. Dort habe ich zwei Bücher gekauft. Am Nachmittag habe ich meine Oma besucht. Wir haben zusammen eine Tasse Kaffee getrunken. Ich bin um vier Uhr zu Hause angekommen. Am Abend sind mein Freund und ich ins Kino gegangen. Wir haben einen neuen italienischen Film gesehen. Der Film hat uns sehr

gut gefallen. Yesterday morning I went into town. I bought two books there. In the afternoon I visited my granny. We drank a cup of coffee together. I arrived home at four o'clock. In the evening my friend and I went to the cinema. We saw a new Italian film. We liked the film very much.

verb practice 4 page 115

1 *a* du wirst kaufen you will buy; *b* sie werden fahren they will travel; *c* Sie werden haben you will have; *d* es wird regnen it will rain; *e* wir werden uns treffen we will meet; *f* ihr werdet vergessen you will forget; *g* ich werde anrufen I will telephone; *h* er wird machen he will do

2 *a* Wann wirst du uns besuchen? When will you visit us? *b* Der Zug wird zehn Minuten Verspätung haben.The train is ten minutes late. *c* Mit dieser App wirst du neue Leute kennenlernen. With this app you'll meet new people. *d* Wir werden nächstes Jahr zurückkommen. We'll come back next year. *e* Hoffentlich wird es dir gefallen. Hopefully you'll like it.

3 *a* Ich meine, dass sie nächstes Jahr an der Uni studieren wird. *b* Ich meine, dass es in achtzig Jahren kein Rohöl geben wird. *c* Ich meine, dass wir ein gutes Restaurant finden werden. *d* Ich meine, dass ich vielleicht nächste Woche gehen werde.

4 *a*-iii, *b*-iv, *c*-v, *d*-ii, *e*-i

verb practice 5 page 131

1 *a* du musst, ihr müsst; *b* ich will, sie wollen; *c* sie darf, ich darf; *d* er soll, wir sollen; *e* er muss, Sie müssen; *f* wir dürfen, ihr dürft; *g* du willst, wir wollen; *h* man soll, du sollst

2 *a* Ich kann keinen Alkohol trinken, I'm not able to drink alcohol Ich soll keinen Alkohol trinken I mustn't/shouldn't drink alcohol (on a doctor's advice); *b* Ich muss es nicht sagen I don't have to say it Ich darf es nicht sagen I mustn't/am not allowed to say it; *c* Was willst du? What do you want? Was möchtest du? What would you like? *d* Wir müssen Deutsch lernen We have to learn German Wir sollten Deutsch lernen We ought to learn German (we feel morally obliged)

4 *a* Ich wollte mit dir sprechen. *b* Konntest du nicht schlafen? *c* Er musste lange warten. *d* Wir wollten mitkommen, aber wir konnten nicht.

answers to questions on how to use a dictionary page 120

1 All of them except sardine

2 Mutter mother, Band ribbon, Herz heart, Tier animal, Wald forest; arm poor, dunkel dark, hoch high, weiß white; brechen to break, kennen to know, aufpassen to pay attention, sein to be

vocabulary builder

A
abbreviation Abkürzung (f)
able: to be able to (can) können
about etwa, gegen, circa/zirka, ungefähr
above über (acc/dat)
absolute absolut
absolutely durchaus, völlig
accept annehmen (pp angenommen)
accident Unfall (m), **(traffic accident)** Verkehrsunfall (m)
accidentally zufällig
accommodation Unterkunft (f)
according to laut (dat)
acquaintance Bekannte(r) (f/m)
across über (acc/dat)
activity Aktivität (f)
actor Schauspieler(in) (m/f)
actually eigentlich
to add hinzufügen
address Adresse (f)
administration Verwaltung (f)
to admire bewundern
adopted: adopted son/daughter Adoptivsohn (m)/Adoptivtochter (f)
adult Erwachsene(r) (f/m)
advance: in advance im Voraus
advantage Vorteil (m)
advice Rat (m)
to advise raten (pp geraten)
afraid: to be afraid Angst haben
afraid: I'm afraid (sorry) leider
after nach (dat)
afternoon Nachmittag (m); **in the afternoons** nachmittags
afterwards nachher, dann
again wieder, nochmal
against gegen (acc)
ago vor (dat)
to agree zustimmen
air Luft (f)
agriculture Landwirtschaft (f)
air conditioning Klimaanlage (f)
airline Fluggesellschaft (f)
air traffic controller Fluglotse (m), Fluglotsin (f)
airport Flughafen (m)
alcohol Alkohol (m)
all alle, ganz
allergic (to) allergisch (gegen) (acc)
to allow erlauben
allowed: to be allowed to (may) dürfen
almond Mandel (f)
almost fast
alone allein(e)
along entlang (acc)
Alps Alpen (pl)
already schon
also auch
alternative alternativ
although obwohl
altogether insgesamt
always immer
amazing (marvellous) toll, herrlich; **(astonishing)** erstaunlich
ambitious ehrgeizig
America Amerika (n)
American national Amerikaner(in) (m/f)
among unter (acc/dat)
amusing lustig
ancient uralt
and und
angel Engel (m)
anniversary Jubiläum (n), Hochzeitstag (m)
to announce melden
annoying ärgerlich
annual jährlich
another ein anderer/eine andere (m/f); noch ein(e)
answer Antwort (f)
to answer antworten
ant Ameise (f)
any: in any case auf alle Fälle, auf jeden Fal
any more mehr
apartment Wohnung (f)
app App (f), Anwendung (f)
to appeal ansprechen (pp angesprochen)
appetiser Vorspeise (f)
appetite Appetit (m)
apple Apfel (m)
apple strudel Apfelstrudel (m)
appointment Termin (m)
apprentice Auszubildende(r) (f/m)
approximately etwa, ungefähr, circa/zirka
April April (m)
archaeologist Archäologe (m), Archäologin (f)
architect Architekt(in) (m/f)
architecture Architektur (f)
are bist/sind/seid (from sein)
area Gebiet (n), Gegend (f)
arm Arm (m)
around (time) so gegen (acc)
to arrange festlegen
to arrive ankommen (pp angekommen)
arrow Pfeil (m)
art Kunst (f)
art gallery Kunstgalerie (f)

arthritis Arthritis (f)
article Artikel (m)
artist Künstler(in) (m/f)
as als, wie, da
be ashamed sich schämen
to ask fragen
to ask for bitten um (acc)
assignment Aufgabe (f)
asthma Asthma (n)
asterisk Sternchen (n)
astonishing erstaunlich
asylum seeker Asylsuchende (m/f)
at an (acc/dat), bei (dat), (time) um (acc)
attack (medical) Anfall (m)
to attack überfallen (pp überfallen)
August August (m)
aunt Tante (f)
Australia Australien (n)
Australian national Australier(in) (m/f)
Austria Österreich (n)
Austrian national Österreicher(in) (m/f)
authority Behörde (f)
autumn Herbst (m)
to be available zur Verfügung stehen (pp gestanden)
average Durchschnitt (m); (on average) im Durchschnitt
to avoid vermeiden (pp vermieden)
away entfernt, weg
awful(ly) schrecklich

B

baby Baby (n)
back Rücken (m)
to back up (computer) sichern
backpack Rucksack (m)
backwater verschlafenes Nest (n)
bad(ly) schlecht, schlimm
bag Tasche (f)
to bake backen (pp gebacken)
balanced ausgewogen
to ban verbieten (pp verboten)
bank Bank (f)
bank clerk Bankangestellte(r) (f/m)
banker Bankier(in) (m/f)
bar Bar (f)
barbecue Grillparty (f)
to have a barbecue grillen
basically im Grunde, grundsätzlich
basil Basilikum (n)
bath Bad (n)
bathroom Badezimmer (n)
battery Akku (m)
Bavaria Bayern (n)
to be sein (pp gewesen)
beach Strand (m)
to beat schlagen (pp geschlagen)
beautician Kosmetiker(in) (m/f)
beautiful schön, wunderschön
because weil
because of wegen (gen)
to become werden (pp geworden)
bed Bett (n)
bee Biene (f)
beer Bier (n)
beer cellar Bierkeller (m)
beer garden Biergarten (m)
before vor (acc/dat); (earlier) zuvor
to begin beginnen (pp begonnen), anfangen (pp angefangen)
behind hinter (acc/dat)
to believe glauben
to belong to gehören
to bend beugen
benefits (state) Sozialleistungen (pl)
beside neben (acc/dat)
best best... (+ ending) (adj); am besten (adv)
all the best (for) alles Gute (zu) (dat)
best of all am besten, am liebsten
best wishes mit freundlichen Grüßen
to bet wetten
better besser
between zwischen (acc/dat)
bicycle, bike Fahrrad (n)
big groß
bill Rechnung (f)
to binge (on) sich vollstopfen (mit)
birthday Geburtstag (m)
birthday card Geburtstagkarte (f)
bisexual bi, bisexuell
bit: a bit ein bisschen
black schwarz
blond blond
blood Blut (n)
blood pressure Blutdruck (m)
to blow wehen
blue blau
boat Boot (n)
boat trip Bootfahrt (f)
book Buch (n)
to book buchen, reservieren
to be bored sich langweilen
boring langweilig
born geboren
to borrow ausleihen (pp ausgeliehen)
boss Chef(in) (m/f)
both beide
to bother stören
bottle Flasche (f)
bought gekauft (pp of kaufen)
bowling: to go bowling kegeln gehen

boy Junge (m)
bracket Klammer (f); in brackets in Klammern
brave mutig
bread Brot (n)
to break brechen (pp gebrochen)
to break in aufbrechen (pp aufgebrochen)
breakdown (car) Panne (f)
breakfast Frühstück (n)
to have breakfast frühstücken
to breathe atmen
breeze Brise (f)
brewery Brauerei (f)
bright bunt
to bring bringen (pp gebracht)
to bring along mitbringen (pp mitgebracht)
Brit, British person Brite/ Britin (m/f)
broken kaputt, gebrochen (from brechen)
brother Bruder (m)
brother-in-law Schwager (m)
brown braun
to browse (internet) surfen
to build bauen
builder Bauarbeiter(in) (m/f)
building Gebäude (n)
building site Baustelle (f)
bus Bus (m)
bus driver Busfahrer(in) (m/f)
bus stop Bushaltestelle (f)
business Geschäft (n); on business geschäftlich
businessman/-woman Geschäftsmann (m)/ Geschäftsfrau (f)
but aber
button Knopf (m)
but yes ja doch
to buy kaufen
by bei (dat), von (dat)
bye tschüs(s), tschau

C

cafe Café (n)
cake Kuchen (m)
to calculate rechnen
calf (leg) Wade (die)
to call (on the telephone) anrufen (pp angerufen)
to call nennen (pp genannt)
called: to be called heißen (pp geheißen)
to calm down sich beruhigen
to camp zelten
campsite Campingplatz (m)
can (to be able to) können
Canadian Kanadier(in) (m/f)
to cancel absagen
canoe Kajak (m)
to canoe Kajak fahren (pp gefahren)
car Auto (n), Wagen (m); by car mit dem Auto (n)
car park Parkplatz (m)
carbohydrate Kohlenhydrat (n)
card Karte (f)
to care for pflegen
careful vorsichtig
to be careful aufpassen
caretaker Hausmeister(in) (m/f)
carnival Karneval (m)
cash Geld (n)
cashpoint Geldautomat (m)
castle Schloss (n)
cat Katze (f)
catastrophe Katastrophe (f)
cathedral Dom (m), Kathedrale (f)
to celebrate feiern
celebration Fest (n), Feier (f)
cellar Keller (m)
central zentral
centre Zentrum (n)
century Jahrhundert (n)
CEO Hauptgeschäftsführer(in) (m/f)
certain bestimmt, sicher
certainly jawohl, sicher
chamber music Kammermusik (f)
champagne Sekt (m)
championship Meisterschaft (f)
chance: by chance zufällig
Chancellor (German leader) Bundeskanzler(in) (m/f)
to change ändern, wechseln
to change (vehicle) umsteigen (pp umgestiegen)
to get changed sich umziehen (pp umgezogen)
to charge laden (pp geladen), aufladen (pp aufgeladen)
charitable karitativ
to chat reden, plaudern, sich unterhalten (pp unterhalten); (in chatrooms) chatten
cheap billig
cheerful heiter
Cheers! Prosit!, Prost!
cheese Käse (m)
cheesecake Käsekuchen (m)
chef Küchenchef(in) (m/f)
chemist's Apotheke (f)
chess Schach (n)
child Kind (n)
childminder Tagesmutter (f), Tagesvater (m)
chilly kühl
chocolate Schokolade (f)
to choose auswählen

choral music Chormusik (f)
choreographer Choreograph(in) (m/f)
Christmas Weihnachten (n)
Christmas market Weihnachtsmarkt (m)
church Kirche (f)
cinema Kino (n)
city Stadt (f)
civil partner Lebenspartner(in) (m/f)
civil partnership Lebenspartnerschaft (f)
to clarify erklären
classical klassisch
clean sauber
to clean putzen, reinigen
to do the cleaning sauber machen
clear(ly) klar
to clear up aufräumen, in Ordnung bringen (pp gebracht)
clergyman/-woman Geistliche(r) (f/m)
clever klug
to click klicken
climate change Klimawandel (m)
to climb klettern
to close schließen (pp geschlossen)
clothes Kleider, Klamotten (pl)
cloud Wolke (f)
cloudy bewölkt
coast Küste (f)
coffee Kaffee (m)
coffee break Kaffeepause (f)
cold kalt; head cold Schnupfen (m)
to have a cold erkältet sein
colleague Kollege/Kollegin (m/f)
colour Farbe (f)
combat sport Kampfsportart (f)
to come kommen (pp gekommen)
to come back zurückkommen (pp zurückgekommen)
to come in reinkommen (pp reingekommen)
comfortable bequem; make yourself comfortable mach es dir bequem
comma Komma (n)
community Gemeinde (f)
company Firma (f), Unternehmen (n)
to compare vergleichen (pp verglichen)
compared to im Vergleich zu (dat)
competent kompetent
complete(ly) ganz
complex Wohnkomplex (m); kompliziert
complicated kompliziert
composer Komponist(in) (m/f)
computer Computer (m)
computer scientist Computerwissenschaftler (in) (m/f)
computer system Computertechnik (f)
to concern betreffen (pp betroffen)
concert Konzert (n)
conclusion Schluss (m); (in conclusion) zum Schluss
conference Konferenz (f)
to confirm bestätigen
conflict: in conflict im Widerspruch
to congratulate gratulieren
congratulations Glückwunsch (m); Congratulations! Herzlichen Glückwunsch!
to connect verbinden (pp verbunden)
connection Verbindung (f)
contact Kontakt (m)
to contain enthalten (pp enthalten)
contemporary heutig, zeitgenössisch
contents Inhalt (m)
to contradict widersprechen (pp widersprochen)
contrary: on the contrary im Gegenteil
convenient günstig
conversation Gespräch (n)
to have a conversation sich unterhalten (pp unterhalten)
cook Koch/Köchin (m/f)
to cook kochen
cool kühl
to cool abkühlen
copy Kopie (f)
to copy kopieren
corporation Gesellschaft (f)
correct richtig; that's correct das stimmt
to cost kosten
could könnte (from können)
counsellor Berater(in) (m/f)
country Land (n)
country(side) Land (n); in the country(side) auf dem Lande
county Grafschaft (f)
couple Paar (n); married couple Ehepaar (n)
courageous tapfer
course (meal) Gang (m); (study programme) Kurs (m); of course natürlich, selbstverständlich
cousin Cousin (m), Cousine (f)
crazy verrückt

cream Sahne (f), Creme (f)
credit (on phone) Guthaben (n)
credit card Kreditkarte (f)
crime novel Krimi (m)
criminality Kriminalität (f)
to cross überqueren
crossword Kreuzworträtsel (n)
crowded voller Menschen
culture Kultur (f)
cup Tasse (f)
curly lockig
customs Zoll (m)
customs officer Zollbeamter/Zollbeamtin (m/f)
to cut schneiden (pp geschnitten); (mow) mähen
cute süß
cycle Fahrrad (n)

D

Dachshund Dackel (m)
daily täglich
dairy products Milchprodukte (pl)
to dance tanzen
danger Gefahr (f)
dangerous gefährlich
to dare wagen
dark dunkel
darling Schatz (m), Schätzchen (n), Liebling (m)
data Daten (pl)
date Datum (n), Wievielte (m)
daughter Tochter (f)
daughter-in-law Schwiegertochter (f)
day Tag (m)
day before yesterday vorgestern
daybreak Tagesanbruch (m)
to deal (with) sich befassen (mit)
dear (informal) liebe(r) (f/m), (formal) sehr geehrte(r) (f/m)
my dear mein Lieber/ meine Liebe (m/f)
December Dezember (m)
to decide sich entscheiden (pp entschieden)
to decorate Tapezierarbeiten machen
decorator Dekorateur(in) (m/f)
to decrease senken
to defeat besiegen
definitely bestimmt, jawohl, sicher
to defrost abtauen
dehydrated dehydriert
delay Verspätung (f)
delayed: to be delayed sich verspäten
delete entfernen
delicious lecker
delight Freude (f)
delightful erfreulich (f)
democracy Demokratie (f)
dentist Zahnarzt (m), Zahnärztin (f)
to depend (on) ankommen (auf) (pp angekommen), abhängen (von)
deputy stellvertretend
to describe beschreiben (pp beschrieben)
despite trotz (gen)
dessert Nachtisch (m)
to develop entwickeln
diabetes Diabetes (m), Zuckerkrankheit (f)
diabetic Diabetiker(in) (m/f); zuckerkrank
dictionary Wörterbuch (n)
to die sterben (pp gestorben)
diet Diät (f), Ernährung (f)
different anders
difficult schwierig
dinner Abendessen (n)
direct(ly) direct
dirty schmutzig
disadvantage Nachteil (m)
to disagree widersprechen (pp widersprochen)
disappointed enttäuscht
disappointing enttäuschend
disappointment Enttäuschung (f)
discount Rabatt (m)
to discover entdecken
discrimination Diskriminierung (f)
to discuss diskutieren
disgusting widerlich, scheußlich
dish Gericht (n)
dishwasher Geschirrspüler (m)
to disturb stören
to dive tauchen
divorced geschieden
DIY Heimwerkerarbeiten (pl)
dizzy schwindlig
do (party) Feier (f), Party (f)
to do tun (pp getan), machen, schaffen
doctor Arzt/Ärztin (m/f), Doktor(in) (m/f)
dog Hund (m)
don't mention it bitte, gern geschehen, keine Ursache
double Doppel (n)
doubt Zweifel (f)
to download downloaden
dozen Dutzend (n)
dreadful furchtbar, scheußlich
to dress (oneself), get dressed sich anziehen (pp angezogen)
to drink trinken (pp getrunken)
driver Fahrer(in) (m/f)
driving licence Führerschein (m)
to drizzle nieseln
drug Droge (f)
dry trocken
dryer Trockner (m)

dumpling Kloß, Knödel (m)
dust Staub (m)
to dust abstauben, den Staub abwischen

E

earlier früher, vorher, vorzeitig
early früh
to earn verdienen
east Osten (m)
Easter Ostern (n)
easy leicht
to eat essen (pp gegessen), (animals) fressen (pp gefressen)
ecological ökologisch
economy Wirtschaft (f)
education Erziehung (f)
eerie unheimlich
egg Ei (n)
elder älter
electricity Elektrizität (f)
elephant Elefant (m)
elevenses zweite Frühstück (n)
email E-Mail (f)
emergency Notfall (m)
emergency services Notdienst (m)
emperor Kaiser (m)
empire Reich (n)
employee Angestellte (m/f)
empty leer
end Ende (n), Schluss (n); at the end am Ende
to end beenden
energy Energie (f)
engaged verlobt
engineer Ingenieur(in) (m/f)
England England (n)
English englisch, (language) Englisch (n)
Englishman/woman Engländer(in) (m/f)
enjoyable lustig
to enjoy oneself sich amüsieren
enormous riesig
enough genug
to be enough reichen
to enter eintreten
entertainment Animation (f)
entire ganz
entry: no entry keine Einfahrt (f)
environment Umwelt (f)
equal opportunities Chancengleichheit (pl)
equality Gleichheit (f), Gleichstellung (f)
equipped ausgestattet
to eradicate beseitigen
estate agent Immobilienmakler(in) (m/f)
etc. usw, und so weiter
euro Euro (m)
Europe Europa (n)
European europäisch
European Union Europäische Union (f)
even sogar
evening Abend (m); in the evenings abends
ever (before) schon einmal
every jede(r), alle; every day jeden Tag; every year jedes Jahr
everyone alle
everything alles
ex, ex-husband/-wife Ex (m/f), Ex-Mann/Ex-Frau (m/f)
exact(ly) genau
example Beispiel (n); for example zum Beispiel
excellent(ly) ausgezeichnet
exceptional(ly) außergewöhnlich, einzigartig
to exchange austauschen
exciting spannend
exclamation mark Ausrufezeichen (n)
excursion Ausflug (m)
excuse me entschuldigen Sie (mich)
to excuse oneself sich entschuldigen
exercise Fitnesstraining (n)
exhibition Ausstellung (f)
exit Ausgang (m)
expensive teuer
experience Erfahrung (f)
to explain erklären
extremely äußerst
eye Auge (n)

F

face Gesicht (n)
facility Einrichtung (f)
fact Fakt (m or n), Tatsache (f); as a matter of fact eigentlich
factory Fabrik (f)
to faint in Ohnmacht fallen (pp gefallen)
fairly ziemlich
faithful treu
to fall fallen (pp gefallen), hinfallen (pp hingefallen)
to fall asleep einschlafen (pp eingeschlafen)
false falsch
family Familie (f)
fan Fan (m)
to fancy (feel like) Lust haben, (imagine) sich vorstellen
fantastic(ally) fantastisch
far weit
Farewell! Leb wohl!/ Leben Sie wohl!
farm Bauernhof (m)
fascinating faszinierend
fashion Mode (f)
fast schnell
fat dick (adj); Fett (n)
father Vater (m)
father-in-law Schwiegervater (m)
favour Gefallen (m)
favourite Lieblings-

February February (n)
feed füttern
feedback Rückmeldung (f)
to feel sich fühlen
to feel like Lust haben
feeling Gefühl (n)
festival Fest (n)
few wenig; a few ein paar, einige
fiancée/fiancé Verlobte(r) (f/m)
fight Kampf (m)
to fight kämpfen
figure Zahl (f)
file Datei (f)
film Film (m)
finally zum Schluss
to find finden (pp gefunden)
to find out erfahren (pp erfahren)
fine gut
to finish beenden
fire Feuer (n)
firefighter Feuerwehrmann/ Feuerwehrfrau (m/f)
firm Firma (f)
first-class erstklassig
first name Vorname (m)
first of all erstens, zunächst
fish Fisch (m)
to fish, go fishing angeln
fit fit
flat Wohnung (f); flach (adj)
flight Flug (m)
flight attendant Flugbegleiter(in) (m/f)
floor Boden (m), Fußboden (m), (storey) Etage (f)
flower Blume (f)
flu Grippe (f)
fly Fliege (f)
to fly fliegen (pp geflogen)
fog Nebel (m)
folder Ordner (m)
to follow folgen, befolgen
food Essen (n)
food shopping Lebensmitteleinkauf (m)
foot Fuß (m); on foot zu Fuß
football Fußball (m)
football club Fußballverein (m)
football match Fußballspiel (n)
footballer Fußballspieler(in) (m/f)
for für (acc), um (acc); (since) seit (dat), (on account of) wegen (gen), (because) denn
to forbid verbieten (pp verboten)
forbidden verboten
foreign ausländisch
foreign policy Außenpolitik (f)
foreigner Ausländer(in) (m/f)
forest Wald (m)
to forget vergessen (pp vergessen)
to forgive verzeihen (pp verziehen)
fork Gabel (f)
formerly früher
fortress Festung (f)
fortunate glücklich
fortunately glücklicherweise
foster parents Pflegeeltern (pl)
frankly offen gesagt, ehrlich gesagt
France Frankreich (n)
free frei; free of charge gratis, kostenlos
free time Freizeit (f)
freedom Freiheit (f)
freelance freiberuflich
freezer Gefrierschrank (m)
French französisch (adj); (language) Französisch (n)
Frenchman/-woman Franzose (m)/ Französin (f)
frequent(ly) häufig
fresh frisch
Friday Freitag (m)
(boy/girl) friend Freund(in) (m/f)
friendliness Freundlichkeit (f)
friendly freundlich
from von (dat), aus (dat)
front: in front of vor (acc/dat)
frozen (computer) abgestürzt
fruit Obst (n)
to fry braten
fuel Brennstoff (m), fossil fuels fossile Brennstoffe
full voll, satt
full-bodied vollmundig
full stop Punkt (m)
full time Vollzeit (f)
fun Spaß (m); to be fun Spaß (m) machen; to have fun Spaß (m) haben
funny lustig
further weiter
furthermore außerdem, zudem
future Zukunft (f)

G

gadget Gerät (n)
gallery Galerie (f)
gambling Sportwetten (n)
game Spiel (n)
garage Garage (f), Werkstatt (f)
garden Garten (m)
garlic Knoblauch (m)
gate Tor (n)
gay homo, schwul
gem Schatz (m)
gender Geschlecht (n)
general: in general im Allgemeinen
generous großzügig
genius Genie (m)

gerbil Rennmaus (f)
German deutsch, (language) Deutsch (n), (person) Deutsche(r) (f/m)
Germany Deutschland (n)
to get bekommen (pp bekommen), werden (pp geworden)
to get off (bus etc.) aussteigen (pp ausgestiegen)
to get on (bus etc.) einsteigen (pp eingestiegen)
to get up aufstehen (pp aufgestanden)
ghost Geist (m)
gigantic riesig
girl Mädchen (n)
to give geben (pp gegeben)
gladly gern(e)
glass Glas (n)
glasses (spectacles) Brille (f)
global warming Erderwärmung (f)
glutton Vielfraß (m)
to go (by vehicle) fahren (pp gefahren), (on foot) gehen (pp gegangen)
to go away (by vehicle) wegfahren (pp weggefahren), (on foot) weggehen (pp weggegangen)
to go back (vehicle) zurückfahren (pp zurückgefahren), (on foot) zurückgehen (pp zurückgegangen)
to go out ausgehen (pp ausgegangen)
to go with (match, suit) passen
goal Tor (n)
God Gott (m)
gold(en) golden
good gut, (favourable) günstig, (well-behaved) brav
goodbye auf Wiedersehen
goodbye (on the telephone) auf Wiederhören
good-looking gut aussehend
goodness: my goodness ach du liebe Güte!
for goodness' sake um Gottes willen
government Regierung (f)
grandad Opa (m)
grandchild Enkelkind (n)
grandchildren Enkel (pl)
granddaughter Enkelin (f)
grandfather Großvater (m)
grandma Oma (f)
grandmother Großmutter (f)
grandparents Großeltern (pl)
grandson Enkel (m)
graphic designer Grafikdesigner(in) (m/f)
grass Gras (n)
great (large) groß; (fantastic) super, toll
Great Britain Großbritannien (n)
great grandfather Urgroßvater (m)
great grandmother Urgroßmutter (f)
greedy gierig
green grün
greetings Grüße (pl)
grey grau
groin Leiste (f)
group Gruppe (f)
to grow wachsen (pp gewachsen)
to grow up aufwachsen (pp aufgewachsen)
to guess raten (pp geraten)
guide (Reise)führer(in) (m/f)
gym Fitnessstudio (n)

H

to hail hageln
hair Haare (pl)
half halb (adj), Hälfte (f)
hand Hand (f); on (the) one hand einerseits; on the other hand andererseits
to hang out (washing) aufhängen
hangover Kater (m)
to happen geschehen (pp geschehen), passieren
happy froh, glücklich
harbour Hafen (m)
hard schwierig
hash sign Doppelkreuz (n)
to hate hassen
to have haben
to have to (must) müssen
hayfever Heuschnupfen (m)
he er
head Kopf (m);
head of department Abteilungsleiter(in) (m/f)
headache Kopfschmerzen (pl)
headphones Kopfhörer (m)
health Gesundheit (f); to your health! zum Wohl!
health and safety Arbeitssicherheit (f)
healthy/healthily gesund
to hear hören
heart Herz (n)
heaven Himmel (n)
heavy schwer (m)
hedge Hecke (f)
hello hallo, (southern Germany) grüß Gott
help Hilfe (f)
to help helfen (pp geholfen)
to help oneself sich bedienen
her ihr (m, n), ihre (f, pl); sie (acc); to her ihr
here hier
to hesitate zögern

hi hallo, (southern Germany) servus
hiccups Schluckauf (m)
to hide verstecken
high hoch
hike Wanderung (f)
to hike wandern
hilly hügelig
him ihn; to him ihm
to hire mieten
his sein (m, n), seine (f, pl)
historian Historiker(in) (m/f)
historic(al)(ly) historisch
to hold up aufhalten (pp aufgehalten)
hole Loch (n)
holiday Urlaub (m); on holiday im Urlaub; public holiday Feiertag (m); holidays Ferien (pl)
home: at home zu Hause; from home von zuhause; to my/your etc. home nach Hause
homesick: to be homesick Heimweh haben
honest ehrlich
honey Honig (m)
to hope hoffen
hopefully hoffentlich
hops Hopfen (m)
horrible widerlich, scheußlich
horror film Horrorfilm (m)
horse Pferd (n)
hospital Krankenhaus (n)
host(ess) Gastgeber(in) (m/f)
hot heiß
hotel Hotel (n)
hour Stunde (f); for hours stundenlang
house Haus (n)
household Haushalt (m)
housework Hausarbeit (f)
how wie
how are you? wie geht's?, (formal) wie geht es Ihnen?
how much, how many wie viel, wie viele
however aber, allerdings, jedoch
HR Personalbereich (n)
huge ungeheuer
human right Menschenrecht (n)
humid feucht
hungry: to be hungry Hunger haben
hurry: to hurry sich beeilen
hurt verletzt
to hurt wehtun (pp wehgetan)
husband Mann (m)
hyphen (Binde)strich (m)

I

I ich
ice cream Eis (n)
ice-skating: to go ice-skating Schlittschuh laufen (pp gelaufen)
idea Ahnung (f), Idee (f)
identity card Ausweis (m)
if wenn, (whether) ob
to ignore ignorieren
ill krank
illegal illegal
to imagine sich vorstellen (dat)
immediately sofort
immigrant Einwanderer/Einwanderin, Migrant(in) (m/f)
immigration Einwanderung (f), Immigration (f)
impolite unhöflich
important wichtig
to impose verhängen
impossible unmöglich
impressive beeindruckend
to improve verbessern
in in (acc/dat)
increase Zuwachs (m)
to increase erhöhen
indeed in der Tat, tatsächlich, wirklich, wohl
indefensible unvertretbar
industrial industriell
industrial estate Industriegebiet (n)
inflamed entzündet
information Informationen (pl)
in-laws Schwiegereltern (pl)
to install installieren
institute Institut (n)
instruction Anweisung (f)
instructor Ausbilder(in) (m/f)
insurance Versicherung (f)
intelligent intelligent
to interest interessieren
interested: to be interested in sich interessieren für
interesting interessant
intern Praktikant(in) (m/f)
internet Internet (n)
to interrupt unterbrechen (pp unterbrochen)
interruption Unterbrechung (f)
intolerable unerträglich
to introduce vorstellen
invitation Einladung (f)
to invite einladen (pp eingeladen)
Irish irisch
Irishman/-woman Ire/Irin (m/f)
to iron bügeln
island Insel (f)
IT EDV, elektronische Datenverarbeitung
it er (m nom), ihn (m acc) sie (f nom and acc), es (n, nom and acc); to it ihm (m, n), ihr (f)
Italian italienisch
its sein ihr (m, n), seine, ihre (f, pl)

J

January Januar (m)
job Arbeitsstelle (f), Beruf (m), Job (m)
joke Witz (m)

jolly lustig
journalist Journalist(in) (m/f)
journey Reise (f)
July Juli (m)
to jump springen (pp gesprungen)
June Juni (m)
just mal

K
keen begeistert
to keep halten (pp gehalten), (delay) aufhalten (pp aufgehalten), (stay) bleiben (pp geblieben)
key (door) Schlüssel (m), (keyboard) Taste (f)
keyboard Tastatur (f)
kilo Kilo (n)
kilometre Kilometer (m or n)
kind freundlich, lieb; (type) Art (f)
kiss Kuss (m)
to kiss (each other) (sich) küssen
knee Knie (n)
knife Messer (n)
to know (people and places) kennen (pp gekannt), (things and facts) wissen (pp gewusst); to get to know kennenlernen

L
label Etikett (n)
Ladies and Gentlemen meine Damen und Herren
lake See (m)
to land landen
landscape Landschaft (f)
lane Gasse (f)
language Sprache (f)
laptop Laptop (m)
large groß
last letzt
to last dauern
late spät
later: see you later bis später
latest neuest... (+ endings)
to laugh lachen
laundry Wäsche (f)
law Gesetz (n)
law and order Ruhe und Ordung (f)
lawyer Rechtsanwalt/ Rechtsanwältin (m/f)
lawyer's office Kanzlei (f)
lazy faul
to lead führen, leiten
to learn lernen
least am wenigsten; at least mindestens
to leave verlassen; (a message) hinterlassen, (leave something behind) lassen (pp gelassen), (train) abfahren (pp abgefahren), (go away) wegfahren (pp weggefahren), weggehen (pp weggegangen)
lecturer Dozent(in) (m/f)
left: on the left links
leg Bein (n)
legal legal
to legalise legalisieren
lesbian lesbisch
leisure Freizeit (f)
less weniger
to let lassen (pp gelassen)
to let (someone) know Bescheid sagen
letter Brief (m), (alphabet) Buchstabe (f)
level Niveau (n)
to lie (to be situated) liegen (pp gelegen); (tell a lie) lügen
to lie down sich hinlegen
life Leben (n)
lifeguard Rettungsschwimmer(in) (m/f)
light (adj) hell, leicht; Licht (n)
lightning: there's lightning es blitzt (from blitzen)
like: What is ... like? Wie ist ...?
to like mögen; (taste) schmecken; would like möchte (from mögen to like)
to like ... ing ... gern(e); I like mir gefällt (gefallen); like ... best am liebsten
likewise ebenfalls
to listen zuhören
literature Literatur (f)
to live wohnen, leben
lively lebendig
to load beladen (pp beladen)
local lokal
located: to be located sich befinden (pp befunden)
to log in/on einloggen
to log off/out ausloggen
long lang; for a long time schon lange
to look (have the appearance) aussehen (pp ausgesehen); to look after sich kümmern um; to look at gucken, ansehen (pp angesehen); to look for suchen; to look forward to sich freuen auf; to look like ähnlich sehen (pp gesehen)
lorry Lastkraftwagen, LKW (m)
to lose verlieren (pp verloren)
to lose weight abnehmen (pp abgenommen)
lot: a lot viel
loud(ly) laut
to love lieben; love (from) (informal) liebe Grüße
lovely lieb, schön, wunderschön

loyal treu
luck Glück (n)
lucky glücklich
luggage Gepäck (n)
lunch Mittagessen (n); to have lunch zu Mittag essen (pp gegessen)
lunchtime: at lunchtime mittags

M
machine Maschine (f)
madam gnädige Frau (f)
made-up geschminkt
main Haupt-
main role Hauptrolle (f)
main street Hauptstraße (f)
to make machen, schaffen
malt Malz (n)
man Mann (m)
manager Geschäftsführer(in) (m/f), Manager(in) (m/f)
mango Mango (f)
manners Umgangsformen (pl)
many viele
March März (m)
mark Note (f)
market Markt (m)
married verheiratet; to get married/marry heiraten
martial arts Kampfsport (m)
marvellous herrlich, wunderschön
match Spiel (n)
matter: it doesn't matter macht nichts; what's the matter? was ist los?; matter of opinion Ansichtssache (f)
May Mai (m)
may: may I? darf ich?
maybe vielleicht
me mich; to me mir
meal Mahlzeit (f)
mean (unkind) gemein
to mean bedeuten
meantime: in the meantime mittlerweise
meat Fleisch (n)
media office Pressebüro (n)
medication Medikament (n)
to meet treffen (pp getroffen), kennenlernen; to meet up with someome sich treffen (pp getroffen)
meeting Besprechung (f)
memory Gedächtnis (n), (computer) Arbeitsspeicher (m)
mention: don't mention it bitte (schön), nichts zu danken
menu (Speise)karte (f), (computer) Menü (n)
mess Durcheinander (n)
message Nachricht (f)
metre Meter (m or n)
midday Mittag (m)
midnight Mitternacht (f)
midwife Hebamme (f), Geburtsspfleger/ Geburtshelfer (m)
migrant Migrant(in) (m/f)
mild mild
milk Milch (f)
milky coffee Milchkaffee (m)
million Million (f)
millionaire Millionär(in) (m/f)
mind: I don't mind das ist mir egal
ministry Ministerium (n)
minority Minderheit (f); ethnic minority ethnische Minderheit
minute Minute (f); in a minute gleich
miracle Wunder (n)
to miss, to be missing fehlen
Mr Herr (m)
misunderstanding Missverständnis (n)
to moan jammern
mobile phone Handy (n)
model Model (n)
modern modern, heutig, zeitgenössisch
moment Augenblick (m)
Monday Montag (m)
money Geld (m)
month Monat (m)
mood Laune (f)
to mop aufwischen
moral(ly) moralisch
more mehr
what's more außerdem, zudem
morning Morgen (m), Vormittag (m); morning; in the morning vormittags
mosquito Mücke (f)
most: the most die meisten
mostly meistens
mother Mutter (f)
mother-in-law Schwiegermutter (f)
motor vehicle Kraftwagen (m)
mountain Berg (m)
mountain climbing: to go mountain climbing bergsteigen (pp berggestiegen)
mountainous bergig
mouse Maus (f)
mouth Mund (m)
to mow mähen
MP Abgeordnete(r) (f/m)
Mrs Frau (f)
much viel
mud Schlamm (m)
muddy schlammig
muggy schwül
mulled wine Glühwein (m)
muscle Muskel (m)
museum Museum (n)
music Musik (f)
musician Musiker(in) (m/f)
must (to have to) müssen
my mein (m/n), meine (f/pl)

N
name Name (m)
to name nennen (pp genannt)
nanny Kindermädchen (n but applies to women), Kinderpfleger (m)
narrow eng
nasty gemein
naturally natürlich
nature Natur (f)
near in der Nähe von
nearby in der Nähe
nearly fast
necessary nötig
to need brauchen
to need to (must) müssen
neglected verwahrlosen
neighbour Nachbar(in) (m/f)
nephew Neffe (m)
nerves: to get on my nerves mir auf die Nerven gehen
nettle Nessel (f)
never nie, nimmer
never before noch nie
new neu
New Year's Eve Silvester (m)
next nächst... (+ endings);
next to neben (acc/dat)
NGO NRO (Nichtregierungs-organisation) (f)
nice nett, sympatisch
niece Nichte (f)
night Nacht (f)
no, (none) kein (m, n), keine (f, pl)
nonsense Unsinn (m), Quatsch (m)
no one niemand
noodles Nockerl (n)
normally normalerweise
north Norden (m)
north-east Nordosten (m)
not nicht
not at all gar/überhaupt nicht; gern geschehen
not yet noch nicht
nothing nichts
to notice bemerken
November November (m)
now jetzt
now and then ab und zu, dann und wann, mitunter
nuclear power Atomkraft (f)
number Zahl (f), Nummer (f)
nursery Kindergarten (m); (garden centre) Gärtnerei (f)
nut Nuss (f)
nutshell: to put it in a nutshell kurz gesagt

O
o'clock Uhr (f)
obviously offensichtlich
October Oktober (m)
of von (dat)
of course natürlich
offer Angebot (n)
to offer anbieten (pp angeboten), bieten (pp geboten)
office Büro (n)
office worker Büroangestellter (f/m)
often oft
oil Öl (n)
old alt
old town Altstadt (f)
old-fashioned altmodisch
OMG Mein Gott!
on (date/day) am = an dem (dat); on (top of) auf (dat)
once einmal
once in a while ab und zu, dann und wann, mitunter
one (I, we, you) man
one and a half anderthalb
onion Zwiebel (f)
only nur
onto auf (acc)
open offen
to open öffnen
opera Oper (f)
opinion Ansicht (f), Meinung (f)
opposite Gegenteil (n); gegenüber (dat)
option Wahlmöglichkeit (f)
or oder
order Ordnung (f)
to order bestellen
organisation Organisation (f)
to organise organisieren
other ander... (+ endings); on the other hand andererseits; the other day neulich
otherwise sonst
our unser(e) (m, n/f, pl)
out of aus (dat)
outrageous unverschämt
outside draußen
oven Ofen (m), Backofen (m)
over über (acc/dat)
overcast bedeckt
overnight: to stay overnight übernachten
to owe schulden
own: on my/your own allein(e)
oyster Auster (f)

P
page Seite (f)
pain Schmerz (m)
to paint malen
painter Maler(in) (m/f)
parents Eltern (pl)
park Park (m)
to park parken
parking permit Parkausweis (m)
parking place Parkplatz (m)
part-time Teilzeit (f)
particularly besonders
partner Partner(in) (m/f)
party Feier (f), Party (f)
pass Ausweis (m)

passenger Passagier(in) (m/f)
passport Pass (m)
password Passwort (n)
past Vergangenheit (f), Vorzeit (f)
past (prep) nach (dat)
path Weg (m)
patience Geduld (f)
patient geduldig
pavement Gehweg (m)
to pay (for something) (be)zahlen
peaceful ruhig
peanut Erdnuss (f)
to peel schälen
pensioner Rentner(in) (m/f)
people Leute (pl)
pepper Pfeffer (m)
per cent Prozent (n)
perfect perfekt
performance Auftritt (m), Spektakel (n), Vorstellung (f)
perhaps vielleicht
permit Ausweis (m)
person Mensch (m)
personal(ly) persönlich
pet Haustier (n)
petrol: to fill up with petrol tanken
pharmacy Apotheke (f)
to phone anrufen (pp angerufen)
phone number Telefonnummer (f)
photograph Foto (n)
to photograph fotografieren
photographer Fotograf(in) (m/f)
piano Klavier (n)
to pick up abholen
picnic Picknick (n)
picture Bild (n)
piece Stück (n)
pigeon Taube (f)
pilot Pilot(in) (m/f)
pity: what a pity! wie schade!
pizza Pizza (f)
place Ort (m), Stelle (f)
to place stellen
to take place stattfinden (pp stattgefunden)
to play spielen
playground Spielplatz (m)
pleasant angenehm
to please gefallen (pp gefallen)
pleased to meet you freut mich, dich/Sie kennenzulernen, sehr erfreut
to be pleased (about) sich freuen (über) (acc)
pleasure Freude (f), Vergnügen (n); my pleasure gern geschehen
plenty viel
plumber Klempner(in) (m/f)
point Punkt (m)
police Polizei (f)
police officer Polizist(in) (m/f)
police station Polizeirevier (n)
polite höflich
political politisch
politician Politiker(in) (m/f)
politics Politik (f)
pollution Verschmutzung (f)
pony Pony (n)
pool Schwimmbad (n)
poor arm
pop music Popmusik (f)
pop singer Popsänger(in) (m/f)
popular beliebt, populär
possibility Möglichkeit (f)
possible möglich
to post (internet) posten
post office Post (f)
postman/-woman Briefträger(in) (m/f)
to pour gießen (pp gegossen)
poverty Armut (f)
practical praktisch
practice Übung (f)
to practise üben
precise(ly) genau
to prefer lieber (+ verb), bevorzugen, vorziehen (pp vorgezogen)
pregnant schwanger
to prepare vorbereiten
present Geschenk (n)
president Präsident(in) (m/f)
pretty hübsch
price Preis (m)
primary school Grundschule (f)
prime minister Premierminister(in) (m/f)
to print drucken
printer Drucker (m)
private privat
probably wahrscheinlich
problem Problem (n)
products (food) Lebensmittel (pl)
profession: by profession von Beruf (m)
professor Professor(in) (m/f)
programme Programm (n)
programmer Programmierer(in) (m/f)
to prohibit verbieten (pp verboten)
to promise versprechen (pp versprochen)
to pronounce aussprechen (pp ausgesprochen)
to protect schützen
psychologist Psychologe/Psychologin (m/f)
pub Kneipe (f), Lokal (n)
public öffentlich
public relations Öffentlichkeitsarbeit (f)
to pull ziehen (pp gezogen), (muscle) zerren
punctual(ly) pünktlich

purse Portemonnaie (n)
to push drücken
to put stellen

Q
quality Qualität (f)
quality control Qualitätskontrolle (f)
quarter Viertel (n)
question Frage (f)
question mark Fragezeichen (n)
quick(ly) schnell
quiet ruhig, leise, (reserved) zurückhaltend
to quit aufhören
quite (completely) ganz, (fairly) ziemlich

R
rabbit Kaninchen (n)
radiologist Radiologe/ Radiologin (m/f)
rain Regen (m)
to rain regnen
to ramble wandern
rambling: to go rambling wandern gehen
rarely selten
rather (would rather) verb + lieber, (quite) ziemlich
to read lesen (pp gelesen)
ready fertig
realistic realistisch
really echt, ehrlich, super, tatsächlich, wirklich
reasonable günstig
to receive bekommen (pp bekommen), erhalten (pp erhalten)
recipe Rezept (n)
to recognise erkennen (pp erkannt)
to recommend empfehlen (pp empfohlen)
to recycle recyceln
red rot
to reduce reduzieren
to reflect (think about) sich überlegen (dat)
refreshing erfrischend
refugee Flüchtling (m)
to refuse verweigern
regardless trotzdem
region Gegend (f), Gebiet (n)
regular(ly) regelmäßig
(the river) Rhine Rhein (m)
relationship Beziehung (f)
relative Verwandte(r) (f/m)
to relax sich entspannen
reliable zuverlässig
to remember sich erinnern an (acc)
remote entfernt
to renew erneuern
renewable erneuerbar
to rent mieten
to repair reparieren
repair shop Werkstatt (f)
to repeat wiederholen
reply Antwort (f)
to report berichten
reputation Ruf (m)
research Forschung (f)
researcher Forscher(in) (m/f)
reservation Reservierung (f)
to reserve reservieren, buchen
reserved (quiet) zurückhaltend, reserviert
resort Ferienort (m)
responsible zuständig
rest Rest (m)
to rest sich ausruhen
restaurant Restaurant (n)
retail Einzelhandel (m)
retired person Rentner(in) (m/f)
to return zurückkommen (pp zurückgekommen)
rich reich
ride: to ride a bike Rad fahren (pp gefahren); to go riding reiten gehen (pp gegangen)
ridiculous lächerlich
right Recht (n); richtig; on the right rechts
right now gleich
to be right Recht haben
that's right das stimmt
road Straße (f)
to rob berauben
room Zimmer (n)
rose Rose (f)
round Runde (f)
to row rudern
rubbish Müll (m)
rucksack Rucksack (m)
rude unhöflich
to run laufen (pp gelaufen), (lead) reiten, führen
run-down heruntergekommen
rush hour Stoßzeiten (pl)
sabbatical year Sabbatjahr (n)
sad traurig
to sail segeln
salesman/-woman Verkäufer(in) (m/f)

S
salt Salz (n)
salty salzig
same derselbe/dieselbe/ dasselbe (m/f/n); gleich; at the same time gleichzeitig
sandwich Brot (n)
sandy sandig
satisfying befriedigend
Saturday Samstag (m), Sonnabend (m)
sauce Soße (f)
sausage Wurst (f); fried sausage Bratwurst (f)
to save (computer) speichern
to say sagen; to say du to each other sich duzen
scared: to be scared Angst haben
scary gruselig
scenery Landschaft (f)

schnapps Schnaps (m)
school Schule (f)
science Wissenschaft (f)
scientist
Wissenschaftler(in) (m/f)
Scot Schotte/Schottin (m/f)
Scotland Schottland (n)
screen Bildschirm (m)
sea Meer (n), See (f)
search Suche (f)
to search for suchen
search engine
Suchmaschine (f)
to season würzen
secondly zweitens
secretary Sekretär(in) (m/f)
sector Bereich (n), Sektor
(m)
security Sicherheit (f)
security guard
Wächter(in) (m/f)
to see sehen (pp gesehen)
to seek suchen
to seem scheinen
(pp geschienen)
seldom selten
self selbst
self-employed
selbstständig
to sell verkaufen
to send schicken, senden
sensitive sensibel
to separate trennen
separated getrennt
lebend
September September
(m)
series Serie (f)
serious ernsthaft
seriously im Ernst
several mehrere
to sew nähen
shadow Schatten (m)
shady schattig
shall we? wollen wir?
to share teilen
sharp scharf
sharp-tasting herb
she sie
shed Schuppen (m)
to shine scheinen
(pp geschienen)
shirt Hemd (n)
shoe Schuh (m)
to shoot schießen (pp
geschossen)
shop Geschäft (n), Laden
(m)
shopping: to go shopping
einkaufen gehen
(pp gegangen)
shopping centre
Einkaufszentrum (n)
short kurz, (of person)
klein
shortcut Abkürzung (f)
should sollte(st/n/t) (from
sollen)
shoulder Schulter (f)
to show zeigen
shower Dusche (f),
(weather) Schauer (m);
to have a shower sich
duschen
to shut down (computer)
abschalten
shy schüchtern
siblings Geschwister (pl)
sick übel
side Seite (f)
sight Anblick (m)
sights Sehenswürdigkeiten
(pl)
signal Signal (n)
silly blöd
simple einfach
since seit (dat)
to sing singen (pp
gesungen)
singer Sänger(in) (m/f)
single ledig, unverheiratet
single father
alleinerziehender Vater (m)
single mother
alleinerziehende Mutter (f)
sir mein Herr (m)
sister Schwester (f)
to sit down sich setzen
to be situated sich
befinden (pp befunden)
situation Lage (f),
Situation (f)
to ski Ski laufen/fahren
(pp gelaufen/gefahren)
skinny dünn
skittles: to play skittles
kegeln
sky Himmel (m)
slash (keyboard)
Schrägstrich (m)
to sleep schlafen
(pp geschlafen)
to fall asleep einschlafen
(pp eingeschlafen)
slim schlank
slow(ly) langsam
small klein
to smell (of) riechen
(pp gerochen) (nach) (dat)
to smile lächeln
to smoke rauchen
snack Zwischenmahlzeit
(f), Imbiss (m)
to snatch reißen
(pp gerissen)
snow Schnee (m)
to snow schneien
so so; or so (approximately)
ungefähr, etwa, circa/zirka
solution Lösung (f)
some einige, manche
someone jemand
something etwas
sometimes manchmal
son Sohn (m)
song Lied (n)
son-in-law
Schwiegersohn (m)
soon bald
sore throat
Halsschmerzen (pl)
sorry: I am sorry (es) tut
mir leid
sort Art (f); what sort of?
was für ein(e)? (m/f)
soup Suppe (f)
south Süden (m)

south-east Südosten (m)
southwestern südwestlich
space (on keyboard) Leerzeichen (n); (outer space) Weltraum (m)
spare time Freizeit (f)
sparkling wine Sekt (m)
to speak sprechen (pp gesprochen)
spectacular spektakulär
to spell buchstabieren
to spend (money) ausgeben (pp ausgegeben)
to spend (time) verbringen (pp verbracht)
spicy scharf
spider Spinne (f)
spite: in spite of trotz (gen)
to split aufteilen
spoon Löffel (m)
sport Sport (m)
sports centre Sportzentrum (n)
spot on genau, haargenau
spring Frühling (m)
square (in town) Platz (m)
stable(s) Pferdehof (m)
stadium Stadion (n)
star Stern (m)
to start anfangen (pp angefangen)
starter Vorspeise (f)
state Staat (m); (in Germany) Land (n)
station Bahnhof (m)
stay Aufenthalt (m)
to stay bleiben (pp geblieben), wohnen
stay-at-home father Hausmann (m)
stay-at-home mother Hausfrau und Mutter (f)
to steal stehlen (pp gestohlen)
steep steil
stepdaughter Stieftochter (f)
stepson Stiefsohn (m)
still immer noch
stockbroker Börsenmakler(in) (m/f)
stomach Magen (m)
stomach ache Magenschmerzen (pl)
stone Stein (m)
stony steinig
to stop (quit) aufhören, (put a stop to) beenden
storm Sturm (m)
story Geschichte (f)
straight (hair) glatt; (heterosexual) hetero
straightaway gleich
straight on geradeaus
Strasbourg Straßburg
street Straße (f)
stress Stress (m)
stressful stressig
strict streng
to stroll bummeln
strong stark, kräftig
stubborn stur
student Student(in) (m/f)
to study studieren
to stuff oneself sich vollfressen
to stumble stolpern
stupid dumm
sturdy fest
style Stil (m)
to subsidise subventionieren
success Erfolg (m)
to suggest vorschlagen (pp vorgeschlagen)
suggestion Vorschlag (m)
suitable: to be suitable passen
summer Sommer (m)
sun Sonne (f)
sunburn Sonnenbrand (m)
Sunday Sonntag (m)
sunglasses Sonnenbrille (f)
sunny sonnig
sunset Sonnenuntergang (m)
superb erstklassig, wunderschön
supermarket Supermarkt (m)
supervisor Vorarbeiter(in) (m/f)
supper Abendessen (n); to have supper zu Abend essen (pp gegessen)
to support unterstützen
suppose: I suppose wohl
supposed: to be supposed to sollen
sure(ly) sicher
to surf surfen
surgery Arztpraxis (f)
surname Familienname (m)
surprise Überraschung (f)
surrounding area Umgebung (f)
to swap wechseln
sweet süß
sweet dreams! träum(t) was Schönes! (du/ihr)
to swim schwimmen (pp geschwommen)
swimming pool Schwimmbad (n)
Swiss man/woman Schweizer(in) (m/f)
to switch off abschalten, ausschalten
to switch on anschalten
Switzerland Schweiz (f)

T

table Tisch (m)
to tackle angehen (pp angegangen)
to take nehmen (pp genommen); (medication) einnehmen (pp eingenommen)
to take place stattfinden (pp stattgefunden)
to take photos fotografieren
talented talentiert
to talk reden
taste Geschmack (m)
to taste schmecken, probieren

tattoo Tätowierung (f)
tax Steuer (f)
tea Tee (m)
to teach unterrichten
teacher Lehrer(in) (m/f)
technician Techniker(in) (m/f)
telephone Telefon (n), (mobile) Handy (n)
to telephone anrufen (pp angerufen)
telephone number Telefonnummer (f)
television: to watch television fernsehen (pp ferngesehen)
to tell erzählen
temperature Temperatur (f), Fieber (n)
tendon Sehne (f)
tennis Tennis (m)
tennis court Tennisplatz (m)
terrace Terrasse (f)
terrible furchtbar, fürchterlich, schrecklich
to text per SMS senden
text message SMS (f)
than als
to thank danken, sich bedanken
thank you danke, ich bedanke mich
that dass, diese(r)(s) (f/m/n)
theatre Theater (n)
their ihr (m, n), ihre (f, pl)
them: to them ihnen
then dann, (at that time) damals
theory Theorie (f)
in theory theoretisch
therapist Therapeut(in) (m/f)
there da, dort
these diese
thin dünn
thing Ding (n)
to think denken (pp gedacht), meinen
to think about (consider) sich überlegen (dat)
this diese(r)(s) (f/m/n)
thirsty: to be thirsty Durst haben
those diese
though allerdings, jedoch
thousand tausend
through durch (acc)
to thunder donnern
Thursday Donnerstag (m)
ticket Karte (f)
to tidy (up) aufräumen, in Ordnung bringen (pp gebracht)
time Zeit (f), Mal (n); at that time damals; (at) what time? um wieviel Uhr?
to have a good time sich amüsieren
tiny winzig
tired müde
to (town, country) nach (dat), (time) vor (dat) (building) zu (dat)
to you (informal, sing) dir, (formal sing and pl) Ihnen, (informal, pl) euch
to your health! zum Wohl!
today heute
together zusammen
toilet Toilette (f)
tomorrow morgen
tone Signalton (m)
too zu; auch
tongue Zunge (f)
toolbar Werkzeugliste (f)
tooth Zahn (m)
toothache Zahnschmerzen (pl)
topic Thema (n)
touch: to get/be in touch kontaktieren, sich melden
tour Fahrt (f)
tourism Tourismus (m)
tourist Tourist(in) (m/f)
touristy touristisch
towel Handtuch (n)
town Stadt (f)
town centre Stadtzentrum (n)
town hall Rathaus (n)
town map Stadtplan (m)
trade fair Messe (f)
trader Kaufmann/Kauffrau (m/f)
tradition Tradition (f)
traditional traditionell
traffic Verkehr (m)
trafficking Handel (m)
train Bahn (f), Zug (m); by train mit dem Zug
to train trainieren
trainee Auszubildende(r) (f/m), Praktikant(in) (m/f)
trainer Sportschuh (m)
tranquil ruhig
to travel reisen, fahren (pp gefahren)
travel agent Reiseverkehrskaufmann/ Reiseverkehrskauffrau (m/f)
trip Ausflug (m), Fahrt (f), Reise (f)
to trip stolpern, ausrutschen
true wahr
trustworthy zuverlässig
to try versuchen, probieren
Tuesday Dienstag (m)
tummy ache Magenschmerzen (pl)
Turkey Türkei (f)
Turkish türkisch
turn Reihe (f)
twice zweimal
twilight Dämmerung (f)
twins Zwillinge (pl)
type Art (f)
typical typisch

U

ultra über
umpteen zig
unbelievable/ unbelievably unglaublich

uncanny/uncannily unheimlich
uncle Onkel (m)
under unter (acc/dat)
Underground (train) U-Bahn (f)
underscore Unterstrich (m)
to understand verstehen (pp verstanden)
undervalued unterbewertet
to undo (computer) zurücknehmen (pp zurückgenommen)
undoubtedly zweifellos
undressed: to get undressed sich ausziehen (pp ausgezogen)
unemployed arbeitslos
unemployment Arbeitslosigkeit
unexpected unerwartet
unforgettable unvergesslich
unfortunate unglücklich
unfortunately leider
United Kingdom Vereinigtes Königreich (n)
United States Vereinigte Staaten (pl)
university Universität (f)
to unload entladen (pp entladen)
unlucky unglücklich
unpleasant unangenehm
until bis (acc)
unusual(ly) ungewöhnlich
up-and-coming aufstrebend
up to bis zu (dat)
to upload hochladen (pp hochgeladen)
urban städtisch
(to) us uns
to use gebrauchen
useful nützlich
usual(ly) gewöhnlich, normalerweise
to vacuum staubsaugen

V

variety Sorte (f)
various verschiedene
vegan Veganer(in) (m/f)
vegetables Gemüse (n)
vegetarian Vegetarier(in) (m/f); vegetarisch
vehicle Kraftwagen (m), Kraftfahrzeug, Kfz (n)
Venice Venedig
venison Reh (n)
very sehr
vicinity: in the vicinity of in der Nähe von (dat)
Vienna Wien
view Aussicht (f), Blick (m)
village Dorf (n)
vineyard Weinberg (m)
visa Visum (n)
to visit besichtigen, besuchen
visitor Besucher(in) (m/f)
voice Stimme (f)
voluntary freiwillig

W

wacky verrückt
wage Lohn (m)
to wait warten
waiter/waitress Kellner(in) (m/f)
to wake up aufwachen
walk Spaziergang (m)
to go for a walk spazieren gehen (pp gegangen)
to wallpaper tapezieren
to want wollen, Lust haben (auf)
war Krieg (m); world war Weltkrieg (m)
warehouse Lager (n), Lagerhaus (n)
warm(ly) warm
to wash waschen (pp gewaschen)
to wash up abwaschen (pp abgewaschen)
washing (laundry) Wäsche (f)
washing machine Waschmaschine (f)
wasp Wespe (f)
waste Abfall (m)
to waste verschwenden
to watch TV fernsehen (pp ferngesehen)
water Wasser (n)
water sport(s) Wassersport (m), Wassersportarten (pl)
wavelength Wellenlänge (f)
way Weg (m)
we wir
weak schwach
to wear tragen (pp getragen)
weather Wetter (n)
weather forecast Wettervorhersage (f)
web page Webseite (f)
website Website (f)
wedding anniversary Hochzeitstag (m)
Wednesday Donnerstag (m)
week Woche (f)
weekend Wochenende (n)
to weigh wiegen (pp gewogen)
weird komisch
welcome herzlich willkommen; you're welcome bitte
welcoming (gast)freundlich
well gut
well (then) also, na ja
well-being Wohlbefinden (n)
well-equipped gut ausgestattet
Welshman/-woman Waliser(in) (m/f)
west Westen (m)
wet nass
what was; what a ...! was für ein(e) ...! (m, n/f); what sort of? was für ein(e)? (m, n/f)

what's more außerdem, zudem
wheat Weizen (m)
when wann, (talking about past) als
whenever wenn
where wo
where from woher
where (to) wohin
which welche(r)/(s) (f/m/n)
while Weile (f)
whipped cream Schlagsahne (f)
to whisk schlagen (pp geschlagen)
white weiß
who wer
whole ganz; on the whole im Allgemeinen
wholeheartedly voll und ganz
whom wen, wem
why warum
widowed verwitwet
wife Frau (f)
wifi WLAN (n)
to win gewinnen (pp gewonnen)
wind Wind (m)
window Fenster (n)
to windsurf windsurfen
windy windig
wine Wein (m); mulled wine Glühwein (m); wine tasting Weinprobe (f)
winery Weingut (n)
winter Winter (m)
winter sport Wintersportart (f)
wish: good/best wishes herzlichen Glückwunsch
to wish wünschen
with mit (dat); with pleasure mit (dem größten) Vergnügen (n)
to withdraw ziehen (pp gezogen)
to withdraw money Geld abheben
without ohne (acc)
woman Frau (f)
wonderful wunderbar, wunderschön
wood(s) Wald (m)
word Wort (n)
work Arbeit (f)
to work arbeiten
world Welt (f)
world war Weltkrieg (m)
to worry Sorgen machen; don't worry about it keine Ursache
worse schlechter, schlimmer
wounded verletzt
to write schreiben (pp geschrieben)
writer Schriftsteller(in) (m/f)
wrong falsch, los; what is wrong? was ist los?
to be wrong sich irren, Unrecht haben

Y

year Jahr (n); next year nächstes Jahr; this year dieses/in diesem Jahr
yearly jährlich
yeast Hefe (f)
yellow gelb
yes ja, (on the contrary) doch
yes indeed jawohl
yesterday gestern; the day before yesterday vorgestern
yet noch
you (informal, sing, nom) du (informal, sing, acc) dich, (informal, pl, nom) ihr, (informal, pl, acc) euch, (formal, sing and plural, nom and acc), Sie; to you (informal, sing, dat) dir, (informal, pl, dat) euch, (formal, sing and plural, dat) Ihnen
you're welcome keine Ursache (f), gern geschehen
young jung
your (informal, sing,m/n, f) dein, deine, (informal, pl, m/n, f) euer, eure, (formal, sing and plural, m/n, f) Ihr, Ihre
youth Jugend (f)
youth hostel Jugendherberge (f)